GEOGRAPHY

GEOGRAPHY

HISTORY AND CONCEPTS: A STUDENT'S GUIDE

FOURTH EDITION

ARILD HOLT-JENSEN

Los Angeles | London | New Delhi
Singapore | Washington DC

First published 2009

SAGE Publications Ltd
1 Oliver's Yard
55 City Road
London EC1Y 1SP

SAGE Publications Inc.
2455 Teller Road
Thousand Oaks, California 91320

SAGE Publications India Pvt Ltd
B 1/I 1 Mohan Cooperative Industrial Area
Mathura Road, Post Bag 7
New Delhi 110 044

SAGE Publications Asia-Pacific Pte Ltd
33 Pekin Street #02-01
Far East Square
Singapore 048763

Library of Congress Control Number 2009924585

British Library Cataloguing in Publication data
A catalogue record for this book is available from the British Library

ISBN 978-1-4129-4649-0
ISBN 978-1-4129-4650-6 (pbk)

Typeset by C&M Digitals (P) Ltd, Chennai, India
Printed and bound in Great Britain by TJ International Ltd, Padstow, Cornwall
Printed on paper from sustainable resources

Mixed Sources
Product group from well-managed
forests and other controlled sources
www.fsc.org Cert no. SGS-COC-2482
© 1996 Forest Stewardship Council
FSC

CONTENTS

PREFACE

Geography is intriguing because it is there all around you; the world that is an inextricable part of your everyday life. The fascination of the discipline is that it gives you keys which can help you to understand and explore that everyday world. To explain this fascination further I will briefly outline my own personal road to involvement with the discipline.

I started primary school in 1944 when Norway was closed off from the rest of the world as a result of German occupation. It was forbidden at that time to own a radio and to listen to the Norwegian broadcasts from London. My father, however, somehow managed to keep track of the changing war frontiers, which he marked with a thread of wool thumb-tacked to an old map of Europe. Then came May 1945, when Monty's young soldiers, who had actually taken part in the movement of that frontier thread, paraded our streets on National Day (May 17), wading through flowers thrown by citizens who thronged the pavements to greet them. Russian prisoners held in my home town were set free and, before leaving, German soldiers befriended us children by distributing sweets. Europe happened once more around us and the world opened, as witnessed by the first American lorry (a 'Fargo') to arrive in our schoolyard and the docking of the first boat loaded with bananas. Then, in the summer of 1945, five volumes of *National Geographic Magazine* arrived which my father had subscribed to before the war. I had learnt to read Norwegian but not yet English. I could, however, 'read the maps' that were included in every second issue. Capital cities were marked with a star and these 'star cities' I learnt by heart! We were no longer geographically excluded; the world was once more ours to explore.

Maps of the Pacific Ocean were particularly intriguing in 1947. In that year Thor Heyerdahl and his crew (including a crewman from my home town) drifted on a balsa-wood fleet from Peru to French Polynesia Heyerdahl's book, *The Kon-Tiki Expedition*, was the first 'grown-up' book I read. My road to geography, however, was for a while diverted to botany: my school herbarium acquired some really good additions as a result of a hiking tour I undertook with my mother into the Norwegian mountains. So my university studies started with botany and an MA in that discipline seemed inevitable. Only to complete my BA I would study geography. It was then I really struck lucky: until the year I started to study geography, the university geography in Norway had been divided in two separate disciplines – physical and cultural geography. In 1959, the year when I started, these were amalgamated into a so-called 'basic discipline' of unified geography. And thus we learnt to understand the landscape around us as the result of the combined forces of humanity and nature.

At first, physical geography was the easier to understand; cultural and human geography seemed much more vague and were more difficult to get to grips with. At Kolsås, a mountain close to Oslo, I got my first thrill of understanding. Here I realized that the layers of rocks I climbed over, created 600–300 million years ago and hence before the age of dinosaurs, still had an important bearing on the landscape of today. I learnt to interpret the geomorphologic features of the landscape. Travelling became much more interesting. Having learnt something of oceanography and climatology, it became clear how the Humboldt Current could transport the Kon-Tiki fleet across the Pacific as well as provide the crew with all the fish they needed.

Geography had fired my imagination – even more so after Pierre Gourou and Torsten Hägerstrand had visited us as guest lecturers, and they were both human geographers. Gourou lectured in French, which I could not speak and could hardly understand. Even so, I can still recall his lecture on Belgium because of its gradual, systematic progression, documenting Belgium's problematic political geography and the multifaceted divisions between Wallonia and Flanders. Hägerstrand brought exciting new ideas on research methods, including the simulation of geographical diffusion employing advanced statistical tools. Silly me, why hadn't I studied statistics!

In 1962, midway through my work towards my MA thesis, I was lucky enough to obtain a grant to attend a student geographical conference in Saarland. During conference excursions we became acquainted with the German School of landscape geography and hence learnt to use our eyes to interpret the cultural features of the landscape. (Manure heaps in front of barns meant active agriculture; barns converted to new uses meant commuting and 'social fallow'.) More importantly, we had to present our thesis work as a paper and in oral form. My rather traditional regional geography approach elicited some very useful comments from an English student: 'Why don't you build up a hypothesis from the background features you explained in the introduction, and follow that as a thread all through?' This gave me the clue I was looking for. I found the hypothetic-deductive method very useful for my thesis: not because my general hypothesis of population decline was proven in the mountain farming district I was studying, but rather because this marginal region also showed some population increase as a result of contingent, local circumstances that I had to explain.

When I started my career as a young geography lecturer in Bergen in 1965, the small staff of our geography department shared responsibilities for a staff seminar on Peter Haggett's book *Locational Analysis in Human Geography* (1965). A whole new world of models and statistical techniques was opened up to us. At the same time, I had to teach a wide variety of courses in 'basic geography' to the yearly intake of new students. As the only one in faculty with a natural science background in biology and with some knowledge of mathematics, I had to teach biogeography as well as cartography, geomorphology, oceanography and regional geography – all of which were outside my own specialism of applied human geography. But this broad teaching experience was very useful and an experience I deeply deplore that new staff do not receive these days. As the faculty acquired new specialist staff I, too, ceased to have such a broad-based involvement, but the problem remains that strictly specialized research-based teaching tends to give students a rather fragmented basis from which to tackle the necessarily specialist research frontier. The aim of this book, therefore, is an attempt to keep this fragmented landscape of geography together in one piece. This is a book on geography, not on physical or human geography. It has tried to widen its scope beyond the Anglo-American world and it intends not only to cover the history of the discipline but also to explore basic elements of science theory, current ideas and concepts which have and are influencing geographical thinking and research. Because of this broad scope all specialists will, quite correctly, comment that this book does not cover their specialism properly. But this book was not written for them; it is an introductory textbook that has the intention of guiding students into the exciting world of geography.

The book also has one other basic intention that needs more lengthy explanation. We need to go back to 1968, the year when student uproar hit Paris and 'flower power' and the anti-Vietnam war movement hit San Francisco and other American cities. Bergen University had a whole week of 'critical discussions' led by the students. As a young lecturer who enthusiastically promoted the Haggettian approach to geography, this debate took me quite unprepared. At a meeting attended by other social science disciplines, I presented geography's spatial science achievements. The critical students dismissed me as hopeless, aiming their attacks instead at the well-known Norwegian political scientist Stein Rokkan, who was also present. His models and his use of the hypothetic-deductive method were challenged fiercely, and I was shocked at this.

However, I learnt two things. The first was Rokkan's truly academic attitude. Even though the criticism was devastating, he liked it. He liked the discussion and the criticism because it helped him to develop new ideas. He was a true supporter of Karl Popper's stand that an active and progressive science should be in a constant state of revolution. This is what distinguishes scientific discourse from political and other debates.

The other thing I learnt was that I had to have a better understanding of the positivism debate that had started earlier in sociology and political science but that was largely absent from geography. This led me to new reading, followed by lectures for my students and, eventually, to the first Norwegian edition of this book in 1976. The first English edition came, with considerable additions and alterations, in 1981. New directions and discussions within geography followed in the 1980s, which resulted in the second English edition in 1988, the second Norwegian edition in 1990 and the third English edition in 1999. In 1992 a Spanish edition even appeared, based on a translation from the second English edition, and lately I received a 'pirate edition' in Persian, edited in Teheran. In the ten years since the third English edition was published, new geography students (as witnessed by continuing sales) have apparently found the book useful. On the other hand, I myself have increasingly found the 1999 edition unsatisfactory. To some degree it has become outdated as the discipline continues its progression through a constant state of revolution. To some extent I also feel there were some aspects of the text that needed to be clarified and that pedagogically some parts needed restructuring. As all authors must feel, a book is never finished and complete; when a book is finally published, you have moved on, and have possibly learnt new things.

As an observer of academic development during the more than 40 years since 1968, it was, however, sad to see so many of those young student critics of 1968 come to adhere to new orthodox trains of thought. They had not the stamina of Rokkan and Popper, but built academic fortresses around their revolutionary gains, admitting into their fortresses only disciples of the 'true belief'. Since the 1980s poststructuralism and postmodernism have come to the fore in human geography. This, in principle, means the death of all orthodoxies and an openness to basic criticism, including self-criticism in all fields of inquiry. But it may also lead to scientific impotence: a situation in which we do not dare to continue an investigation, present its results or write it up as a thesis because we can see all its weaknesses and the potential for criticism from others. This frustrating situation must, of course, be avoided. But how can we proceed? This is the second basic intention of this book: a kind of solution, summarized in three points:

1) *Every scientific presentation is a simplification.* It is not the truth in itself, only a possible part-truth as seen through the disciplinary lens of the scientist. Simplification is necessary if we are to convey to an audience an understanding it can get to grips with. This is, of course, particularly the case with a textbook such as this: an introductory work has to simplify (and shorten) in order to be readable and comprehensive.

2) *You should not believe that something written in a textbook or presented by senior academics is true simply because they say it is true.* You should only believe it when you have had the opportunity to test the postulates yourself. This may seem very difficult for a young student but it is, at the very least, a plea to keep an open mind and to remain sceptical to any form of orthodoxy. This is also a warning. When writing a thesis, it is too easy to hide behind references to leading iconoclasts or to hide in the fogs of obscure academic concepts. You must feel free to declare whatever findings and perspectives you can offer! It is hoped that you will be aided in this by those who adhere to the next point.

3) *Criticism should be positive and constructive rather than negative.* This, I think, is difficult for most academics when assessing and marking dissertations or student essays. It is easy to recognize failures, missing perspectives and misunderstandings and to focus one's assessment and criticism on these. Students find it equally easy to criticize a lecturer for delivering a lousy lecture that was 'so badly structured'. Assessment, however, has a human side too. You are stuck with that lecturer and no one performs better if he or she only hears negative criticism. When a teacher supervises student theses, this becomes very obvious. You have to find something positive to say so that the students will perform to the best of their abilities. Look for positive points first: Did I learn something new from this chapter or lecture? Was a new perspective or approach presented? Was the structure logical and consistent? Sum up the positive points first; then consider any deficiences.

These points are as equally important when we assess the history of the discipline in this book. One-sided, negative criticism often leads to a new orthodoxy because such criticism is defensive; it is not open to fruitful discourse in which one continues to learn new things. And this is the whole point: the world of everyday environments is ours, and geography should help us to explore it. I suggest you look twice at Robert Sack's diagram (Figure 1.9 in this book). To ordinary citizens living 'somewhere', the geographic environment is conceptually a unified 'one'. It consists of nature, social relations and meanings (i.e. your own personal 'roots' in a place). There is no division between human and physical geography. As researchers, however, we take on a certain paradigmatic perspective when learning in academia. We look through an academic lens from 'nowhere' to the 'somewheres' of geographic everyday life. The important point is that any lens only conveys a part, perhaps even a distortion, of geographic reality. This should warn us against any kind of academic self-righteousness: 'we alone know'. I wish you luck with your further exploration of the 'somewheres' in this world of ours. And I hope you proceed further than I have during a lifetime in geographic academia.

When reading the book it is a benefit if you have some basic understanding of geography in advance. If you start from 'scratch' it might be an idea to read John A. Matthews and David T. Herbert's small book *Geography: A Very Short Introduction* (2008) in advance. An alternative is Alistair Bonnett's *What is Geography?* (2008). For first-year Scandinavian students in geography I have written a similar simple introductory book, *Hva er geografi?* (Holt-Jensen, 2007), that fills the same function.

TO THE TEACHER

The aim of this book is both to give a presentation of geography as a science, its history from atiquity to the present day, and to give basic insight into discourses within philosophy of science which have had major influence on geographic research. This fourth edition of *Geography: History and Concepts* has been completely revised and rewritten to include new developments in geographical thought and methods. Those who have used the third edition will find that the framework of the book is changed, primarily to make it easier to read and use as a student text. One criticism of the third edition from students has been that some schools of thought in the discipline were presented in bits and pieces in different chapters. The factual history of geography and its different schools of thought are for this reason now mainly covered in Chapters 2, 3 and 6, while Chapters 4 and 5 cover such basic philosophy of science issues as paradigm theory, general scientific epistemologies and the positivism debate, and relate these discussions to geography. The account of newer trends within the discipline could, of course, only be covered after the philosophy of science had been presented in Chapters 4 and 5, so newer schools of thought within geography are discussed in the last part of Chapter 5 and in Chapter 6.

Chapter 1 sets the framework of the book. It has been rewritten to give a broader, general presentation of the discussions contained within the discipline, its subdivisions and its general position among the sciences. The aim of this chapter is to arouse the interest of the student for further travel into the history of the discipline in order to understand the juxtaposition of different views. Chapters 2 and 3 provide a historic encounter of the scientific development of the discipline from antiquity to the 1980s, focusing on the growth of scientific tools and the tasks in the wider society. Chapters 4 and 5 are structured on the same pedagogic idea, starting with a presentation of a dicotomy which, through the following discussions, is shown to be too simple; in short, it is a practical exercise in dialectics. Chapters 4 (on paradigms and revolutions) looks at whether the history of geography follows the Kuhnian model of ruling paradigms and revolutions or not, with a special focus on the spatial science school. Chapter 5 starts with a juxtaposition of positivism and its critics, and analyses to what extent the positivism discourse has influenced the discipline and its gradual change. The last part of this chapter examines the growth of schools that was directly related to the positivism debate: humanist approaches, behavioural and welfare geography and structuralism. The newer schools of thought are, however, given a broader coverage in the completely new Chapter 6, which covers structuration theory, realism, actor-network theory, poststructuralism, postmodernism and feminist geography. A basic coverage is also presented of new tools in geographic research, such as satellite photos and GIS. And of course, finally, what tasks are there for geography as a discipline in the future, as split in human and physical geography, or as a united discipline?

A feature of the book are the text boxes, which elucidate particular research examples and, in some cases, the life histories of leading geographers. They also clarify particular research concepts and methods.

This edition, like the third, also contains a glossary, in which central concepts are defined and explained. The personality index contains, as in former editions, short biographical notes as far as it has been possible to find such information.

A new feature in this edition are lists of questions for the students at the end of each chapter which can be used for student seminars and revisal.

These features emphasize the fact that this book is intended as a textbook for students that should be useful in the first or second year of study.

For the work with the previous editions I was greatly indebted to senior lecturer Brian Fullerton, formerly at the University of Newcastle upon Tyne, for his cooperation in providing a text in readable and clear English. He was unable to take any responsibility for this new edition. The responsibility for any defects or false conclusions rests, of course, wholly with the author. Citations from German texts are translated by the author.

For work on this new edition I must particularly acknowledge the debts I owe to Ralph Jewell and Britt Dale, who read and commented upon the complete manuscript. Jewell, who is a British-born Senior Lecturer in Philosophy at the University of Bergen, commented upon and corrected the parts of the book related to the philosophy of science as well as correcting my English in some cases. Britt Dale, Professor in Geography at the University of Trondheim, who has used the previous edition in her teaching, gave suggestions for restructuring, clarifications and additions throughout the manuscript in order to provide a better student text. I have followed their recommendations to a very large extent. Professor Robert David Sack has also read the preliminary manuscript and given positive comments. I am also indebted to Tor Halfdan Aase, who provided me with material for two 'boxes' and who helped me with the section on semiotics, to Jostein Bakke for providing the text for Box 6.6 and to Anne Lucas, who provided a box on the use of GIS. I would also like to thank my students for criticisms and comments on previous editions. Comments and advice on the former editions have also benefited this one, and my thanks go to Ove Biilmann, Moshe Brawer, Olavi Granö, Jens Chr. Hansen, Torsten Hägerstrand, Jan Lundquist, Michael Morgan, Richard Morrill, Hans Skjervheim and Wolf Tietze. Some of the illustrations in this edition are new, and they have been drawn by Kjell Helge Sjøstrøm, design technician at the Department of Geography, University of Bergen. And finally, lots of thanks to Robert Rojek at Sage for comments, encouragements and patience throughout the process of writing!

Arild Holt-Jensen
Bergen, Norway, June 2009

ACKNOWLEDGEMENTS

The author and the publishers would like to thank the following for permission to reproduce copyright material:

Walter de Gruyter, Publishers, for Figure 1.2, from Schmithüsen, J., *Allgemeine Geosynergetik,* 1976; and Figure 1.10, adapted from Hard, G., *Die Geographie, eine wissenschaftstheoretische Einführung,* 1973.

Polity Press for Figure 1.4, from Duncan, S.S. and Goodwin, M., *Uneven Development and the Local State,* 1988, p. 50

Blackwell Press for Figure 5.3, from Stoddart, D.R. (ed.), *Geography, Ideology and Social Concern,* 1981, p. 24

Verlag Franz Deuticke, for Figure 1.5 from Weichhart, P., *Geographie in Umbruch,* 1975, pp. 11, 99 and 104.

Harper & Row, for Figure 1.6, from Haggett, P., *Geography: A Modern Synthesis,* 1983.

Westermann Lernspielverlag, for Figure 1.7, from Leser, H., *Geographie, Das Geographische Seminar,* 1980, pp. 68–9.

Edward Arnold for Figure 4.2, from Harvey, D., *Explanation in Geography,* 1969; for Figure 3.4 from Haggett, P., *Locational Analysis in Human Geography,* 1965 and for Figure 3.5 from Haggett, P., Cliff, A.D. and Frey, A., *Locational Analysis in Human Geography,* 1977.

Random House UK Ltd, for Figure 4.3, from Popper, K.R., *The Logic of Scientific Discovery,* 1972, p. 243; and Figure 6.2, from Sayer, A., *Method in Social Science: A Realist Approach,* 1984, p. 215.

Studentlitteratur, Sweden, for Figure 4.5, from Alvesson, M. and Sköldberg, K., *Tolkning och reflektion. Vetenskapsfilosofi och kvalitativ metod,* 1994, p. 45.

Elsevier Science Ltd., for Figure 4.8, from Forer, P., *Progress in Human Geography,* Vol. 2, 1978, p. 247.

Henk Meijer, for Figure 3.3, from *IDG: Zuyder Zee-Lake Issjel,* 1981.

Geografforlaget, for Figure 3.6, from Reenberg, A., *Det Katastroferamte SAHEL,* 2nd ed., 1984, p. 15; and for Figure 2.1, from Biilmann, O. *Geografi, tradisjoner og perspektiver,* 1981.

University of Trondheim, for Figure 5.1, from Löfgren, A. *Om kvalitativ metod och fältarbete i geografi. Arbeider fra Geografisk Institutt, New Series* C, no. 4., 1996.

Curzon Press, for Figure 6.4, from Manger, L. (ed.) *Muslim Diversity: Local Islam in Global Contexts,* 1999; and Figure 6.5, from Madsen, S. Toft (ed.), *State, Society, and the Environment in South Asia,* 1999.

H. Meesenberg, for Figure 6.8, from *Geojournal,* 1996, Vol. 39, pp. 143–52.

Johns Hopkins University Press, for Figure 1.8, adapted from Sack, R.D., *Place, Modernity and the Consumer's World,* 1992.

Figure 6.6, from Dorling, D. and Fairbairn, D., *Mapping: Ways of Representing the World,* 1997.

Oxford University Press, for Figure 6.7, from Matthews, J.A. and Herbert, D.T. *Geography: A Very Short Introduction,* 2008

Swedish Society for Anthropology and Geography, for Figure 1.11, from Jones, M., *Geografiska Annaler,* 1988, Vol. 70B, pp. 197–204.

Every effort has been made to trace the copyright holders but if any have been inadvertently overlooked the publishers will be pleased to make the necessary arrangement at the first opportunity.

1 WHAT IS GEOGRAPHY?

INTRODUCTION

> Of course the first thing to do was to make a grand survey of the country she was going to travel through. 'It's something very like learning geography,' thought Alice, as she stood on tiptoe in hopes of being able to see a little further. (Lewis Carroll (1872), *Through the Looking-Glass and What Alice Found There*)

Alice started from 'some-where' in her family garden in Oxford when she decided to follow the White Rabbit. But was she going 'no-where'? A number of different perspectives are juxtaposed in her experiences in Wonderland:

> 'Will you tell me, please,' she said, 'which way I must go from here?'
> 'Yes,' said the Cat, 'but mustn't you tell me where you want to go?'
> 'Well, any place – 'Alice began.
> 'Then you can go any way,' the Cat said.
> '– if it is a place,' Alice said.

After pointing out the Hatter's house, the Cat explained that as every one in Wonderland was mad, Alice must be mad too. The Cat did not go away, but it was still not there anymore. It just disappeared, its big grinning mouth the last to go. Space and time do not matter in Wonderland. At the Hatter's house, the watch does not tell the time because it is always tea-time, and Alice is told there is no place for her although there are many empty chairs. And strange doors and paths appear at the most unlikely places. Luckily she has pieces from both sides of the mushroom to eat to get smaller or bigger when it pleases her. This comes in handy when she enters the rose garden to play croquet with the Queen of Hearts. This is the Queen's **territory**, over which she seems to have total control, shouting 'Off with his or her head' every time someone displeases her. But heads were not cut off, as it was difficult to find the head of a playing card or the body of the Cheshire Cat. The trial before the Queen's tribunal is fearsome as long as Alice is the size of a small girl; but as she swallows a 'get bigger' bit of mushroom the assembly is reduced to a pack of fifty-two small playing cards.

This strange children's book gives us some clues to the concept of **relational space**. All through the book, competition over territory is demonstrated, as well as the fear and attraction of unknown spaces behind closed doors. Gradually, Alice gains control over relational space and her fears disappear as she learns how to change her size. Her relational space, her relationship to the physical and social realms as well as the realm of meanings in Wonderland, is changed (see also Figure 1.8, p. 20).

Since Alice started on her journey into the unknown land more than 130 years ago, the discipline of geography has travelled a long way. A hundred years ago the geographer's job was the 'grand survey' – mapping the landscape, the **absolute space**, as seen from a balloon or a hilltop – to guide subsequent travellers through it. On the basis of this surveillance, curiosity would lead on naturally to the basic geographical question: '*Why* is it like that here?' Alice did not pose that question; she took in the 'strangeness' of life on the other side as a matter of fact. Geographers, on the other hand, have had problems with this question since ancient times, having had problems in finding appropriate methods to analyse the *why* of the things observed.

Box 1.1	**The popular notion of geography**

The scene was typical of that extraordinary ritual known as the Cocktail Party. – Groping for something else to fill the silence, she got in her word first. 'And what do *you* do?' she said. 'Oh,' I said, grateful for the usual filler, 'I'm a geographer.' And even as I said it, I felt the safe ground turning into the familiar quagmire. She did not have to ask the next question, but she did anyway.

- 'Oh really, a geographer ... and what *do* geographers do?'

It has happened many times, and it seldom gets better. That awful feeling of desperate foolishness when you, a professional geographer, find yourself incapable of explaining simply and shortly to others what you really do. One could say, 'I look at the world from a spatial perspective, in a sense through spatial spectacles,' or 'Well, actually I'm a spatial analyst,' both of which would be true up to a point. But such phrases convey no meaning to most people, and leave them suspecting that you need a new oculist, or perhaps an analyst of a different sort. – In a desperate attempt to build a bridge with familiar words, one ends up saying, 'Well, actually, I teach geography.' 'Oh really?', and laughing. 'What's the capital of North Dakota?' (From Gould, 1985, pp. 4–5)

Most people have vague notions about the content of scientific geography. School geography may have left many with bad memories of learning the names of rivers and towns by rote. It is still common to meet people who think that geographers must have to learn a mass of facts, must know the population of towns all over the world and can name and locate all the states in Africa. This idea of geography as an encyclopaedic knowledge of places is illustrated when a newspaper rings up its local department of geography to find out how many towns there are in the world called Newcastle, or when readers write in to settle bets as to which is the world's longest river. Recently, the Norwegian State Television phoned me and I thought this would be on my international research in social housing geography, but they wanted me to delimit 'Northern Europe' in a programme on 'Northern attractions'! A whole TV crew came to record me drawing up different possible borders on a map of Europe.

People have an idea that geography has something to do with maps. Less cynically than Swift:

So geographers, in Afric-maps
And o'er unhabitable downs
With savage-pictures fill their gaps
Place elephants for want of towns.

Geographers are thought to be people who know how to draw maps and are somehow associated with the Ordnance Survey or the US Coast and Geodetic Survey.

Another opinion is that geographers write travel descriptions – a reasonable belief for anyone who reads reviews of the year's books and sees that many of those listed under 'geography' are accounts of exciting expeditions to the Amazon, sailing trips around the world or something similar.

Each of these popular opinions as to what geography is has some truth in it. Place names, locations of towns, land use, topography and other spatial features you may observe on maps, air and satellite photos are facts for geographers of the same order as dates are facts for historians. They are the basic building blocks of the subject, but they are not the subject itself. Maps representing collection of such data are very important specific tools for geographers.

Different types of **thematic maps** are also important means of expression in geographical research, along with tables, diagrams and written accounts. Today, geographers are increasingly using **Geographical Information Systems (GIS)** and computer mapping, rather than the traditional maps (see pp. 187–93). Geospatial technologies have definitely changed the methods in geography; by combining, for instance, data from satellite images with other spatial data, computer mapping has become a powerful tool for description, analyses and often a basis for decision-making. As stated by Bonnett (2008, p. 94), 'the satellite and aerial data collected for Google Earth promise to allow anyone, anywhere, a God-like ability to see everything'. With access to the Internet you can start to explore the world. But to be able to analyse and make sense of what you see, you need to learn more geography.

The art of visual expression and analyses is much more closely associated with geography than with other social and natural sciences. Observations recorded during travel and **fieldwork** still provide essential data for geographers. A cultivation of the power of observation is therefore an important objective in the education of a geographer. Geographical training aims to develop the ability to 'see geographically', to observe and interpret a natural or cultural landscape in the field and/or through the study of maps, aerial photographs, satellite images and other visual representations. But in general we travel through landscapes that have been discovered and mapped by others before us.

EXPLORATION AND THE COSMOGRAPHIC TRADITION

Until the end of the nineteenth century, however, voyages of discovery and the mapping of formerly unknown lands *were* closely associated with geography. Wayne K. Davies (1972, p. 11), for instance, maintained that geography enjoyed its strongest relative position among the sciences during the so-called 'golden age' of exploration from the fifteenth to the nineteenth centuries. This was not due to the academic status of the subject during this period but to the work of a number of people who were actively involved with the mapping and description of the new lands being discovered. To the extent that they were working scientifically, they would, however, be better described as cosmographers rather than geographers. **Cosmography**, as termed by Schmithüsen (1976, p. 10), included not only geography and cartography but also natural sciences like biology, geology and geophysics, and social sciences like anthropology, which only achieved their independent academic standing towards the end of the nineteenth century. Exploration, and all these other fields of cosmographic activity, were also regarded as being part of geography by the general public because they were carried out, to a large extent, under the auspices of the **geographical societies** (see Box 2.3, p. 47).

Geography developed as an academic discipline partly on the basis of a cosmographic philosophy that was developed to give coherence to the different activities of the geographical societies. Gradually, theoretical studies made an increasing contribution to the advancement of a specific geographical methodology. The chief emphasis remained, however, on geography as a science of **synthesis**, a science linking humanity and environment and creating a bridge between the social and natural sciences. Later parts of this book will show that **geographical synthesis** is not an easy task. Some even argue that it is impossible. We will, however, leave these critics for the time being, and present some of the synthesizing features that characterize geography.

A SCIENCE OF SYNTHESIS

As a student you will notice that geography has no obvious place in the traditional classification of the sciences by faculty. In Eastern Europe, geography is in general located in the faculty of natural sciences, in other countries you find geography in the faculty of social sciences or even arts. Only at some universities, like in Utrecht, the Netherlands, the problem is solved with a separate faculty for the 'geosciences'. Some parts of geography have their strongest affiliations with mathematics and natural sciences, others with history, philosophy and social sciences. Other sciences study distinctive types of phenomena: geologists study rocks, botanists plants, sociologists social groups, and so on. The work of geographers involves several types of phenomenon, each already studied by another science. Are geographers, therefore, 'jacks of all trades and masters of none'? Representatives from some other disciplines, such as the historian Peter Bowler (1992), maintains that geography is a classic example of a subject that can disappear as a separate discipline and be split up in its different specialities.

Geographers would argue that although the subject-matter is shared with other disciplines, it is treated in a different way for geographical purposes. Many maintain that the subject-matter of geography is exclusive; geographers alone study **places**.

To clarify this point we may look at the position of geography as seen by Hartshorne (1939) (Figure 1.1). The diagram shows that the specialized, systematic branches of geography, such as vegetation geography, climatology, geomorphology, economic geography and social geography, analyse phenomena that were closely connected to some systematic science. Hartshorne (ibid.) stated, however, that 'geography does not border on the systematic sciences, overlapping them in common parts on a common plane, but is on a trans-verse plane cutting through them'. For every systematic science there is a corresponding systematic branch in geography, but the perspectives and the questions asked are different. Geomorphology uses knowledge from geology, but the aim is to understand how the physical landscape we observe in a particular location has been shaped. The geographer studying climate is interested in how the average weather (climate) characterizes an area, not in the weather in the coming days, which is the task of the meteorologist. The **vegetation geography** focuses on the plant societies that form forests and grasslands, not the single plant species. Political geography is concerned with how forms of governments and power relations differ from country to country, from place to place, not on how decision-making functions. The economic geographer focuses on the mapping of and changes in the local-ization of economic activities, not on macroeconomic models for consump-tion growth, purchasing power, interest rates, inflation and wage levels. Social geographers are more interested in where the different social groups are living, in segregated neighbourhoods or mixed, than in social relation-ships. There are also clear relationships between the different branches of **systematic geography**. It is easy to see, for example, that the relationship between climate and soil type must have an important bearing on condi-tions for agricultural production and that the development of industry in an area may not be due only to economic factors but also to the natural resources of the area, its population potential and its historical and political development. Hartshorne (ibid.) concluded that the interaction of all these factors can primarily be studied within definite areas or regions, and argued that geography should cultivate its core, **regional geography**, 'as a safeguard against absorption by other sciences'. Regional geography is defined as the study of areas in their total composition or complexity. In most cases, regional geography would, however, focus on the relationship between humanity and

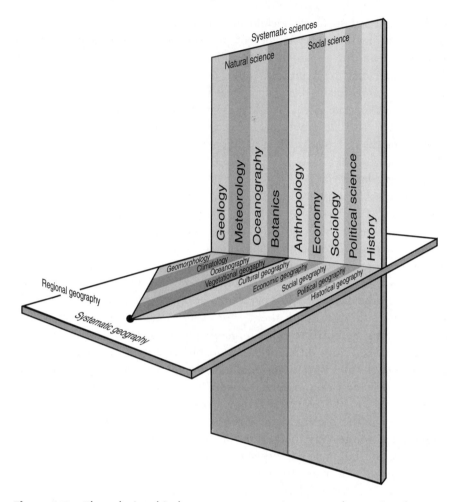

Figure 1.1 The relationship between systematic geography, regional geography and the systematic sciences

Source: Adapted from Richard Hartshorne's 'The nature of geography', 1939

its habitat, or another theme that makes an illuminating presentation of the region possible. Hartshorne made it quite clear that each region should not necessarily be studied in the same way. For any particular region at a particular time a special pattern is woven, linking a selection of systematic threads. A regional presentation then needs to find the special features that character-ize the area and seek the relevant systematic data that explain them. In the philosophical discussion in Box 1.2 on categories of basic reasoning in **regional geography** is related to **total–special reasoning** (the 'D' corner). Hartshorne's regional geography cannot, however, be placed at the top 'D' corner of the tetrahedron in Figure 1.2. The model, as are all models, is too simple. Regional geography is *inside* the tetrahedron, somewhat close to the top of 'D'. As it is impossible to cover everything in a region, the 'total-special' ideal cannot be reached.

Box 1.2	**Categories of basic reasoning, or arguments for a chorologic, regional approach**

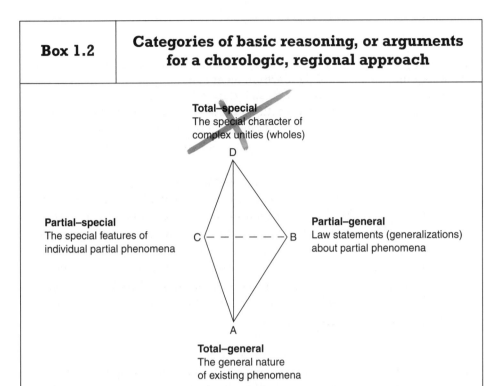

Total–special
The special character of
complex unities (wholes)

D

Partial–special
The special features of
individual partial phenomena

C

Partial–general
Law statements (generalizations)
about partial phenomena

B

A

Total–general
The general nature
of existing phenomena

Figure 1.2 The four categories of basic reasoning (after Schmithüsen, 1976). The use of the tetrahedron stresses that it is not necessary to choose only one of the four categories of basic reasoning. Most scientific reasoning involves more than one category

Joseph Schmithüsen, in his **Allgemeine Geosynergetik** (1976), attempts to establish a philosophical base for geography as a science, arguing that all scientific research is based upon four different categories of basic reasoning, which are characterized by the following pairs of concepts: total–general, partial–general, partial–special and total–special (Figure 1.2). **Total–general reasoning** implies a holistic understanding of objects with the intention of making general statements about them. The questions asked are about the nature or essence of the objectives of science. This is the type of reasoning undertaken by the philosophers of science.

Partial–general reasoning implies a study of the parts as such, with the ultimate aim of presenting general statements, such as laws in physics. Scientific reasoning in physics thus corresponds to B in Figure 1.2. **Partial–special reasoning** is concerned with the understanding of individual phenomena, such as 'why was Hadrian's Wall built across Britain?' This form of reasoning is also termed **idiographic**.

Total–special reasoning, on the other hand, tries to understand the complex features of particular unities, for example, landscapes or regions in geography. According to Schmithüsen (1976, p. 22), the methodological

(Continued)

(Continued)

peculiarity of geography is that it seeks to understand the complexities that exist together in a part of the earth in its spatial integration. This is, in his opinion, the basis of geography as an independent science. No other discipline concerns itself with the earth's surface and its spatial parts in their totality: with the association of phenomena in particular spaces or regions.

While there is some truth in the assessment that many geographers have lost their geographical identity to other subjects when working on specialized systematic themes, any fear of absorption by other disciplines seems rather strange today. We may instead stress the point made by Ackerman (1958, p. 3) that geography is 'a mother discipline' from which other specialized disciplines, like geodesy, meteorology, soil science, plant ecology and regional science, have emerged. Geography has become an outward-looking discipline that has frequently created new specializations. This multidisciplinary perspective may be regarded both as our *raison d'être* and our life-raft in the sea of knowledge (Capelle, 1979, p. 65). If the periphery seems interesting, why not explore it; this will only widen the 'circle of geography'.

The systematic branches of geography are breaking much new ground. Admittedly, useful knowledge from other disciplines can be fitted to the procedures used in geography, but no other specific procedures are designed or followed in order to reveal the intricacies of spatial relations. Economic geographers are, for instance, concerned with structural changes in the **localization** of industries and the **spatial factors** that may explain these changes, while economists are generally less interested in spatial factors and distributions, preferring to concentrate on the factors which determine economic development on the national scale. Recently, some of world's leading economists have, however, acknowledged the value of contributions from economic geographers. *Journal of Economic Geography*, which was founded in 2001, has become an exciting meeting-place for new research contributions from both geographers and economists. The research in the borderland between the two disciplines has had great impact on the understanding of global processes in trade and industry, and has also to a large extent influenced planning and urban policies. These must be regarded as fruits of geographical thinking, although many inputs come via economy and regional science. A good reference is Peter Dicken's *Global Shift* (1986, 5th edn, 2007), now regarded as one of the classics in human geography. As economy has become increasingly globalized, the value of a geographical perspective is becoming more crucial.

In principle, there is a difference between social geography and sociology, but particularly within the field of urban studies, with a focus on social exclusion, urban deprivation and housing, cross-disciplinary cooperation has become more and more important. New international projects involving geographers, sociologists and planners have been given priority, for instance in the NEHOM (Neighbourhood Housing Models) project which I coordinated for the European

Union in 2000–04 (Holt-Jensen et al., 2004). Geographers have also been invited as coauthors in leading textbooks in urban sociology (Savage et al., 2003). Among sociologists, it has been noted that the leading British sociologist Anthony Giddens (1984) has acknowledged the inspiration he has received from geographical theory on space and place.

We may note that there are even differences between botanists specializing in plant distribution and geographers interested in vegetation. In most cases, geographers will concentrate on vegetation types and their distribution, carrying their relevance to human geography somewhere at the back of their mind. Botanists, on the other hand, are more interested in the distribution of single plant species or grouping of species; vegetation as part of the landscape picture and its importance to humanity recede into the background; rare and inconspicuous flowers are often of greater interest to them than common and landscape-forming trees. But research within the protection and maintenance of cultural landscapes has created very fruitful cross-disciplinary projects and cooperation. Botanists have come to realize the value of the broad geographical focus on human behaviour and its impact on the living landscape. So maybe Hartshorne's model of the transverse planes needs some revision; two planes may indicate that we are living in separate academic worlds. In any case, the crucial message is that the geographical perspective is increasingly becoming more important and recognized by the systematic disciplines. As noted by Bonnett (2008, p. 4), this is due to two interconnected themes which are in the main media focus: environmental (for instance **global warming**) and international (as **economic** and **cultural globalization**) change. These are themes clearly associated with geographical knowledge.

We now proceed to look at a couple of the basic approaches to geographic study that have been at the forefront of discussion in the last fifty years.

A model-oriented approach

Geography exists to study variations in phenomena from place to place, and its value as an academic discipline depends on the extent to which it can clarify the spatial relations and processes that might explain the features of an area or a place. Geographical curiosity starts with the question, 'Why is it like this here?' Peter Haggett (1972, 2001) illustrates an approach to geographical inquiry by discussing the starting points of different scientists who might all be studying the same beach full of people bathing and sunning themselves (see Box 1.3). The geologist would be interested in the sand particles and the zoologist in the marine life along the shore. The sociologist might study the behaviour of the groups using the beach and the economist might well be concerned with the marginal costs of the different ice-cream sellers. For a geographer, one interesting field of inquiry would be to study the variations in population density on the different parts of the beach by mapping the location of each person. The geographer would find it difficult to work on the ground and might want a general oversight, perhaps using a helicopter to cover the situation by taking aerial photographs.

Box 1.3	On the beach – a spatial science approach

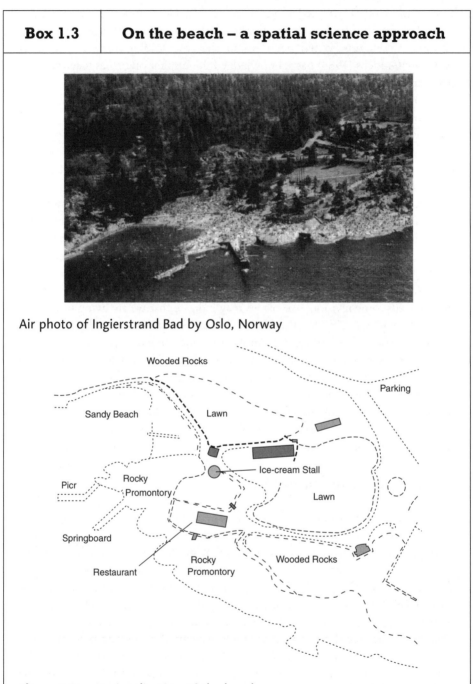

Air photo of Ingierstrand Bad by Oslo, Norway

Figure 1.3a Regionalization of the beach

Air photographs make good starting points for geographers. A sequence of air photographs can show population densities at different times of the day. The study area can be reduced to a scale that is easy to work with later. While many scientists like to enlarge objects in order to study them,

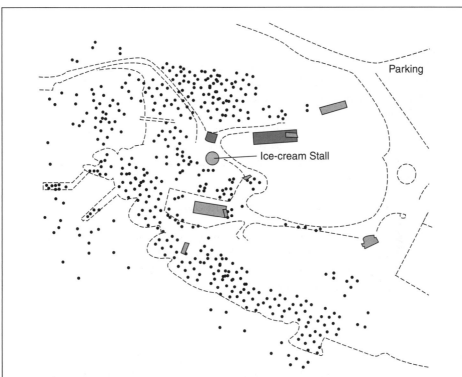

Parking

Ice-cream Stall

Figure 1.3b   Map of the beach. Each dot represents the location of a person when the air photo was taken

geographers often prefer to reduce the scale of complex phenomena through maps and photographs. Figure 1.3 shows a bathing beach in Norway on a fine summer's day. Haggett (1972) used a beach on Cape Cod, USA, as an example in his book, but added in later editions (2001) also photos from a Norwegian Beach (Sjøsanden, Mandal), a Chinese beach and historical maps of the changing beach at Orford Ness, UK. Our photo and maps are from Ingierstrand Bad close to the Norwegian capital Oslo. The **natural landscape** here consists of a small sandy beach with rocky promontories: grass fields and woodlands around. We can also see it as a **cultural landscape** with many physical objects created by humans: roads, restaurants, a springboard and a pier, and we see people in the sea and sunbathing, queuing up at the ice-cream stalls and walking around.

The first reaction of geographers would presumably be to map accurately the exact location of each activity and map the changing population density during the day. At the second stage, geographers would try to systematize what they observed on the photographs or maps into some sort of geographical pattern, for instance, by dividing the beach into zones of different population density. The third task would be to explain how the geographical pattern of density distributions came about. That explanation would consider a range of distinctive factors, including natural factors like exposure to

(Continued)

(Continued)

sunshine and shelter provided by the topography, as well as cultural factors, such as the distance from restaurants, car parks and toilets. A crucial factor would be the *process of change*; each picture of the 'settlement pattern' on the beach would depend on what time of the day the photo was taken.

The beach is, of course, a microcosm; geographers usually work with larger areas, analysing population densities by counties or the distribution of agricultural land across the world. However, studies of large areas are basically similar to those used to study the beach. The analysis of geographical patterns requires:

1 an understanding of maps, projections and scales and of how maps are made;
2 knowledge of the statistical methods available to sort out those factors which might explain the patterns observed; and
3 an appreciation of the techniques which might elucidate the dynamics of changing geographical patterns.

Source: Based on Haggett, 1972, 2001

This example illustrates a working sequence in geographical research generally related to the **spatial science** school and the concept of **relative space** (see pp. 30–1, 116–18): *localization → geographical pattern → explanation*. We start to locate spatial phenomena and use different mapping methods to discover specific geographical patterns, which we set out to explain. Because geographical patterns in general change through time, an understanding of the processes of change is crucial to the explanation of a specific geographical pattern. This working sequence is still rewarding as an educational device, but other models for research work have become more prominent.

Local responses to global processes: deviations from the models in focus

Today a geographical research project often starts with the presentation of a social or natural process which seems to be related to geographical factors or have spatial relevance. Examples would be changing patterns of manufacturing or changing extensions of glaciers. Analysing and perhaps focusing on general trends of change, we may find that there are geographical differences in the patterns of change. While the ice caps of Antarctica and the North Pole are diminishing, the glaciers in Norway may at the same time be increasing. While textile mills have been closed down all over Britain, there are still some pockets where the industry thrives in this country. How can we explain such geographical differences? To what extent do local factors matter in global processes of change? As exemplified in Box 1.4, we are here making use of the following work sequence: *process → variations of geographical change → explanation*.

Box 1.4	**Pit and place: reflections on the geographical patterns of the miners' strike of 1984–85**

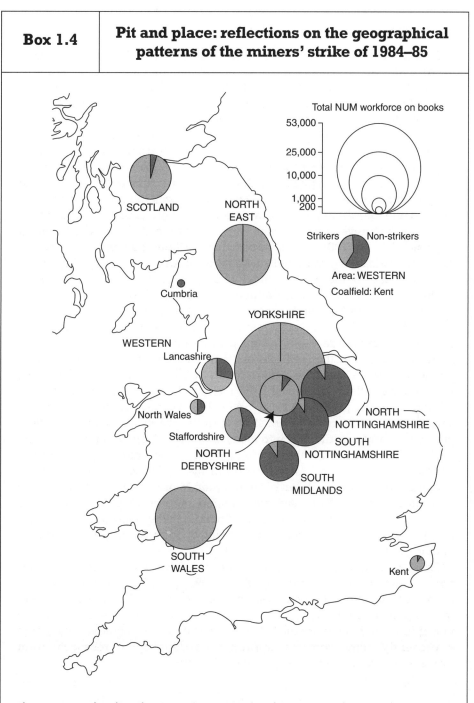

Figure 1.4 The distribution of support for the NUM strike in September 1984

Source: Duncan and Goodwin, 1988, p. 50; Johnston, 1991

(Continued)

(Continued)

In March 1984 the National Union of Mineworkers (NUM) called its workers to strike as a protest against the government plan for extensive pit closures. The strike lasted till March 1985, at which time the strikers went back to work, although no settlement was reached. The strike was a very important symbolic fight between the union and the Conservative government, a fact that should support full solidarity between the miners. In addition, coal mines are generally located outside the main industrial conurbations with strong bonds between workplace, home and social life: a society very much based on solidarity. Emphasis on the crucial importance of the pit for the local community, its economic and social life, was the main argument in the strike leaders' campaign. What interests us here is that, in spite of this, there was an uneven geographical support for the strike. In some mining regions, NUM got 100 per cent support throughout the year-long dispute; in others, the backing was small and coal continued to be mined. Figure 1.4 gives a picture of the geographical variability of the participation in the strike at one date – approximately halfway through its duration. Willingness to strike could to some extent be related to regional variations in the prospects of pit closures: South Yorkshire, north Nottinghamshire and north Derbyshire recorded surpluses and had good prospects for future working. But the 'self-interest' explanation fails as the strike had strong support in Yorkshire though not in Nottinghamshire. So the pattern must rather reflect long-established cultural differences between the mining districts. Johnston (1991, pp. 121–3) points out that the special system of subcontracting established in Nottinghamshire, at an early date, created a workforce divided into many small, relatively independent units each with its own wage rate – creating no miner solidarity of the type developed in Yorkshire. An 'aftermath of the strike was the formation in Nottinghamshire of the Union of Democratic Miners (UDM), which was not federated with the NUM and was denied membership of both Trades Union Congress and the Labour Party. Turning to the *politics of the community,* the Dukeries [in north Nottinghamshire] again stands out as atypical among British coalfields' (ibid., p. 129).

This example illustrates that local, geographically contingent determinants matter or, in the words of Peet (1998, p. 135), 'that the historical dynamics of socio-economic systems can be comprehended only in the geographical context because spatially specific circumstances limit the possibilities of human actions'. At the same time, the example elucidates a presently more common approach in geographic research: from processes in space to geographical explanation.

AN ORGANIZATIONAL PLAN OF GEOGRAPHY

The number of branches of systematic geography could be argued indefinitely. Earlier accounts even included 'mathematical geography', which has long been regarded as part of astronomy. Uhlig (1971, p. 15) limits the field of

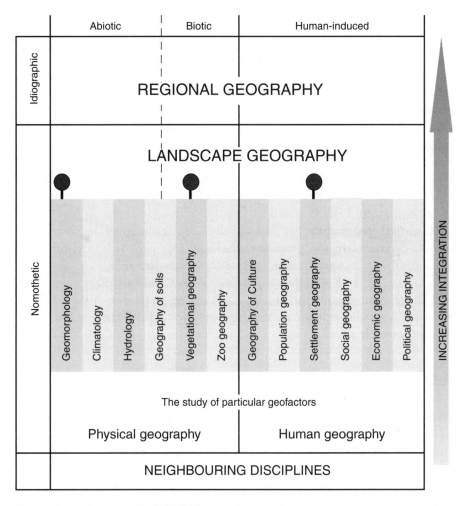

Figure 1.5 An organizational plan of geography

Sources: Uhlig, 1971; Weichhart, 1975

Note: Landscape geography is also known as Landschaftkunde

geographical inquiry to five aspects of the physical environment and five aspects of human life (Figure 1.5). Uhlig uses the term **social geography** in the German sense of integrative human geography rather than in the Anglo-American usage as a specialized branch of human geography. Of more significance is Uhlig's location of **landscape geography** at a higher level of integration than the systematic branches. In the German geographical tradition, landscape geography (***Landschaftskunde***) forms a transition or bridge between systematic geography and regional geography (***Länderkunde***), which is the most complex form of geographical integration. The landscape is seen as the product of the interaction of **geofactors** and only such features as are repetitive and appear in accordance with certain rules or laws are taken into account. The landscape concept represents an integration of human and physical geography that considers elements and properties (or characteristics) which form landscape types (Weichhart, 1975, p. 9). The aim of **landscape geography** is therefore to present and explain a typology of landscapes which most often focus on three aspects in the landscape: geomorphological landform features, vegetation cover and settlement patterns (marked with 'bulletpoints' on Figure 1.5). Regional geography, on the other hand, seeks to give a total, integrated presentation of a specific area. Whereas landscape geography is concerned with the **nomothetic** (law-based) aspects of a certain area, the real research interest of regional geography lies in those aspects that make a region specific. Such **singular** aspects that have arisen in the course of history are the results of individual decisions through time and mould each region in a way peculiar to itself (ibid., p. 16).

Regional geography has traditionally been regarded as the core of the subject. **Systematic geography** is then the area in which scientific laws are formulated and regional geography becomes the field in which such laws are tested, and which also provides a **synthesis** of the physical and human phenomena within an area or region (Hettner, 1927). It has, however, been difficult for regional geography to fulfil these roles in the field of research.

A NEW SYNTHESIS?

Haggett (1972/1983, 2001) has tried to develop a new form of synthesis which diverges from the traditional division of the subject (Figure 1.6). He emphasizes that the historical divisions are important if only because universities still often use them as a basis for their courses. But it is more valuable, he thinks, to divide the subject up in relation to the way in which it analyses its problems. His three main groups are defined as follows:

1) *Spatial analysis* concerns itself with the variations in the localization and distribution of a significant phenomenon or group of phenomena; for instance, the analysis of variations in population density or poverty in rural areas. Which factors control the distribution pattern? Which processes led to this pattern? How can these patterns be modified so that the distribution becomes more effective or just?

2) *Ecological analysis* concerns itself with the study of connections between human and environmental variables. In this type of analysis we are studying the relations within particular bounded geographical spaces, rather than the spatial variations between regions.

3) **Regional complex analysis** combines the results of spatial and ecological analysis. Appropriate regional units are identified by areal differentiations. Connecting lines and flows between the individual regions may then be observed.

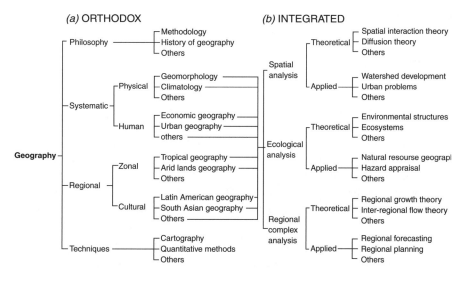

Figure 1.6 The internal structure of geography

Source: From Haggett, 1972/1983, p. 764

The advantage, maintains Haggett (2001, p. 765), 'of looking at geographic problems in terms of these three approaches rather than the orthodox divisions is that they stress the unity of physical and non-physical elements rather than their separation'.

Weichhart (1980) has also attempted to provide a better organizational plan for the discipline in order to promote geographical synthesis. He refutes the notion that 'geography as human ecology' or ecological analysis can form a leading concept for the whole of geography. Questions relating to humanity and its environment can only be a part of the research field – but need to become a more important part. Returning to Uhlig's (1971) organizational plan (Figure 1.5), Weichhart (1975) classifies the **geofactors** that are the important elements of the **geosphere** into three groups: abiotic, biotic and human–induced. **Abiotic** factors are geology, soil, climatic features, ocean currents, etc.; **biotic** factors include vegetation, animal life and humans as biological creatures; and human–induced factors are settlement, transportation, industry, social structures, etc. Weichhart (1975, p. 99) envisaged three groups of complex system relations for geographical analyses:

- It is possible to study the system relations between all or a number of the abiotic or biotic geofactors – geography as a physical geographical synthesis. The leading threads might include a nomothetic-orientated typology of natural landscapes or a process-orientated description of the evolution of the landscapes in a certain region.

- On the human side, we may study the system relations between all or a number of the human-induced factors.

- The catalogue of relevant problems would, however, be incomplete without consideration of the interrelations between abiotic, biotic and human-induced factors which constitute the human-environment system. Weichhart (1975, p. 98) makes the point that this does not imply that the totality of geofactors is brought into consideration. Geographical research has shown that the abiotic and biotic parameters needed to describe and explain the patterns of physical nature or human geography are not identical to those needed to explain and describe the complex of relations between humanity and nature. Relief structures recede into the background; soil, vegetation and hydrological features become more important. Among human-induced factors, there are also some that may have less significance for the relations between humanity and nature. The study of humanity–environment relations is therefore not the same as a total synthesis of all the geofactors.

This understanding of geographical research is exemplified in Box 1.5, in which focus is on specific geographical investigations within each of the three groups of study.

Box 1.5	Simplified examples of analysis models of geographical synthesis within physical geography, ecogeography and human geography

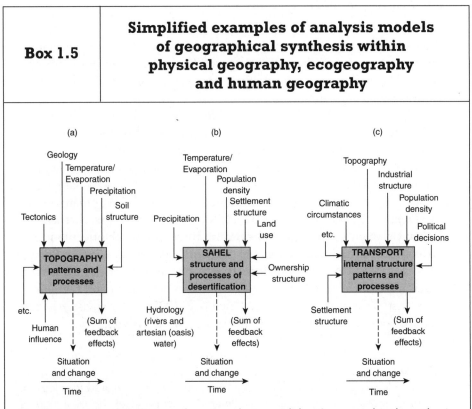

Figure 1.7 Simplified examples of analysis models of geographical synthesis within physical geography, ecogeography and human geography

Source: Leser, 1980, pp. 68–9

Figure 1.7 illustrates some of the factors that have to be taken into account in the geographical study of the three concrete research themes:

(a) The study of the topography of the Grampian Mountains, Scotland, in **physical geography** has to build on a syntheses of different natural factors and processes, but human influence can also be of great importance. The topography of the Scottish Highlands are not so easily changed by human action, whereas the topography of the sandy shores on the Danish west coast (see p. 203) is to a large extent dependent on human actions. And where there are heavy precipitations in the form of rain and snow the landforming processes are different from where there are deserts. Shifts in temperatures between freezing and melting have great influence on the denudation/erosion in the Grampians, whereas in deserts high evaporation may result in rivers drying up and losing their dredging and transport capacity. The local geology, the occurrence of hard and soft rocks, influences the results of erosion, while new landforms are created by volcanic activities and faulting of the continental blocks (**tectonics**). The landforms in an area as we see them today represent the results of a sum of factors and processes which may be different from place to place. A study of landforms is based on a synthesis focusing *mainly* on the natural factors.

(b) The study of desert structure and **desertification** processes, for instance in the Sahara region (SAHEL) in Africa, in **ecogeography** will have to focus on a mix of natural and human influences (see Figure 3.6, p. 96). Global warming created by human activities as well as natural climatic processes have to be taken into account. Land ownership structures, population development and agricultural practices are other factors that have to be considered. Some natural factors, such as geology, may have less impact, while social practices are of much greater importance than in the study of landforms. Here focus has to be on a man–land synthesis.

(c) A study of transport patterns and processes in **human geography** calls for a focus mainly on human-induced factors. But we also have to consider natural conditions. In Norway we definitely know that topography and climate are crucial factors for the road and rail connections, particularly in winter, crossing the mountains. How dense a network is needed depends on the population density, the industrial activity and the ability to cover the costs of transport. Political decisions are also very important, for instance when it comes to the development of main roads. So here we see a synthesis of politics, power, settlement and industrial structures as well as considerations of natural conditions.

(Continued)

(Continued)

In all three fields of research both human and physical geographic factors have to be considered, but to different degrees. In ecogeography the integrative task is crucial, but we should note that this does not mean we will need to integrate all the human and physical factors that are included in either purer physical and human geographical research.

Weichhart's organizational plan provides a useful framework for the applied research projects that are of growing importance in geography. Many German departments use the threefold division to provide a framework for degree courses in geography.

More fundamental than the suggestions for new organisational structures for the discipline is, however, a basic, philosophical underpinning of geography as a science that has been presented by Robert David Sack in his book *Homo Geographicus* (1997).

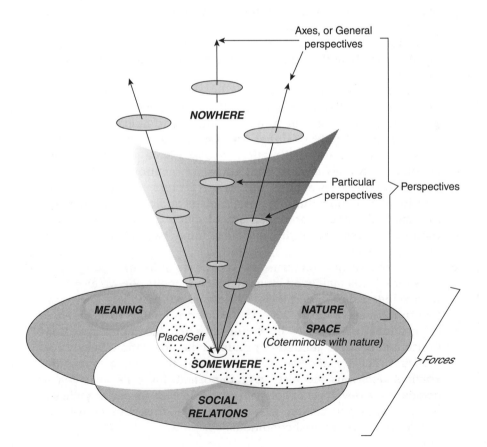

Figure 1.8 The relational geographical framework

Source: Sack, 1992, improved by Sack, 1999

HOMO GEOGRAPHICUS

What does it mean to be 'a geographical human being'? Is it something that is reserved for the specially educated geographers? No, Sack's message is that every one of us are *homo geographicus*, that our geographical relations are intrinsic parts of our life projects. This can be linked to **existentialism** and Heidegger's philosophy (see Box 1.7). To enter these philosophical discussions we need briefly to consider the basic geographical terms **place**, **space**, **territoriality** and **globalization**.

All human actions involve space and place. The world is full of *places*, from mountain tops and forests to towns, streets and houses. When we travel fast in a car or by train and only briefly observe the places passing by, we conceptually recognize it as travel through *space*. Distances recognized as kilometres, travel time or as psychologically felt distance become more important than the places we pass by. We may also recognize during our travel in space that in the modern world many differences from place to place are disappearing. Globalization leads to 'McDonaldization' (Ritzer, 2007), with the same architectural style all over the world. Globalization makes places look more alike. Some call this 'placelessness' (Relph, 1976). On the other hand, we experience in the contemporary world a counter-current of **postmodernism** which aims at preserving or creating places of special meaning. This includes, on the one hand, architects like Christian Norberg-Schultz (1984), who argues that physical planners needs to take care of **'genius loci'**, the spirit of place, which is conveyed to us in the old towns of Praha and Jerusalem, but is absent in new suburban housing estates. On the other hand, it includes social scientists like Pierre Bourdieu, who in a number of books attacked neo-liberal modernism and through the concept **'habitus'** defined conditions for a social sense of place (see Hillier and Rooksby, 2005). As increasingly more and more millions of people today see international travel and awareness as normal parts of ordinary living the place-specific becomes much more interesting than the placeless features of modernity.

And in these geographical expeditions of ours, place becomes much more than the visible – the buildings and landscapes we see. Places are to a great extent the social constructions we form in our heads and that are created through our social relations in places. A pub is a physical place which can have pleasant interior furnishings in an old building, but it is of interest only if it is the place where we meet our friends. A place can also have *meaning* for you if you experienced something special there, for instance if it was where you met your boyfriend or girlfriend for the first time. So if we link 'genius loci' and 'habitus' we see that we have to understand place as something combining physical nature (which also includes houses and streets), social relations and meaning. These are three basic concepts in Sack's figure (Figure 1.8). Before returning to the concepts 'nowhere' and 'somewhere', we have also to consider the concept **territoriality**.

An agricultural field is a place, but it acquires meaning as an area that needs ploughing, weeding, sowing and harvesting to produce what the farmer has decided for it. When using the power of decision in this way, we create territories. This is the equivalent of using geographical power. Territoriality creates places designated for specific functions, and thus places of distinct meaning as living-room, home, school. We all need territories we feel we can control. A child, growing up, will try to push the boundaries, but perceptions of 'safe' and 'unsafe' areas are always there to set limits. As adults we may have developed such self-confidence and so strong a personality that we dare to move almost anywhere. But this depends on what kind of person you are, your gender, physical strength, social status, age, ethnicity, education, and so on. Territorial safety also depends on whether you are an 'outsider' or an 'insider' in a place, and a command of international and local languages is a good asset (Box 1.6 gives a concrete example).

| **Box 1.6** | **Territories of a Sri Lankan tourist resort** |

A tourist hotel sited between palm trees on a sandy beach in a Third World country seems a 'Shangri-La' of wealth and affluence in a world of general poverty. Such a place attracts beggars, fortune-tellers, taxi drivers and youngsters selling T-shirts – all in the hope of earning big money. The hotel wants to protect its guests from these 'fortune-seekers', partly because it does not want competition on the territory reserved for the hotel shops. So the hotel's territory is guarded as a place only for the guests, hotel employees and entertainers who have been invited in by the manager. Even the native bus-drivers who transport the tourists from hotel to hotel have to sleep in poor accommodation in a part of the building that does not allow them access to the hotel's facilities. Between the palms, guards are posted to keep the beggars out, while inside fat middle-aged Europeans are served drinks at their beach chairs.

The hotel is a pleasant oasis but, at the same time, a tourist 'ghetto' – the guests do not dare break out. When they do so, on foot through the main entrance, they are at once offered taxis and guided tours and have to break through a phalanx of other offers and appeals for help. If the tourist manages to refuse all these requests and walks a couple of hundred metres from the hotel, he or she will find him- or herself in another territory. Here there might be a small child or two asking for a 'pen' but, principally, the tourist will be left to look around, to sit undisturbed on a bench or to walk around the marketplace.

The ring of fortune-seekers around the hotel is also a territory, and this might be divided up into smaller territories. Each beggar (or family group) has carved out a definite small territory of his or her own. There might be competition over boundaries and zones of ambiguity, but the beggars, pimps and prostitutes have territories of action they try to control. Only those with a great deal of self-confidence and strong personalities can afford not to bother about these territories and to trespass anywhere.

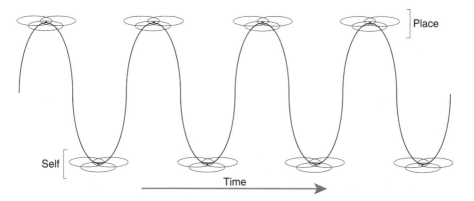

Figure 1.9   The dialectical relations between 'self' and place through time. From birth our 'self' is influenced by the place in which we grow up. Gradually we also make some influence, particularly on the social relations, in the places we move to. And new experiences from places we later in life live in or visit influences our 'self'.

Source: Adapted from Sack, 1997, p. 132

Our experience of territoriality, our ability to control the territory around us, is an important part of what we call our **relational space** – the understanding and feeling of spatial relations which we carry in our mind and on which our actions are based. The concepts place, space and territoriality are key concepts in geography, but also basic elements in any human's life.

You can possibly agree that place consists of 'nature' or physical surroundings, the social contacts we have there and the meaning the particular place have for us. Figure 1.8 from Sack's book *Homo Geographicus* (1997) shows this, but also that place and 'self' are closely related. The growth of our own 'self', our identity, builds on our relations to the realms of 'nature', 'social relations' and 'meaning' connected to places. All the time we must relate to the physical world, to existing things which we use and to distances between things. Our social relations take place and lead on to social influence and the establishment of territories, at least in our own room or home. The realm of meaning is connected with symbols, for instance 'roots' that connects us to places through our lives. A place means something because we relate special events to it. Place then constitutes and integrates forces from the **realms** of nature, meaning and social relations. Sack points out that, in addition to these three, it is possible to talk of a fourth realm, the realm of **agency**. This is based on the claim that the forces from the other realms are not determinate; we have power to choose for ourselves, we have 'free will'. This realm, however, is not included in Figure 1.8 as it cannot be seen separately from the other three.

The structural similarities between place and 'self' are based on the fact that both are weaving together elements of nature, meaning and social relations (see Figure 1.9).

We have a physical body, we are dependent on social relations with others and we need to find meaning in our life. This mix of physical nature, social relations and meaning is understood primarily because it involves activities in place and space. Place becomes an active agent in the forming of our 'self'. There is a reciprocal (or dialectic) relation between 'self' and place. We start our life as children in a parent's home and a hometown which influences the formation of our 'self' in the first instance. But then we may move to another place to study or we start travelling in the world. We have our 'roots', but the development of our 'self' is influenced through new experiences in new places. To some extent we also influence the places we come to, particularly the social life around us, friends and lovers, definitely the 'meaning' of others and sometimes even the physical structures. If we become farmers, housebuilders or politicians this is definitely the case.

If you accept this argument, you also have to accept that place as a focus in life and research is basic and necessary; we cannot understand human life and activity without a conscious relation to places, their physical properties, social activities and interpreted meaning (a deeper philosophical basis is presented in Box 1.7).

Box 1.7	**Existentialism, Heidegger and 'being' in the world**

Basically, many scientists see **existentialism** as 'anti-intellectual philosophy on the grounds that one of its central tenets holds that reality and existence can only be experienced through living and cannot therefore be made the object of thought' (Walmsley and Lewis, 1993, p. 117). On the other hand, existentialism – particularly through the philosophy of Martin Heidegger (1889–1976) – is crucial for an understanding of relational space as presented by Sack (1997). The central concept in Heidegger's philosophy is **Dasein** (i.e. 'being here'), a German word meaning a human subject's existential 'being' in the world. As human beings, we are, on the one hand, interwoven with the environment and processes that make up the world and, on the other, we 'step out of this unity to observe, experience, reflect on and choose between possible ways of being in the world. This duality means that everyone is, to varying degrees, estranged, alienated from the world. A schizophrenic seems to live in a deep existential fear that alienates him or her from a meaningful being in the world. We are all located on a scale between 'being' and 'not-being' in the world. The human struggle against estrangement is essentially connected to our existence in space/place (being) and time (becoming). Every human tries to eliminate detachment through the creation of meaning in places of 'being' in the world and through a meaningful future life of 'becoming'.

The world is a structure of meaningful relations in which the individual exists and which he or she partly creates. Heidegger distinguishes between three aspects of the world: the physical, the social and the subjective. We can link these three aspects to the realms of nature, social relations and meaning in Sack's figure (Figure 1.8). As human beings, we are 'thrown' into the physical world or realm of nature with the conditions set by the place we live in and the material conditions that set frames for our future. An important part of 'being' in the world relates to how we manage to cope with these conditions.

Another crucial part of being is our relations to, and dependencies on, other human beings. Basically, however, we are all alone: no one else can live my life or die my death, so to be in the world we need a subjective meaning for our existence.

As place and space are intrinsic parts of our being in the world, our individual **relational space** is the basis for our actions. If we are to understand how this relational space influences humanity's being and becoming in the world, we need to encounter people and situations in an open, intersubjective manner.

In intellectual life – in the scientific division of labour – the realm of nature, the social realm and the realm of meaning are, however, separated, somehow creating an intellectual deadlock. Most scientists analyse primarily phenomena within one of the three realms while phenomena or influences from the other two are seen as 'background facts' or are simply overlooked. Most natural science research does not consider human behaviour. Natural science and medicine normally focus on physical processes. When the focus is on humans they are rather seen as part of nature and are exposed to its forces. A medical examination finds out whether you are sick or not through blood tests and other physical indicators, while sickness *can* be related to your personality and your social situation.

Research within sociology and political science are generally not concerned with nature and have less room for humanistic interpretation. Social scientists may maintain that our social relations guide our thoughts and our organisation in the physical world and that our physical environment is socially constructed. Often it is maintained that social relations also guide 'meaning' as our ideas, values and belief are formed by our social roles. 'Tell me who you associate with, and I will tell you who you are and how you think!' The assertation that social relations guide our opinions also concern the meaning we ascribe to nature, including the **metaphors** (conceptions) we use to define nature as something separate from humans and our scientific models and theories about the natural realm.

Researchers working with intellectual history or literary interpretation focus to a small degree on social relations and the physical world. Humanists may maintain that social relations and nature concern our interpretation of the interplay between signs and symbols and that meaning and ideas motivate our actions. The world and the self are therefore mentally, not socially constructed. Research within social science, natural science and humanities will generally assume that the chosen realm is the most important and superior to the other. Natural scientific, social scientific and humanistic research provide three different perspectives and basic interpretations of the world, but none give the whole and full 'truth'. Here, maintains Sack (1997, p. 15), the concepts of space and place are essential categories that incorporate all the realms. The geographic approach and understanding of place and 'self' bind the different perspectives and geography together as a science of synthesis, and thus have a crucial role in academia as well as for man in general.

The cone in Figure 1.8 (starting in 'somewhere' and extending out to 'nowhere') is intended to indicate two things:

1) 'Somewhere' (indicating **insidedness**) and 'nowhere' (indicating **outsidedness**) are limiting cases and are never in themselves completely attainable. 'Somewhere' is the personal perspective of the 'ego', whereas various degrees of public, abstract or objective 'outside' perspectives are located further up the cone.

2) There are many paths from 'somewhere' to 'nowhere', even though they are interrelated. The lenses in the cone represent such different paths or perspectives. A religious, moral lens may, for instance, be located rather close to 'somewhere'. A scientific, abstract lens closer to 'nowhere' could draw attention to place as a location in space, whereas a less abstract lens further down on the same axis could be analysing a personal sense of place (ibid., p. 18). Throughout the history of geography, most approaches have been close to 'nowhere'.

The discussion on concepts as 'nowhere' and 'somewhere' are directly related to the methods we use in scientific investigations, **quantitative** versus **qualitative methods** and to the discussion between **spatial science** and humanistic geography which will be presented later in this book. Based on the discussion above we will, however, now conclude this chapter with some inputs in a discourse that is as old as the discipline: should geography narrow its field of investigation to make us less 'a jack of all trades' or is the broad pluralism of geography the main asset of the scientific discipline? Note: our aim is *not* to give a 'blueprint answer' to this important question; rather, throughout the book the aim is to stimulate discussion by juxtaposing opinions!

SPECIALIZATION AND PLURALISM

The broad field of inquiry traditionally attributed to geography requires that research workers in the subject deploy a wide variety of skills. It also requires that research workers recruited to the discipline have experience in mathematics, statistics, biology and geology, as well as in history, sociology and economics. As no one individual can hope to cover more than a couple of these fields, it has been necessary to build up a staff of specialists in each of the branches of geography so that the whole discipline can be presented to students. The adage that 'geographers specialize in not being specialists' in no way applies to the staff of university geography departments. Research workers must specialize in order to create something worthwhile. In the normal course of events, an individual will work in a field that interests him or her and in which he or she has a fair amount of background knowledge. As an individual's specialization develops, he or she will resent the imposition of any kind of **paradigm**, understood as a framework for what the geographer should investigate and what methods should be used.

James Bird (1979, p. 118) observes that there 'certainly are basic strains within geography, and if one paradigm is plastered across the subject, it will soon be broken by the disjunctions below'. It is, he believes, a hopeful sign at present that the idea of a ruling paradigm (which is similar in effect to an imposed orthodoxy) has been more or less discarded. Alternative schools of thought coexist, and this diversity is a good thing because it offers understanding with wider dimensions.

Gerhard Hard (1973, p. 237) suggests that, with our increasing awareness of the multitude of scientific traditions that are pursued within the framework of geography, we might begin to doubt the extent to which there has ever been a single former geographic discipline. The *history of geography* is the focus of this book; the following chapters will both try to present a cumulative story as well as discuss whether we can identify paradigms and substantial changes within the discipline. We also need to take into consideration that our perspective on a discipline's history is always more or less influenced by the norms and outlook of the present generation. We see history in the terms of the present. Whether we emphasize the continuity and gradual growth of a science or dwell on its discontinuities and changes, we tacitly assume a single line of progression to our present situation. Perhaps we should stress geography's heterogeneity – its many-faceted and rich traditions?

In an argument on the traditional German understanding of regional geography, Hard (1973) posed the following question: are real geographers only those who integrate all the branches of the discipline into their research? If so, he maintained, there are very few 'real geographers'. Hard uses Venn diagrams to develop his argument (Figure 1.10). His first example, though simple, is not totally unrealistic. The term 'real geographer' may here only be applied to those who are committed to (a) geomorphology or (b) cultural landscape morphology, or both (shaded in Figure 1.10 (I)). If, however, synthesis is the sole aim of geography, a 'real geographer' must study both the physical and the cultural morphology of the landscape to qualify (Figure 1.10 (II)). If we consider the research themes actually pursued by self-styled geographers, the figure expands (Figure 1.10 (III)) to include climatologists, geomorphologists, biogeographers, ecogeographers and landscape geographers of different sorts, as well as economic geographers, location theorists, behavioural geographers, and so on. It is too restrictive (Figure 1.10 (IV)) to include among the 'real geographers' only those ecogeographers who are attempting a synthesis of natural and human factors.

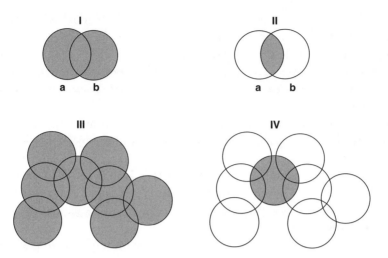

Figure 1.10   Different definitions of a 'geographer' (shaded). The circles symbolize closely connected research themes: (a) geomorphologists; (b) landscape morphologists; I–IV are explained in the text

Source: Adapted from Hard, 1973, p. 235

Hartshorne (1939, pp. 243–5) described geography as an 'integrative' discipline, but that is not the same as regarding it as an 'integrated' discipline. There is an integrative task to transmit impulses from branch to branch within the structure, but there is no need to withdraw from the periphery. We may still postulate a core or nerve centre, but to regard regional geography as this core is no longer helpful. The core in **spatial science** terms was defined by Ackerman (1963, p. 433) as 'thinking geographically':

> To structure the mind in terms of spatial distributions and their correlations is a most important tool for anyone following our discipline. The more the better. If there is any really meaningful distinction among scientists, it is this mental structuring. The mental substrates for inspiration differ, however, from field to field within the discipline.

The observable spatial structures need to be in focus, but we need to proceed below the surface appearance of spatial distributions and analyse processes and actions that lead to events in space and place. Our concern will be to analyse processes and how they are linked to both structural necessities and local, place-bound factors. We will be interested in how our relational space is formed in our everyday life. Both Sack's presentation of *Homo geographicus* (1997) and Jones's (1988) approach to the study of the cultural landscape, as presented in Box 1.8, may help to illustrate this.

Box 1.8	The cultural landscape – functional, intentional and structural modes of explanation

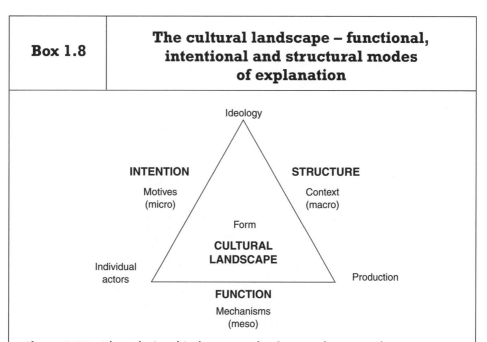

Figure 1.11 The relationship between the factors that contribute to an explanation of the cultural landscape

Source: Jones, 1988

Geography is a field-study discipline that has a keen interest in the relations between humanity and nature as these may be studied in the everyday cultural landscapes that surround us. One focus of investigation (promoted by, among others, Carl Sauer – see Box 2.10) has been the study of changes in the cultural landscape, in land tenure, land use, building culture and settlement form (that is, very much a focus on physical changes and their explanation).

However, Jones (1988, p. 203) points out that in such a study we need three modes of explanation: functional, structural and intentional (see Figure 1.11) to explain the form and patterns of the cultural landscape. This can be represented as a triangle in which the three sides represent the three modes of explanation and the associated geographical scales (micro, meso and macro). At the corners are phenomena which appear to provide a link between them: the individual actor as the link between intention and function; production as the link between function and structure; and ideology as the link between structure and intention.

As an example of this we might consider a study of a farming landscape, with all its infields and outfields, forests and farm buildings. The *functional* mode of explanation focuses on the landscape's functions in human terms. This is more or less a traditional geographical perspective in which modes of production are related to natural resources, buildings, property structures, market possibilities, etc. Such studies tend to draw their inspiration

(Continued)

(Continued)

Figure 1.12   A traditional Norwegian farm

from the natural sciences and they work mostly at the mesoscale – the cultural landscape of a region.

In the *intentional* mode of explanation, a particular feature of a cultural landscape (such as land use) can be explained 'in a chronological-biographical sense in relation to the needs, motives, preferences, decisions and actions of individual persons' (ibid., p. 200). A building may be explained through its history and through the needs and aspirations of the farmer. Here we see the farmer's practice as **'agency'**, acting on the basis of personal intentions and his or her interpretations of the functional resources at hand as well as the structural forces at the macroscale (for example, the threats of globalization and of changing national policies).

Whereas the intentional mode of explanation focuses at the microlevel on the individual agent, *structural* explanations try to explain changing landscape features as adjustments to agricultural policies, technological innovations or market forces. Hence explanation is sought here at the macrolevel in relation to socioeconomic structures and related ideologies.

We need all three modes of explanation to understand such a basic and simple geographical object of study as the cultural landscape. But we must, of course, accept that the individual researcher may focus his or her research project on only one of these modes. Aasbø (1997) points out that there is currently an increasing interest within geographical research in the intentional mode. There is a tendency to push this perspective further towards the study of identity and meaning in the cultural landscape. Insiders (e.g. farmers using the landscape) and outsiders (e.g. environmental planners and tourists) have conflicting perspectives on the identity and meaning contained within a cultural landscape which might lead to misunderstandings and antagonistic policies.

One reason for this new focus in the research seems to be the economic changes that have transformed our society in the last hundred years. Before 1900 when the influential French approach to **regional geography** was developed by Paul Vidal de la Blache and others (see pp. 66–70), it was possible to study cultural landscapes as dominated by local agricultural conditions, the features of the cultural landscape could be understood locally as results of the **vertical connections** between humanity and the natural conditions in that landscape. Hence a **chorological** perspective based on the notion of **absolute space** was not problematic.

The growth of manufacturing industry meant the breakdown of local dependencies, making a focus on **relative space** more fruitful. The cultural landscape could now be understood better in terms of transport cost – as a result of the physical distances between factors of production, of the location of raw materials and markets, and of the availability and location of labour. Geography became a 'discipline in distance'.

The 'third industrial revolution' (which is, rather, the advent of a postindustrial society, in which only a fraction of the population really produces goods) has created new and less directly explicable landscape features. Figure 1.12 shows a traditional Norwegian farm surrounded by its infields and forests. Looking at the picture, you might overlook the people when trying to work out why the farm buildings are built as they are, and consider the farm's production potential and its market possibilities. However, the picture attracts our attention for a quite different reason. There are a lot of people sitting on the sloping field watching a scene where young people are performing traditional folk dances. And in front of the barn there is a van containing a TV crew. Even though it is raining slightly (as witnessed by the umbrellas), people have paid money to be here. This is a *media-dominated landscape*. The farmer may receive income from this activity, but the farm and the farm buildings function only as a stage set! I took this photo during my MA fieldwork in upper Telemark (see p. viii in Preface) in the summer of 1962 at a folk festival held there. Now almost fifty years later the economy and landscape in my field study area are to an even larger degree dominated by the tourist industry and new kinds of service activities. Amazing to visitors, this small 'rural community' (1,800 inhabitants) has successfully managed to integrate some 50 asylum seekers from Somalia into their workforce!

This brave new world of ours is continuously throwing up new tasks and problems for the geographer to solve. Humanity and nature are still dependent on each other but local connections are no longer so easy to see. The global dependencies between humanity and the fragile environment of the earth become, however, more and more clear. We have to think globally, as stated in the World Commission on Environment and Development (WCED) report *Our Common Future* (1987), but the necessary local actions are often obscured by the diffuse effects of these dependencies on the global, and even local, environment.

Through this introductory chapter we have tried to expose a variety of inputs from geography as an academic discipline. We have as well introduced a number of concepts and discourses that need a deeper explanation, so you have to proceed through the following chapters to get a better basis for further discussion. The hope is, however, that this introductory chapter has spurred your curiosity to learn more and to go on to explore the history of scientific geography. The next chapter tells the story of the discipline from antiquity to the Second World War.

Questions for Discussion

1. Describe some of the popular notions of geography that you have heard. How would you describe in few words the scope and aims of geographic research to somebody that has not at all studied it?
2. Define the concepts absolute, relative and relational space.
3. Define systematic and regional geography and discuss the relations between them and systematic sciences.
4. Give an account of the different research processes in spatial science school and newer approaches.
5. Discuss the organizational plans for geography presented in Figures 1.5, 1.6 and 1.7. How are these reflected in the study structures at your university?
6. Define the concepts space, place and territoriality.
7. Discuss Sack's illustration in Figure 1.8. Do you agree with Sack in his presentation of the different realms that constitute place (somewhere) and that all humans are *homo geographicus?*
8. How can we understand the relations between place and 'self'?
9. Explain and discuss Figure 1.11 and the factors that explain development of the cultural landscape.

2 THE FOUNDATION OF GEOGRAPHY

GEOGRAPHY IN THE ANCIENT WORLD

Interest in geographical problems, and writings on subjects we can recognize as geographical, began long before the introduction of the subject into universities. It is difficult to imagine how there were ever people who did not think geographically, who never considered the conditions under which they lived, and never wondered how people lived in other places. In this sense geographical thinking is older than the term *geography* (literally meaning 'earth description', from the Greek geo = earth and grafein = to draw), which was first used by scholars at the Museum in Alexandria about 300 BC.

Herodotus

The ancient Greeks made the first major contribution to the development of geography. Scholarly writers produced **topographical** descriptions of places in the known world, discussing both natural conditions and the culture and way of life of the people who lived there. The best known of these was Herodotus (*c.* 485–425 BC). He was first and foremost a historian, but he placed historical events in geographical settings. Some of his writings are truly geographical in character. He not only described geographical phenomena such as, for example, the annual flow of the Nile, but also attempted to explain them.

Herodotus had no interest in the mathematical and astronomical problems that later became associated with geography – the measurement of the circumference of the earth, mapmaking and the establishment of exact locations for places. He accepted the Homeric view of the earth as a flat disc over which the sun travelled in an arc from east to west. The belief that the earth was a sphere was discussed at that time but it was Aristotle, about a century after Herodotus, who provided arguments, based on observations, for a spherical form of the earth. The scholars at the important Hellenistic learning centre, the Museum in Alexandria, were then able to establish the foundations for the calculation of latitude, longitude and the size of the earth.

Eratosthenes

Eratosthenes (276–194 BC), who was chief librarian at the Museum, succeeded in calculating the circumference of the earth with remarkable precision. Of equal importance was his development of systems of coordinates for the world, i.e. latitude and longitude, which he used to locate places and to measure distances. This made it possible for him to draw the first passably accurate maps.

Box 2.1	**How Eratosthenes calculated the size of the earth**

Eratosthenes learned that the rays of the mid-day sun penetrated to the bottom of a well at Syene (Assuan) at the summer solstice (Syene is located on the Tropic of Cancer). At the same time and day he observed that the obelisk in front of the Museum in Alexandria cast a shadow. He used a plumb line to measure the angle of the sun's rays in Alexandria at that time and day, which turned out to be 1/50th of a circle. The north–south distance from Syene to Alexandria must then be 1/50th of the circumference of the earth. The story goes that he sent some reliable slaves to Syene, travelling on an ox-cart with a lump on each wheel. They counted the jolts from the lumps to arrive at the number of wheel turns and, knowing the circumference of the wheel, calculated the distance from Alexandria to Syene. From this measurement, Eratosthenes calculated the circumference of the earth to be 252,000 stadii (a stadium equals 157.5 m) or 39,700 km. Modern measurements show the actual circumference to be 40,000 km. If you look closer at a map of Egypt you will find that Alexandria is located 7.80 north of the Tropic of Cancer, 1/50 of the circle or 7.20 is thus inaccurate. The road along the Nile does not go straight north–south, and the slaves may have counted incorrectly. The result may have been achieved by some luck, but in any case this is one of the first geographical research projects we know of.

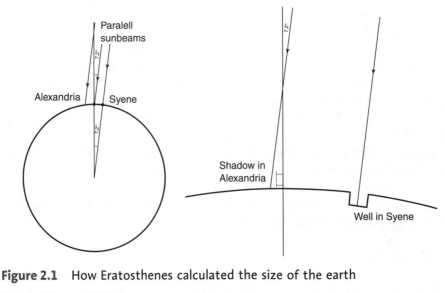

Figure 2.1   How Eratosthenes calculated the size of the earth

Source: Biilmann, 1981

Ptolemy

Eratosthenes' cartographical work was later developed by his students and successors at the Museum in Alexandria. Ptolemy (AD 90–168) wrote a major work in eight volumes which is now known as Ptolemy's *Geography*. The first volume explained the principles for calculating the dimensions of the earth, its division into degrees, calculations of latitude and longitude, and a discussion of map **projections**. The eighth volume contained maps of different parts of the world. Other volumes included tables of latitude and longitude for 4,000 places.

Although it was widely known how to calculate geographical latitude from the altitude of the sun in Ptolemy's time, calculations had only been made for a handful of places. The calculation of longitude was, however, only possible by estimating the length of journeys from one place to another, and so many of Ptolemy's locations for places were erroneous. His biggest mistake was to underestimate the size of the earth, rejecting the almost correct estimate of Eratosthenes in favour of a reckoning made by Posidonius in about 100 BC. Posidonius reckoned the circumference of the earth to be 180,000 stadii against Eratosthenes' estimates of 252,000 stadii. Because calculations of longitude had to be based on rather unreliable travel distances, Ptolemy's otherwise remarkably accurate map of the known world included too many degrees east–west. The map extended from a prime meridian in the Canary Islands to a 180 meridian which crossed inner China. The actual distance between these places is only 120 degrees.

Strabo

The topographical tradition of Greek geography, represented by Herodotus, was carried forward into Roman times. Strabo (64 BC–AD 20) wrote a work of 17 volumes called *Geographica*. This was largely an encyclopaedic description of the known world whose chief value was that it preserved for posterity many writings which he annotated and cited. *Geographica* also included attempts to explain cultural distinctiveness, types of government and customs in particular places. The significance of natural conditions for cultural development was discussed in relation to a number of places, especially in the description of Italy.

Greek and Roman geographers concerned themselves with three basic issues:

1) The detailed topographical description of places and their history, which Ptolemy called **chorography**.

2) The measurement of the earth and the production of maps.

3) A more philosophical interest in the relations between humanity and the environment, which involved the beliefs that the earth demonstrates an order and purpose which has been designed by a deity, that the environment influences people and that people can only to some extent modify their environment.

These ideas had an important bearing on the later development of geography.

MIDDLE AGES AND THE RENAISSANCE

The Middle Ages were a dark period for the development of science in Europe. At best, scholars made accurate but sterile copies of the works of the ancients, rejecting anything that did not conform with the dogmas of the Christian Church. Such an intellectual environment stifled any development of scientific investigation. The earth became a flat disc with Jerusalem at its centre.

Arab geographers

Ancient learning was, however, carefully preserved in the Islamic countries at the Arab schools in Spain, north Africa and the Middle East. Arab traders travelled widely and gathered information which could be used by scholars to fill in the gaps on Ptolemy's original map. The best known of these travellers was Ibn Batuta (1304–68), who travelled as far east as Beijing in China, and sailed far south of the equator along the east coast of Africa. This particular trip showed that Aristotle had been wrong in believing that it was too hot here for human habitation, in what the Greeks had called the 'torrid zone'.

But already by the twelfth century, Al Idrisi (1099–1180) had shown that the Greek division of the world into five climatic zones (two cold, two temperate and one torrid) did not correspond to reality, and had suggested a more sophisticated world climatic system. He wrote a descriptive geography to accompany a large silver map of the world that had been constructed for Roger II of Sicily. His connection with this mighty Christian king made it possible for him to give an account of Europe in the first half of the twelfth century that is unrivalled (Unwin, 1992, p. 57).

Al Muqaddasi (945–88) was the most eminent Arab geographer of the Middle Ages, according to Scholten (1980). Before his time, geographers had generally based their topographical descriptions on compilations of second-hand sources. Muqaddasi was a pioneer of **fieldwork** and stated in his book *The Best Divisions of the Study of Climate* that he would not present anything as fact to his readers unless he had seen it with his own eyes. His book was based on extensive travels within the Islamic world.

The last great Islamic geographer of the Middle Ages was Ibn Khaldun (1332–1406). He established the foundation for historical geography in writings which analysed the rise and fall of empires. He suggested that warlike nomads often founded large states, but after a while the nomads were absorbed by their permanently settled subjects. As peasants and townspeople, the rulers lost their warlike spirit and eventually their kingdoms fell apart. Ibn Khaldun both predicted and lived to see the collapse of the Islamic state in which he lived. At the fall of Damascus in 1400 he actually met Tamerlane, the Mongolian conqueror and devastator. It was unfortunate that the works of the Arab scholars were not translated into Latin or any other language until the nineteenth century; as a result, scholars in other parts of the world were unable to make use of their observations.

Europeans

The journeys undertaken by Europeans during the Middle Ages made little significant contribution to the development of geographical knowledge. Around AD 1000 the Norsemen sailed across the North Atlantic to Greenland and North America but the sagas of these adventures were only passed on by word of mouth and written down long afterwards in isolated Iceland. That the Norsemen were in America more than 400 years before Columbus has been proved by archeological excavations in the 1960s of a settlement at L'Anse Aux Meadows on the northern coast of Newfoundland. The settlement had been used in a period around AD 1000, but the Norse settlement on Greenland which sent out the expeditions was to small to sustain a new colonization. The Black Death, 350 years later, even eradicated the Norse settlement on Greenland. Similarly, the Irish sailors who may have crossed the Atlantic during the same period made little impact on geographical understanding about the world. The Irish tales of St Brendan's journeys have not been proved, but there were without doubt Irish youngsters on the Norse ships that sailed west to Greenland and America. This we know from a large Icelandic DNA and chromosome investigation, which revealed that almost half of the females and a fourth of the males that followed the Viking ships west were of Irish blood. But only on one occasion is an Irish girl mentioned in the Islandic sagas; they were forgotten because they were slaves captured by the Norsemen on their way west. The majority were girls, and they brought with them the Catholic faith so that even the first settlers on Greenland built churches.

China

Meanwhile, exploration and learning flourished in China. Actually, Europe and India were 'discovered' by Chinese travellers long before Europeans reached the Orient. In the period between the second century BC and the fifteenth century AD, Chinese culture was the most efficient in the world in applying knowledge of nature to useful purposes. The study of geography was advanced well beyond anything known in Europe at this time. Among other things, the Chinese used coordinates and triangulation to produce beautiful maps of China and neighbouring countries. When, however, the Italian Marco Polo (1254–1322) wrote an account of his travels to China, describing the high level of Chinese learning, his book was widely discounted as a fictitious adventure.

The Renaissance

The Renaissance brought about a renewed interest in the geographical knowledge of ancient times. A copy of Ptolemy's *Geography*, which had been preserved in a monastery in Byzantium (Istanbul), was discovered and brought to Italy where it was translated into Latin in 1406. After the invention of printing in the 1450s, copies of this book, including reconstructed maps, were printed in Bologna, Rome and Ulm, and made a great impact on contemporary scholars (Bagrow, 1945). Columbus and other expeditionary leaders relied on Ptolemy's calculations (see p. 35), but some of their more famous discoveries disproved the latter's calculations and changed the world picture he had established. There were new developments in cartography – new **projections**, especially that of Mercator in 1569, were invented; the first globes were made; and new world maps were published. The rediscovery of classical cartography played a significant role in the European expansion of political and economic power in the fifteenth and sixteenth centuries.

Few European explorers or scholars regarded themselves as geographers. They preferred the term **cosmography** (the descriptive science of the globe and its relation to the universe), which was used in a number of treatises, often modelled on the works of Strabo and Ptolemy.

The Renaissance saw a revival of another branch of ancient geography, that of topographic description. Accounts of voyages provided raw material for encyclopedic works on the world, or on parts of it, often called chorographies. The jumble of information related to place-names included in such chorographies (where notes on natural and physical conditions were juxtaposed beside miscellaneous information on folklore, etymology and history) places them outside the field of science as we understand it today. The popularity of these works in their own time might well puzzle us until we realize that we

> are often prisoners of contemporary logic and cannot see those qualities of old works which cannot be integrated into our system ... at the time it had just as much relevance as what continues to interest us today: it was part of what the episteme of the time indicated was knowledge.
>
> (Claval, 1980, p. 379)

Above all, geography retained in the fifteenth and sixteenth centuries a practical importance; it provided better maps and information which was essential for statesmen and merchants working towards the European domination of the globe. But as a science it was diffuse; there was no need to define disciplinary boundaries. Later disciplinary discussions on the content of the discipline have, however, been influenced by this early development. Geography could be defined as the all-embracing **cosmography**, the science of the globe, or it could be **chorography**, the descriptive science of single regions (Box 2.2).

VARENIUS

Strabo (64 BC–AD 20) had made a rough definition of the study of geography when he said that

> wide learning, which alone makes it possible to undertake a work on geography, is possessed solely by the man who has investigated

things both human and divine. ... The utility of geography ... regards knowledge both of the heavens and of things on land and sea, animals, plants, fruits, and everything else to be seen in various regions – the utility of geography, I say, presupposes in the geographer the same philosopher, the man who busies himself with the investigation of the art of life, that is, of happiness.

(Cited in Fischer et al., 1969, p. 16)

He considered that geographers should study both human activities and natural conditions, a reasonable conclusion so long as geography was regarded as a descriptive discipline. The role of geography was to describe the earth and its different places, and in such descriptions both humanity and nature would play a role. After the Renaissance, as the natural sciences developed analytical methods, some scholars began to argue that the respective methodologies of physical and human geography should be different. In studies of natural phenomena, including climate, geology and landforms, it is possible to use the methods of the natural sciences and to draw conclusions with a large measure of scientific precision. The methods of natural science, however, do not lend themselves very well to the study of social and cultural phenomena. Our generalizations about human groups must be limited in time and space, and must relate to statements of probability rather than certainty.

Bernhard Varenius (1622–50), whose *Geographia Generalis* was published in Amsterdam in 1650, was one of the first scholars to suggest these essential differences in the character of physical and human geography. His book includes

Box 2.2	-Graphy or -Logy?

Well into the seventeenth century, geographical writing was profoundly influenced by Greek and Latin classical writers, and a number of classical Greek words were used to define aspects of the subject. Thus 'geography' combines *geo* (the earth) with *graphos* ('drawing' and, by extension, 'description'). 'Cosmography' involved the description of the universe (*cosmos*) and included what later developed as biology, cartography, geography, geophysics and also anthropology. *Chorography* (*choros* = place) described places in general and larger areas, whereas 'topography' was concerned primarily with the physical features of particular places at a smaller scale.

Words ending in *-logy* incorporate the Greek word *logos*, which signifies a rational principle or structure. (*Logos* is the 'Word' which was 'from the beginning' in the first chapter of St John's Gospel.) So *logos* implies explanation rather than the description, which is implied by *graphos*. 'Chorology' suggests some explanation about places, just as **'chronology'** deals with time and how historical events can be seen as logical outcomes of a course of previous events.

much material which today would be treated as mathematical geography or as astronomy. The *Geographia Generalis* is divided into three parts:

1) The absolute or terrestrial section, which describes the shape and size of the earth and the physical geography of continents, seas and the atmosphere.

2) The relative or cosmic section, which treats the relations between the earth and other heavenly bodies, especially the sun and its influence on world climate.

3) The comparative section, which discusses the location of different places in relation to each other and the principles of navigation.

Varenius intended that the *Geographia Generalis* should be followed by what he called, in his Foreword to the book, 'special' geography, in which descriptions of particular places should be based upon

- 'celestial conditions', including climates and climatic zones;

- terrestrial conditions with descriptions of relief, vegetation and animal life; and also

- human conditions, including trade, settlement and forms of government in each country.

In fact he showed little enthusiasm to embark on the study of human geography as it was not possible to treat it in an exact way. He explained that he had included this last group of conditions as a concession to traditional approaches to the subject. Unfortunately, he did not have the opportunity to write on special geography since he died at the early age of 28 (Lange, 1961).

Varenius made two major contributions to the development of geography. First, he brought together contemporary knowledge of astronomy and cartography and subjected the different theories of his day to sound critical analysis. Secondly, his partition of geography into *general* and *special* sections originated what we now call **systematic** and **regional geography**. His *Geographia Generalis* dealt with the whole world as a unit, but was restricted to physical conditions which could be understood through natural laws. **Special geography** was primarily intended as a description of individual countries and world regions. It was difficult to establish 'laws' in the special (regional) part, for the explanation must be descriptive where people are involved. Preston James (1972, p. 124) points out that the general (systematic) and special (regional) parts of Varenius's work complement each other, and that Varenius saw **general** and special **geography** as two mutually interdependent parts of a whole.

THE PHILOSOPHER, IMMANUEL KANT

The lectures on physical geography given by Immanuel Kant (1722–1804) in Königsberg (now Kaliningrad) were of great significance for the later development of geography. The course, which was given more than 40 times, was one of his most popular. It was not a course on physical geography as we now understand it, because it also discussed human racial groups, their physical activities on the earth and natural conditions in the widest sense of the term. Kant regarded geography as only an approach to the knowledge that was necessary for his philosophical research:

> But, finding the subject inadequately developed and organised, he devoted a great deal of attention to the assembly and organisation of materials from a wide variety of sources, and also to the consideration of a number of specific problems – for example, the deflection of wind direction resulting from the Earth's rotation. (Hartshorne, 1939, p. 38)

Kant provided a philosophical foundation for the belief that the subject has a significant scientific contribution to make. He pointed out that there are two different ways of grouping or classifying empirical phenomena for the purpose of studying them: either in accordance with their nature, or in accordance with their position in time and place. The former is a **logical classification**, the latter a physical one. Logical classification lays the foundations for the systematic sciences – the study of animals is zoology, that of the rocks is geology, that of social groups is sociology, and so on. **Physical classification** gives the scientific basis for history and geography: history studies the phenomena that follow one after the other in time (chronological science), while geography studies all phenomena belonging to the same place (chorographic science). This enabled him to argue that as sciences 'geography and history fill up the total span of knowledge; geography namely that of space, but history that of time' (Kant, in May, 1970, p. 261).

Geographers have often appealed to Kant in justifying the existence of the subject and its special character among the sciences. Alfred Hettner (1859–1941), who did most to affirm the significance of Kant's work to geography, admitted (1927, p. 115) that for a long time he had not paid sufficient attention to Kant's exposition of geography but had later rejoiced to discover a close correspondence between the conclusions of the great philosopher and his own. The American geographer Richard Hartshorne closely followed Hettner in his *The Nature of Geography* (1939), which considers that Kant's approach led towards a satisfactory understanding of the nature of geography and answered all its basic questions.

Werlen (1993, pp. 2–3) maintains that Hettner misinterpreted Kant:

> For Kant geography was a descriptive or taxonomic discipline, rather than a science: it only had the status of a propaedeutic discipline. Kant used the word 'chorographic', meaning descriptive, to describe geography. Hettner (1927) transformed this into 'chorologic', which refers to explanation rather than description.

However, in the days when Kant was lecturing in Königsberg, history sought to tell a tale of temporal sequences, while geography described the world and its parts in a systematic way. To suggest, as Werlen does, that Kant would have distinguished between taxonomy and science is about as odd as it is to state that the Swedish botanist Carl von Linneaus (1707–78), who created the taxonomic order of plants in species, families (Latin names), etc., did not think of taxonomy as science. We have to bear in mind that science has changed a great deal since the late eighteenth century. The change in the appellation of geography from a chorographic to a chorologic science by Hettner and Hartshorne must be seen as a consequence of general changes in all the sciences, which took place during the nineteenth and early twentieth centuries. As we shall see later, however, Hettner and Hartshorne were still subsequently attacked for presenting geography as a mere descriptive science.

Today it is widely considered to be impossible, and to some extent philosophically untenable, to draw such sharp divisions between the 'sciences' as Kant, in Hettner's interpretation, did. Understanding of geographical situations is always improved when we consider their development over time. Just as there are geographers who wish to study the cultural landscapes of former times without necessarily using their knowledge to illuminate contemporary conditions, so historians should not neglect the study of differences between places. The individual sciences overlap each other.

Hettner considered that the biggest difference between history and geography

> **does not lie in that geography sets out to study a given time, namely the present, but that in geography the time aspect recedes into the background. Geography does not study development in time as such – although this particular methodological rule is often broken – geographers cut through reality at a distinct point in time and only consider historical developments in so far as they are necessary to explain the situation at that chosen point in time.**
>
> **(Hettner, 1927, pp. 131–2, my translation)**

During the period between the death of Kant in 1804 and Hettner's book in 1927, this 'methodological rule' had not only been broken, but also almost systematically opposed, since Kant's philosophical guidelines for the subject had been virtually forgotten until Hettner and Hartshorne resurrected them. In the nineteenth century, geographical research was closely associated with the *study of process*, that is, the historic development in geographical space.

THE 'CLASSICAL' PERIOD

While Kant gave geography a theoretical justification, it was Alexander von Humboldt (1769–1859) and Carl Ritter (1779–1859) who laid the scientific foundations for geography as a branch of knowledge. These two men had many views in common and were united in their criticism of the casual and unsystematic treatment of geographical data by their predecessors. The similarity of their opinions was not accidental – Ritter regarded himself as a student of Humboldt, and Humboldt described Ritter as 'his old friend'. They differed markedly, however, in temperament and character.

Humboldt

Humboldt was the last of the great **polymaths**. Penck (1928, p. 31) regarded him as a cosmographer rather than a geographer. He mastered a number of disciplines and put all his energy (and fortune) into travel and research in order to understand the whole complex system of the universe. In his great work *Kosmos*, with its subtitle *Sketch of a Physical Description of the World*, he attempted to assemble all the contemporary knowledge of the material world. *Kosmos* was published (1845–62) in five volumes at the end of his life, while the results from his long and important journeys in Latin America (1799–1804) had been published in 30 volumes in Paris (1805–34).

Humboldt had a gift for exceptionally sharp observation, and in **fieldwork** he was unsurpassed. His books and letters demonstrate that nothing escaped his observation. This, together with his training in geology, is shown in a letter he wrote to a Russian minister after a visit to the Urals: 'The Ural Mountains are a true El Dorado', he wrote, 'and I am confident, from the analogy they present to the geological conformation of Brazil, that diamonds will be discovered in the gold and platinum washings of the Urals.' A few days later, diamonds were actually discovered (Tatham, 1951, p. 55). Humboldt was primarily interested in the natural sciences. He undertook a large number of altitudinal measurements during his travels and drew height profiles of the continents. These measurements were used in his studies of climatic and vegetation zones which were of basic importance for later research in biogeography and climatology. He also wrote regional accounts of Mexico and Cuba that are still of interest (Schmieder, 1964).

In contrast to most other natural scientists of his day, Humboldt was not so much interested in discoveries of new species and in collections for natural science museums as he was in understanding the connectivities in the world of nature – a scientific approach he called *physikalische Geographie*. This must not be confused with the more limited concept of '**physical geography**' as used today. The relations between the vegetation, animal life, and also humankind with geographical conditions of climate, topography and altitude were central to Humboldt's interests. In his search for *Oeconomia Naturae*, we find some of the roots of modern ecological thinking. His work is much freer of the **environmental determinism** than the much later studies of Ratzel and Semple (see pp. 63–5).

Humboldt transferred Kant's idea of a threefold division of all the sciences to the natural sciences, dividing them into:

- **physiography** or description of nature;

- *historia telluria*, the geological history of the earth; and

- *geonosia or physikalische Geographie*. (Beck, 1982, p. 90)

Humboldt did not wish to confine his research to any one of these subdivisions. As a cosmographer, he was not interested in becoming a specialist in a particular field. Geography and the natural sciences were not then institutionalized and specialized *disciplines*. Humboldt and Ritter would barely have understood the later division of science into disciplines, the specialized fields of work of scientific institutions or the interminable discussions about the nature or limitations of specific disciplines. They were both, in this sense, cosmographers, although their field of inquiry differed.

Ritter

Ritter's recognition as a geographer dates from the publication (in 1817–18) of the first two volumes of his *Erdkunde* – with a volume on Africa and a volume on Asia. The second edition was published in 19 enlarged volumes in 1822–59. On the initiative of leading politicians, he was established in 1820 as the first professor of geography in Berlin. Although Ritter travelled widely in Europe, he spent relatively more of his time in his study than did Humboldt. The two men can be considered as complements to each other, in that Ritter was chiefly concerned with studies of human geography, and stood somewhat apart from the rapidly advancing research front of the natural sciences. It would be wrong to describe him as a crude **determinist**, as some commentators have done. He believed, as did Vidal de la Blache much later, that 'earth and its inhabitants stand in the closest reciprocal relations, and one cannot be truly presented in all its relationships without the other. Hence history and geography must always remain inseparable. Land affects the inhabitants and the inhabitants the land' (cited in Tatham, 1951, p. 44). This implied that the individual region or continent had a unity, a *Ganzheit* (which may be translated as a 'whole'), which it was the task of the geographer to study. This entity was something more than the sum of its parts – more than the totality of topographical, climatic, ethnic and other circumstances. Ritter's views were shaped by his deeply religious outlook and by the accepted natural philosophy of his time. His ideas on the 'wholeness' of things were in accordance with the writings of the German 'idealist' philosopher Georg W. F. Hegel (1770–1831), whose attitudes amounted to an attempt to comprehend the entire universe, to know the infinite and to see all things in God (Chisholm, 1975, p. 33). **Holistic** views dominated scientific thought throughout the nineteenth century, and Ritter's ideas were in line with the generally accepted biological, geographical and geological understanding.

The scientific stance of Ritter, like Immanuel Kant before him, was *teleological* (Greek *teleos* = 'purpose'). Teleology seeks to understand events in relation to their underlying purposes. **Teleological explanations** are therefore often regarded as the opposite of **mechanical explanations**, where the phenomena and observations are understood as outcomes of prime causes such as the 'laws of nature' (see p. 106). Ritter studied the workings of nature in order to understand the purpose behind its order. His view of science sprang from his firm belief in God as the planner of the universe. He regarded the earth as an educational model for humanity, where nature had a God-given purpose which was to show the way for humanity's development. He did not regard the shape of continents as accidental, but rather as determined by God, so that their form and location enabled them to play the role designed by God for humankind's development.

Ritter's approach to knowledge has been strongly criticized. Hettner (1927, p. 87) said that Ritter's views were in accordance with the spirit of his time, and this reinforced their influence on his generation. This influence, however, was bound to decline when Darwin's *Origin of Species* inaugurated a new philosophy of science.

Ritter combined a basic teleological standpoint with a very critical scientific precision: 'My system builds on facts, not on philosophical arguments', he said in a letter (cited in Tatham, 1951, p. 46). The collection of facts was not an end in itself; the systematization and comparison of data, region by region, would lead to a recognition of unity in apparent diversity. God's plans, which give purpose and meaning, could only be discovered by taking into account as objectively as possible all the facts and relationships in the world. In this, he followed the advice of Immanuel Kant that the scientist must, on the one hand, continue to explore the universe along mechanistic lines, and should never abandon this approach yet, on the other hand, should bear in mind that organic life can best be understood by minds like ours in terms of the principle of natural teleology (Greene, 1957, p. 68).

Ritter's significance as a scientist lies in his thorough and critical study of sources and in his ability to systematize extensive material. In these respects his work is in the same tradition as that of Humboldt. While earlier regional descriptions had consisted to a large extent of the accumulation of unsystematized data about particular places, Humboldt and Ritter effected a clear structuring of such material and, through deliberate research into both the similarities and the differences between countries and regions, they sought to compare the different parts of the world with each other.

Ritter was, according to Hassinger (1919, p. 66), 'the founder of the **comparative method** in regional geography, the victor over every dead aggregate presentation of geographical knowledge. He gave our science unity and coherence' through his use of historical development as its leading thread. Ritter himself, however, regarded Humboldt as the founder of the comparative method (Schültz, 1980, p. 44). The basis for Ritter's comparative studies was the physical layout of the land – the area and character of river basins, for example. In this way he could present a land classification or a set of physical regions. The most important part of his work, however, would be to explain the relationships between humanity and nature in the different regions through the history of humankind. Ritter believed that thorough research into the historical development of culture and its relations to physical regions would demonstrate the physical layout of the land as God's educational home for humankind. He therefore made historical development in geographical space the main theme of his educational task. For a long time afterwards geography followed this tradition, including the period of its **institutionalization** as a specific discipline from the 1870s on.

Subsequent writers have commented on the differences between Humboldt's and Ritter's religious and scientific outlooks, and have somewhat exaggerated them. Both men laid great stress on the unity of nature. They both believed that the ultimate aim of research was to clarify this unity and, in this respect, were in accord with the idealistic philosophies of their time. Humboldt did not pursue **idealism** in the same way as Ritter, for his concept of the unity of nature was more aesthetic than religious. In this respect he had more in common with Goethe than with Ritter. Unlike Ritter, he saw no reason to explain unity and order in nature as a God-given system to further humanity's development. Humboldt was very much engaged in the gradual development of natural sciences, and his greatest contributions lay in the field of **systematic** physical geography. Many regard him as the founder of **biogeography** and **climatology**. Ritter was, on the other hand, to a considerable extent a **regional** geographer.

The geography Ritter and Humboldt represented was designated as '*classical*' by Hartshorne (1939) because it dominated the foundation – or perhaps we should rather say the pre-foundation – period of the subject, since the discipline's institutionalization came much later.

FROM COSMOGRAPHY TO AN INSTITUTIONALIZED DISCIPLINE

No geographer, before or since, has enjoyed a more central position in science and society than Humboldt and Ritter. It might be thought that, in Germany at least, this would have led to a real breakthrough for geography as a scientific discipline. Quite the contrary: with the death of both Humboldt and Ritter in 1859 the 'classical' period came to an end; there were no real successors. The personal professorship Ritter had held ceased with his death, and new university chairs in geography were not established until c. 20 years later.

Geographical societies

An important reason for this lack of progress was the cosmographic character of Ritter's and Humboldt's achievements. At this time, 'geography' was still not related to an institutionalized university discipline. It remained an umbrella concept for a variety of expeditions and other activities within the natural and social sciences, to a large extent supported by **geographical societies** (see Box 2.3) which were flourishing at this time.

| Box 2.3 | **Geographical societies as promoters of expeditions and national interests** |

The founders of the *geographical* societies included prominent members of the middle classes and enthusiastic scientists who sought to widen support for expeditions and research. These societies also received help from governments during the turn-of-the-century period of colonial expansion. Although forerunners of these societies existed during the sixteenth and seventeenth centuries, the first modern geographical society was founded as the Société de Géographie de Paris in 1821. In rapid succession came the Gesellschaft für Erdkunde zu Berlin in 1828, the Royal Geographical Society in London in 1830, then societies in Mexico (1833), Frankfurt (1836), Brazil (1838), the Imperial Russian Geographical Society in St Petersburg (1845), and the American Geographical Society in 1852. By 1885 nearly 100 geographical societies (with an estimated membership of over 50,000) were spread across the world (Freeman, 1961, pp. 52–3).

These societies' most important work was their support for expeditions and their publication of yearbooks and journals, which included maps and other material from expeditions. Many of the societies also supported their respective countries' colonial expansion. Some, such as the societies at Nancy and Montpellier, supported local studies in their home areas. At Nancy, barely 10 km from the Franco-German frontier after the 1870–1 war, the Société Géographique de l'Est pursued studies supporting the return of Alsace-Lorraine to France. During this time geographical societies enjoyed a high profile because of their commitment to popular political causes. Their meetings attracted great public interest, especially when well-known explorers came to give accounts of their discoveries and adventures.

The activities of the geographical societies stood in marked contrast to the development of academic geography at the time. In the 1880s there were fewer than twenty university teachers in geography in the whole world, and there were far fewer university students in the discipline than members of the geographical societies. The universities were, however, reluctant to give geography status as an academic discipline largely because of the cosmographic nature of the investigations promoted by the societies. In the latter part of the nineteenth century, however, the universities promoted the disciplinary division between the sciences. The information brought back by explorers helped to build up the new disciplines at the universities, particularly in the natural sciences. Many scientists who worked in these disciplines depended on the geographical societies for their data-collecting activities, and feared this support would dwindle if geography became established as a separate academic discipline.

Geography becomes an academic discipline

Many academics considered that geography was not a science; it was only sustained by borrowing from others (Schültz, 1980, p. 65). This argument was based on a scientific philosophy that emphasized natural laws and causality (**partial–general reasoning** – see Figure 1.2), which was gradually replacing earlier holistic philosophies. These scientists found it difficult to accommodate a 'cosmographic' geography as a scientific discipline. The year 1859 (in which, incidentally, both Humboldt and Ritter died), saw the publication of Charles Darwin's *Origin of Species*, which provided much of the basis for the new ways of scientific reasoning.

Part of the reason for the lack of new chairs in geography was the fact that the discipline, as expounded by Ritter, was considered by influential academics as merely a subdivision of history or, at best, as a subsidiary subject to it. In his zeal to demonstrate that the earth is a school for humanity, Ritter had become more and more interested in its historical development, and his more influential students concentrated to an even greater extent on historical research. In many schools of geography, especially in France, the subject came to be closely associated with history. In Germany by 1850, geography was a widespread school subject, taught in most cases as an auxiliary subject to history. However, the modern pedagogical principles of the Swiss educationalist Johann Heinrich Pestalozzi (1746–1827) gave geography in Germany, Switzerland and France a somewhat more independent role in compulsory elementary education. Geography was here seen as a means to develop children's power of observation, and the development of academic geography was needed for the education of geography teachers. By 1875 there were geography chairs at three Swiss universities (Capel, 1981, p. 59).

It was after the Franco-Prussian war of 1870–1 that influential politicians in Prussia came to realize that geography could also serve an important political purpose. Geographical education could be used to reinforce and popularize the idea of the nation-state (a commendable objective at that time), and could also provide people with a better understanding of the economic and political possibilities of world trade and development. To achieve these goals, geography teachers needed to have a better education. For this reason, in 1874, the Prussian government decided to establish chairs of geography in all the Prussian universities. By 1880, ten professors had been appointed. For more or less the same reason (Boxes 2.4 and 2.5), other European countries also established geography as a university discipline.

One of the reasons why France had lost the war of 1870–1 was considered to be the superiority of the German educational system, which led to calls for school reform and better teaching of geography. During the 1870s, a handful of chairs of geography were established at French universities, the most significant appointment being that of the young Paul Vidal de la Blache (1845–1918) to the chair at Nancy in 1873 and in 1877 at École Normale Supérieure in Paris (Capel, 1981, p. 60).

Box 2.4	Political arguments for school geography in the nineteenth century: the relations between history and geography

While both history and geography could serve to develop nationalistic sentiments, the relative position of these two subjects in the educational system largely came to depend on the degree to which either seemed more useful in building up the idea of a national identity. In Germany, with its long history of shifting borders and divisions into small states, geographical patterns associated with the German-speaking lands seemed very significant, and so geography was seen as very important. Norway, on the other hand, had developed its educational system during the union of the crowns with Sweden (1814–1905) and it had no disputed borders. Under these circumstances, Norway's national awakening was fostered by teaching about the glorious history of Viking times and about the precious liberal constitution of 1814. Hence history predominated over geography. Finland, however, which had also experienced a union of crowns (in this case with Tsarist Russia), lacked a clearly discernible glorious past and so geography developed as a relatively more important subject. A pioneering research work of great political importance in the Finnish liberation process, the *Atlas of Finland* (first edited in 1899), stressed the uniqueness of the Finnish lands.

Geography at British universities

The political arguments in favour of teaching geography in the universities met with more or less active opposition from within the universities themselves. In Britain, the first personal chair of geography was held by Captain James Machonochie at University College, London, from 1833 until 1836. Permanent university teaching was only established from the 1860s onwards when the Royal Geographical Society began to take a growing interest in education. The Society urged the need to establish chairs in geography at Oxford and Cambridge, pointing out that chairs had been or were being established in German, Swiss and French universities. But the proposals were only taken seriously in 1887, when the Royal Geographical Society offered to cover the main bulk of the costs involved in establishing lectureships at Oxford and Cambridge. This financial support led to the appointment of Halford J. Mackinder to a readership at Oxford in 1887.

Mackinder became an outstanding promoter of geography at both universities and schools. In 1893, together with a group of schoolmasters, he founded the Geographical Association, which did much to encourage and improve geographical education, and although he was elected to Parliament in 1901, he

Box 2.5	Arguments for school geography today

As early as 1885, Kropotkin (1842–1921) suggested that geographical education is ideally suited to promote a sense of mutual respect between nations and people. Geographical knowledge of other cultures, civilizations and ways of life increases our ability to communicate and is a necessary prerequisite for international cooperation and solidarity. These views have been recently re-emphasized by the Commission on Geographical Education of the International Geographical Union in its *Charter on Geographical Education* (1992). This charter particularly addresses the principles of the United Nations, the *World Declaration of Human Rights and the Rights of Children* and the recommendations from UNESCO on education in cross-national understanding, cooperation and peace. The Charter points out that geographical education helps to promote the principles of these charters and declarations.

There are four other main reasons why geography should have a role as a 'key discipline' in school education. A 'key' discipline:

1) should provide students with some basic concepts to enable them to understand the world around them. This is provided by Kant's categories of classification. Place is an elementary and universal key concept, as explained in Chapter 1 (pp. 20–2).
2) should provide students with qualifications to cope with the world around them. Geography teaches the techniques needed for expeditions out in the world. A basic education in geography is needed early in life so as to understand maps, the use of maps, places, peoples and countries. The first task should be to map the path from home to kindergarten or primary school.
3) should explore the possibilities of synthesis. Geography is the only discipline that has constantly sought to build bridges between the social and physical sciences, between humanity and nature. Geographical education provides students with the ability to understand the 'wholeness' of a place and how the landscape evolves as a result of natural processes and human actions.
4) should also provide basic knowledge needed by other disciplines. Geographical facts and the understanding of mapmaking and spatial relations provide essential background knowledge for students of history and the environmental, social and political sciences.

remained an important father figure in British geography. Mackinder firmly believed that geography should help to train future citizens for the 'world stage' upon which, in Mackinder's view, the British Empire was a force for good. Geographical teaching should therefore be 'from the British standpoint':

This is, no doubt, to deviate from the cold and impartial ways of science. When we teach the millions, however, we are not training scientific investigators, but the practical and striving citizens of an Empire which has to hold its place through the universal law of survival through efficiency and effort. (Mackinder, 1911, pp. 79–80)

The first British university geography department was established at Oxford in 1900, but geography only achieved a firm footing at Cambridge after 1908, mainly through the continued financial support of the Royal Geographical Society. During a period of 35 years, the society invested about £7,250 in the Cambridge project and £11,000 at Oxford (Stoddart, 1986, pp. 83–125). 'Hence we have the paradox that in the 1880s and 1890s British geography emerged as a scientific discipline without the benefit of aid from strictly scientific men' (ibid., p. 67).

The reluctant and somewhat hostile attitudes in the universities towards the establishment of geography as an academic discipline were largely due to the rapid growth of the systematic sciences and the increasing need to specialize in scientific work. The image of geography as an all-embracing cosmographic subject did not fit in with academic development at this time. Influential academics argued that the fields of geographical inquiry were already covered by existing disciplines. The historian Edward A. Freeman could not understand how geography could be recognized as an independent university discipline when 'on the one hand a great deal belongs to history but on the other the geologists lay claim to much of its material' (Keltie, 1886, p. 466). McKenny Hughes, a professor of geology at Cambridge, argued that his geology department already did all the necessary lecturing and fieldwork in physical geography. At a university, students should specialize in either history, geology or zoology, drawing on a knowledge of geography already imparted at school (Stoddart, 1986, p. 70). But Mackinder articulated, in a lecture to the Royal Geographical Society in 1887, the need for a geographical science to bridge the gap between the natural sciences and the study of humanity 'which in the opinion of many is upsetting the equilibrium of our culture'. He believed that theories of social evolution, based on Darwinian ideas, would replace the arguments of Ritter (Livingstone, 1992, pp. 190–2; see also Box 2.6, p. 53–4).

The Keltie Report of 1886 (p. 71) was a powerful and comprehensive documentation of the academic and practical value of geography:

It is through geography alone that the links can be seen that connect physical, historical and political conditions; and it is thus that geography claims the position of a science distinct from the rest, and of singular practical importance ... scientific geography may be defined as the study of local correlations.

The USA

In the USA, university teachers of geography included William Morris Davis (1850–1934), who began teaching at Harvard in 1878. The first geography department was established in Chicago in 1903. By the First World War, the discipline was firmly established at a number of North American universities, notably Harvard, Yale, Teachers College (Columbia University), the Wharton School (University of Pennsylvania) and Chicago.

The 'new' geography

The **institutionalization** of geography meant that examinations with national standards had to be organized and the discipline defined as a subject area with a distinct content. This 'new' geography, for which syllabuses and reading lists were drawn up, led to the **professionalization** of people calling themselves geographers. New professional journals were founded, such as the *Geographical Journal* in Britain, *Annales de Géographie* in France and the *Annals of the Association of American Geographers* in the USA.

The new academic geography gradually distanced itself from the geographical societies as university geographers developed a scientific base which the societies lacked. This divergence was, in some cases, widened by the attitudes of prominent members of the societies. The chairman of the Finnish Geographical Society, for instance, maintained the cosmographic view that geography was a collection of different sciences but not a science in itself. This view was of course strongly repudiated by the Finnish professors of geography (Granö, 1986). In the new academic journals (which had often been founded almost in opposition to the geographical societies' journals), geographers set out to justify the new science: they defined its long traditions, its utility and special methods, and delimited geography unequivocally from neighbouring disciplines. A more important function of the academic journals was to publish research that students could use as **exemplary models** (see Chapter 4).

The new geography drew on some of the ideas of Humboldt and Ritter, but was also influenced by developments within the natural sciences which followed the Darwinian breakthrough, and by the political milieu of the period.

DARWINISM

During the late nineteenth century, it was considered important that we learn how to shape human societies from nature; we see a shift from consulting the Bible to consulting the laws of nature. **Darwinism's** influence was strong, not only on social thinking but also on the development of science as such. There are good reasons to purport that, alongside the Bible, no book has had a more profound influence on our ways of thinking than Charles Darwin's *Origin of*

Species (1859). Stoddart (1966) suggests that the following four main themes from Darwin's work can be traced in later geographical research:

1) Change through time or evolution – a general concept of gradual or even transition from lower or simpler to higher or more complicated forms. Darwin used the terms 'evolution' and 'development' in essentially the same sense.

2) Association and organization – humanity as part of a living ecological organism.

3) Struggle and natural selection.

4) The randomness or chance character of variations in nature.

The concept of change over time is, for instance, found in Davis's cyclic system of the development of a landscape through the stages of youth, maturity and old age, which Davis himself described as evolution. The French school of regional geography (pp. 66–70) also used the term in their study of the changing cultural landscape.

Box 2.6	**Evolution and Society**

The philosophical reflections of the Greek and Roman geographers on the relationships between humanity and the environment survived into modern times. The view that the environment had an influence on people and on the development of human society became central to **environmental determinism**. A more positive alternative scenario was **possibilism**, which studied the extent to which people were able to modify their environment. Possibilists also recognized that humankind could have negative influences on the environment (as, for instance, suggested by Marsh and Réclus, see p. 57).

The idea of **evolution**, the gradual or even transformation from lower and simpler to higher and more complicated forms of life, dominated scientific debate in the latter part of the nineteenth century, in both the natural and social sciences. There were fierce debates on whether evolution was strictly governed by inheritance and selection of the fittest through random biological variations, or whether qualities acquired or learnt by an organism during its lifetime could be passed on to its offspring. The latter concept had been promoted by Jean-Baptiste de Lamarck (1744–1829), a gifted French natural scientist who lived before Darwin's time.

Livingstone (1992, p. 187) maintains that geography was influenced more by the social ramifications of the neo-**Lamarckian** version of evolutionary theory than by Darwin's own ideas. Neo-Lamarckian arguments support the belief that social progress can be greatly accelerated by learning and through the acquisition of habits in response to adaptations

(Continued)

(Continued)

to the environment. Biologists eventually agreed that Lamarck had been wrong; an individual's acquired abilities are not passed on to the next generation by biological inheritance. Today, of course, social theory no longer emphasizes the laws of natural science: social environment of mutual learning may be more important than biological inheritance in shaping life for future generations. If you have trained yourself to be an excellent football player, this learnt ability is not transferred in the genes to your offspring; but your interest in the sport will probably be conveyed to your children as a social stimulus for them to be engaged in the sport too.

Social Darwinism became a catch-all term used to characterize a variety of social theories that emerged in the latter part of the nineteenth century. These theories have particularly been associated with the influential philosopher, Herbert Spencer (1820–1903). Spencer's ideas buttressed *laissez-faire* individualism in economic and political life. He believed that the development of civilization was a manifestation of the survival of the fittest, an argument much favoured by big business and imperialists. For instance, John D. Rockefeller, the founder of Standard Oil, saw the growth of big business as the outcome of natural selection of the best fitted individual leaders. Benjamin Kidd (1894), another promoter of social Darwinism, saw the European dominance of the world through imperialism as a reflection of the superior fittedness, energy and efficiency of Europeans.

On the other hand, political liberals used Darwinian language in their assault on aristocratic privilege and landed proprietors, which protected some idle and unproductive members of society from competition with more entrepreneurial individuals. The writer George Bernard Shaw, for instance, suggested that the quality of civilization might be improved by **eugenics**, the 'science' of improving the qualities of the human race by the careful selection of parents. Such ideas developed into Nazi racial ideology, as later voiced by Hitler. A modern version of eugenics have been made possible by medical development in gene manipulation, artificial insemination and by abortion of embryos that, by ultrasound, are found to have deficiencies.

The ideas of association and organization – which Darwin had inherited from earlier philosophers and scientists – have been rather tenacious in geographical research. The influential German geographer Friedrich Ratzel (1844–1904), discusses in his *Political Geography* (1897) 'the state as an organism attached to the land'. Although this **organism analogy** was derived from the natural sciences, its roots may also be traced back to the earlier idealist philosophy and concept of *Ganzheit,* or 'whole', as used by Ritter (see above). The **region** (that particular field of study for geographers) has been regarded as a unique functional complex which, despite a steady stream of material and energy, is in apparent equilibrium and constitutes a 'whole' that is more than the sum of its parts. This idea of the region is to be found in the French school of regional geography, and is also apparent in relatively more recent university textbooks (Broek and Webb, 1973, pp. 14–15). The concept of the region as an

organic unity pervaded British geography in the first half of the twentieth
century. Andrew John Herbertson (1865–1915) used the term 'macro-organism'
for the 'complex entity' of physical and organic elements of the earth's surface
(Stoddart, 1966, p. 691).

The concept of struggle and selection, which had parallels in the contemporary political ideas of both economic liberals and Marxists, is reflected in subsequent geographical research, although no agreement was reached as to whether
variation and development occurred by chance or were predetermined. This
reflects a certain ambiguity in Darwin's thought. In later revisions of his work,
Darwin abandoned the issue of random variation and chance, partly because he
had failed to discover the laws which he had earlier believed to govern chance
variations, and partly as a response to churchmen who sought to reconcile evolutionary process with fundamental direction (Box 2.6).

The scientific method that dominated the latter part of the nineteenth
century was in marked contrast to the **teleological** thinking of the 'classical'
period, which had supported and sustained the pursuit of a cosmographic
science. It was no longer science's objective to be a witness to the existence of
God or to find in His grand plan final causes or purposes in what was observed.
Scientists should seek to determine the laws of nature as prime causes which
might explain observed reality. This change in viewpoint gradually led to the
replacement of **inductive reasoning** by **hypothetic-deductive reasoning**.
Hypothetic-deductive reasoning sets up hypotheses to see how far they can
explain observed reality. If and when the testing of these hypotheses yields
positive results, scientists are on the way to formulating **scientific laws** (see
Chapter 4). Scientists were now in general agreement that religion could not
provide explanations for natural phenomena: some theologians were even
prepared to accept that the Bible was not an authoritative source on scientific
matters. Discussion as to whether or not there was a big idea or a God behind
the laws of nature, or whether natural laws were the means of development
towards a designed end, came to be regarded as unscientific. Questions of belief
and questions of knowledge now occupied two different realms, with science
concerning itself with causes rather than purposes. This increasing belief in the
inherent value of science led to a considerable growth in research into the natural
sciences. There was, however, no agreement on how to interpret the laws of nature
and their roles in shaping the human society. An important discourse was
between social anarchists and social Darwinists, and this is a discourse that for
political reasons have become highly relevant today.

THE SOCIAL ANARCHISTS

Réclus

The French geographer Elisée Réclus (1830–1905) attended some of Ritter's
lectures, but was much more influenced by the new political and scientific
developments of his time. He achieved recognition with a work of systematic

physical geography called *La Terre* (1866–7), but is best remembered for his 19-volume regional geography *Nouvelle Géographie universelle* (1875–94). The clarity and accuracy of this work made it much more popular than Ritter's *Erdkunde*, which had been its exemplar in many respects. Réclus's work became a model for a range of encyclopedic studies of the geography of the world and of particular countries.

Réclus (see Box 2.7) was probably the most productive geographer of all time. Although he was the best-known French geographer of his time, Réclus never held a university chair in France and had to earn a living from his writings and, although most of his books were published by Hachette in Paris, he was obliged to live abroad in exile because of his political activities and hence could only indirectly influence the development of French academic geography.

Box 2.7	**Elisée Réclus (1830–1905) – the life of an idealist**

The French geographer Elisée Réclus was first and foremost an uncompromising idealist. He was expelled from the teacher seminary at Montauban in his very first year because he supported the ideals of the 1848 revolution. When only 20 years old he went to Berlin to study theology, but began to attend the popular lectures of Carl Ritter, which awakened his interest in geography. Returning to France in the autumn of 1851, Réclus resumed his political activity. Resisting the *coup d'état* of Napoleon III in the same year, he was obliged to flee to England with his brother (Dunbar, 1981, p. 155). Réclus then travelled extensively in North and South America, more in order to observe than to do research. Sustained research was, in fact, beyond his means, for Réclus had to make a living from the meagre incomes he could earn as a tutor and worker *en route*. In 1857, he returned to France and befriended the leading anarchist, Mikhail Bakunin (1814–76). From that time onwards, Réclus belonged to the inner circle of the secret anarchist association Fraternité Internationale. In 1871, he took an active part in the Paris Commune but was captured during the first days of fighting. He was held in prison for almost a year. A sentence of deportation to New Caledonia was commuted to ten years' banishment as a result of the active intercession from geographical societies and such leading personalities as Charles Darwin. Réclus chose to settle in Switzerland in his exile. Although promised a readership in geography in the Université Libre in Brussels in 1892, the university reneged on the appointment for fear of demonstrations after an outbreak of anarchist violence in France in the autumn of 1893. A support committee for Réclus started to collect money and eventually founded the New University of Brussels where he was professor for the last years of his life, refusing to take any salary since his modest needs could be satisfied by the income from his books.

Reclus's books, including his major work, *Nouvelle Géographie universelle*, sho̵ ̵ed little evidence of his political beliefs. For this reason they attracted a ̵ adership and provided politicians and leading ̵ ̵ical societies with a model for the geography they ̵ subject in schools and universities. So Réclus had ̵ fluence on the **institutionalization** of geography ̵ ademics saw geography only in its role as a natural science. Like R̵itter, R̵éclus was particularly interested in the human aspects of geography. He had a sharp eye for the inequalities of the human conditions around the world, and made this a central theme of his books. He was also the first European geographer to support the ideas of the American nature conservationist George Perkins Marsh. Marsh had written *Man and Nature, or Physical Geography as Modified by Human Action* in 1864, describing his book as 'a little volume showing that whereas Ritter and Guyot [a student of Ritter who emigrated to the USA] think that the earth made man, man, in fact, made the earth' (cited in Beck, 1982, p. 148). Marsh suggested that humanity had, throughout history, destroyed many natural resources and landscapes and he called for a better management of nature. In his very first work, *La Terre* (1866–7), Réclus acknowledged his debt to Marsh.

Réclus's political views were more directly expressed in his last work, *L'Homme et la Terre* (mostly published posthumously 1905–8), which introduced the concept of **social geography**. Since Réclus devoted his political life to social justice, social conditions were inevitably always discussed in his books. He had made a special study of social geography and his inclusion in a travel guide of a description of poverty and relief among the poor of London broke new ground (Beck, 1982, p. 135). Réclus also established a connection between geography and modern town planning and sociology. He influenced and had close contacts with Frédéric le Play, the French sociologist, and Sir Patrick Geddes, the Scottish biologist, social scientist and planner. Geddes, although no anarchist, became a close friend in the last decade of Réclus's life. He spread Réclus's ideas in Britain and was most interested in his ideas on social geography, in which he found a suitable basis for the development of his work on applied research and planning (see p. 75–7).

Kropotkin

We have emphasized the life and work of Réclus to demonstrate that the old masters still have something to say to us today. The urge for **social relevance** in geographical work is not a recent phenomenon; it was present in the life and work of the anarchist geographers more than 100 years ago. Today Réclus and his fellow anarchist friend and geographer, Count Peter Kropotkin (1842–1921) have aroused renewed interest. The Russian nobleman became famous for his research into the physical geography of northern

Europe and Siberia and was a welcome speaker among the geographical societies of western Europe. Kropotkin also gave Réclus ample help with the sections of *Nouvelle Géographie universelle* that dealt with Siberia and eastern Europe.

Kropotkin voiced his political opinions much more directly than Réclus, trying to revolutionize the discipline of geography in a number of ways. He presented theories of geographical education, the relations between humanity and nature, and of decentralization, which were clearly aimed at discouraging the use of geographical research for exploitative and imperialistic purposes (Breitbart, 1981, p. 150).

Kropotkin's political ideas had developed while he was travelling in Siberia during the 1860s. He was impressed by the Russian peasants' spirit of equality and self-sufficiency, but was disheartened by the negative effects of political centralization and social inequality. In 1871, Kropotkin became an active advocate of **social anarchism** and, as a consequence, had to go into exile. From that time onwards he devoted his life to two revolutions: one in social and economic relations, the other in the discipline of geography itself. Kropotkin's social anarchism sought to demonstrate that people had a capacity to develop a better society on a cooperative basis, provided that the structures of domination and subordination were taken away. He believed that centralized institutions inhibit the development of a cooperative personality, promote inequality and limit economic progress. An important book is his *Mutual Aid: A Factor of Evolution* (1902), a part of which has been republished (2008). Here he maintains: 'Man is no exception in nature. He is also subject to the great principles of Mutual Aid which grants the best chances of survival to those who best support each other in the struggle for life' (Kropotkin, 2008, p. 489).

He advocated small-scale economic activity within and between regions which, he thought, could provide economic development superior to that produced by large-scale industry. Such arguments are advanced today by the 'green' movements, by economists such as Schumacher in *Small is Beautiful* (1974), by urbanists and planners in calls for **governance** and **collaborative planning** (Healey, 1997). Kropotkin suggested that large city regions should be disaggregated into small, more or less self-sufficient townships within which living, working and recreational space might be integrated. Such ideas were later put into practice by the **Garden City movement** led by Ebenezer Howard and Lewis Mumford. Another important connection was to Patrick Geddes (see pp. 75–7).

Most significantly for his time, Kropotkin opposed strongly the dominant interpretation of Darwin's *Origin of Species* (1859), which saw nature as an immense battlefield upon which there is an incessant struggle for life and the extermination of the weak by the strong. He attacked the **social Darwinist** views of the influential philosopher Herbert Spencer (1820–1903). Spencer envisaged human societies as closely resembling animal organisms which must engage in a constant struggle to survive in particular environments. Spencer believed that the 'fittest individuals' would survive best in a free-enterprise system, and thus lead civilization forward. In his 'general law of evolution' he claimed that all evolution is characterized by concentration, differentiation and determination. Kropotkin, on the other hand, wrote (1924, p. vii): 'I failed to find, although I was eagerly looking for it, that bitter struggle for the means of existence between animals of the same species.' The struggle for existence may be hard, but it is not carried out by individuals – rather, by groups of individuals cooperating with each other. In the development of civilization, as in the quest for survival, Kropotkin believed that mutual aid within small, self-contained communities was the best workable solution. He found support for this in his research 'among the barbarian' communities in Central Asia as well as in many other parts of the world. Pointing out how Caucasian Ossetes practised communal rights and mutual aid at critical times of the year, he concludes 'as if to prove how contrary unbridled individualism is to human nature' (2008, p. 497).

Interestingly, in practice, Kropotkin had a stronger political following in the USA than in the UK. This is because mutual help and communality was necessary for the different group of settlers. In the American Midwest there is still a large number of cooperative institutions, schools and churches built and maintained by mutual effort, telephone and farming cooperatives. My second cousin in Montana admitted on my visit in summer 2008 that 'what we have here is almost communism'. The problem in political terms, however, is that the individualistic market liberalism derived from social Darwinism has taken the lead as this shares the scepticism towards top-down government with the social anarchists. What remains on the global political scene is the all too simple dichotomy between socialism and market liberalism; since Kropotkin none has been able to promote the third, social anarchist solution in a convincing way.

Both Réclus and Kropotkin stressed and developed the idea that geography as a discipline should encompass both humanity and nature. Kropotkin was a close friend of Scott Keltie (secretary of the Royal Geographical Society) and strongly supported the arguments that were used to establish geography as a university discipline in Britain (the 'Keltie Report' of 1886). But for Keltie it was essential that science should be politically and socially neutral and value-free – that is, based on the scientific ideals of **positivism** (see Chapter 5). In writing the obituary of Kropotkin, Keltie (1921, p. 319) expressed the view that 'this is not the place to deal in detail with Kropotkin's political actions, except to regret that his absorption in these seriously diminished the services which otherwise he might have rendered to geography'. Réclus and Kropotkin may have had little direct influence on the geographical establishments of their day, but they kept alight a flame of critical social inquiry that has been resurrected today.

MORPHOLOGY AND PHYSIOGRAPHY PROVIDE ACADEMIC RESPECT

During the latter half of the nineteenth century, it was primarily a group of natural scientists with interests in physical geography who won the subject academic respect. A start had been made in Britain by the first prominent female geographer, Mary Somerville (1780–1872), whose *Physical Geography* had been published in 1848. This book gave detailed descriptions of the topography of each continent (without illustrations) and of the distribution of plants, animals and human beings. It was not a simple physical geography since it included the works of human beings, being more an exercise in the **cosmographic** tradition.

The German school of geomorphology

As a result of Darwin's work, geology and biology became the most ambitious branches of the natural sciences. Geology was important because it could, with the aid of **palaeontology** (which interprets fossils), clarify the evolution of plant and animal species. These sciences had been elements within cosmographic geography and their independent development (which led to the establishment of university chairs) was a threat to the universalistic claims of geography. Some opportunities were created for geography, and these were first appreciated by the German, Oscar Peschel (1826–75). In an otherwise scientifically weak book called *New Problems of Comparative Geography as a Search for a Morphology of the Earth's Surface* (1870), Peschel chose the right moment to propose that geographers should study the **morphology** of the earth's surface. Like Ritter, he was interested in the significance of landforms for the development of human society, but he did not share Ritter's religious outlook, being more concerned with causes and effects, as illustrated by the methods of the natural sciences.

Geologists had set themselves such huge tasks – including the development of geological timescales, the systematic mapping of rock types and the analysis of fossils – that they found it difficult to cope simultaneously with the morphology of the earth's surface. Here was a field where geography could carve out a place for itself as a scientific discipline. The study of landforms became the leading field of research for most of the professors appointed to geography chairs in the latter half of the nineteenth century. The biological elements in nature subsequently came to play a relatively small role in the teaching of geography in most countries, making **physical geography** a more appropriate description of what was taught than the term 'geography of nature'.

One important reason for the 'geologification' of geography during the 1870s and 1880s was that the new professors needed academic qualifications, preferably doctorates. Friederich Ratzel (1844–1904) said: 'they told me when I returned from my expeditions that they needed geographers'. So he organized as quickly as possible all the material he had collected on the Chinese migration to the USA and wrote it up as a doctoral thesis, which gained him the chair of geography at Munich in 1875 (Jean Brunhes, 1912, after a discussion with Ratzel in 1904). There were, however, many academics who had a scientific training in geology. Ferdinand von Richtofen (1833–1905) was a well-known geologist and explorer when he was offered the chair of geography in Bonn. Although he did not want to exclude humanity from his teaching of geography, he made the study of landforms the main research field for himself and his students.

Even more influential in this development was Albrecht Penck (1858–1945), a dominating figure in German geography. Internationally, Penck's influence could only be compared with that of the American, William Morris Davis (1850–1934), with whom he was in close contact – despite their very different interpretations of the **cycle of erosion** (Martin, 1985, p. 224). Penck, like von Richtofen, was a geologist by training, but he was primarily interested in the **Quaternary period** and worked on the identification of glacial periods and on **glacial morphology** in general. Early in life, Penck developed his glacial theory, which he used to explain many of the landforms of central and northern Europe. His main work (1901–9) was on the glacial periods in the Alps and their effects on Quaternary sedimentation. His identification of the four glacial periods (Günz, Mindel, Riss and Würm) was a major step in the development of glacial geomorphology. Having been advised by a geologist friend to take his doctorate in geography, Penck was, at the age of 27, appointed to a chair of physical geography in Vienna. He founded an influential school of geography there, but in 1906 moved to Berlin, where he held an influential position until his death.

Penck's work had a major impact in the Scandinavian countries and, for a long time, Scandinavian academic geographers were primarily concerned with the study of the effects of glacial periods on the landscape. The leading professors, generally the first to be appointed, were geomorphologists. Another important contributor to geomorphological research was the Serbian geographer, Jovan Cvijic (1865–1927). His work on the karst phenomena in the limestone regions of his homeland introduced Serbo-Croat words like *dolina* and *polje* into the scientific vocabulary. The word **karst** is in itself a placename from the border region between Slovenia and Croatia (Freeman, 1980, p. 19).

Huxley and Davis

In Britain, no work was more influential in changing the teaching of geography at all levels than T. H. Huxley's *Physiography*, first published in 1877. At this time the term '**geomorphology**' had not yet been invented and only '**morphology**' was in general use. '**Physiography**' has a much wider meaning; it may be defined as a 'description of nature', encompassing the systematic sciences of botany, geology and zoology. One reason for the success of Huxley's book was its demonstration of better and more interesting ways of learning, linked directly with the pupil's own experience. The book begins with the Thames at London Bridge and, working from the local and familiar to the unfamiliar, it ends with the earth as a planet. The characteristic of the book is its emphasis on experimentation and local studies. The idea that geography can only be learnt through local studies, field courses and excursions is, to a large degree, derived from the educational principles of the Swiss educationalist, Heinrich Pestalozzi (1746–1827), and it was these principles that were developed into practice by Huxley.

'**Physical geography**' (renamed '**physiography**' after 1877) became a very popular school subject during the last third of the nineteenth century, accounting for some 10% of the examination papers sat in English and Welsh schools during that time (Stoddart, 1975, p. 26). Physiography was now regarded as an integral, if not the most important, part of geography.

As more specialized earth sciences became established, physiography as a comprehensive subject gradually vanished from the syllabuses. Within geography, its place was filled by the new science of **geomorphology**, which was introduced to Britain in 1895. The American William Morris Davis (1850–1934) became the leading personality in the development of geomorphology in the English-speaking world, although he preferred the term '**physiography**' himself. His organizing principle was not simple causality but rather the idea of regular change of landforms through time, as systemized in his scheme of the **cycle of erosion**.

Based on his investigations of valley formations in Pennsylvania, Davis presented his first systematic exposition of the erosion cycle in 1889. This was an ideal typification of landform processes. Initially, a rapid tectonic uplift created a young landscape, which was immediately attacked by the destructive agents of erosion that would, in time, reduce the landscape to its ultimate old-age form, a low flat plain termed a **peneplain**. Davis argued that most places had gone through several complete cycles of erosion, and that present-day high mountain plateaux were merely remnants of former base levels.

The success of physical geography, variously termed physiography, morphology or geomorphology, led the German Georg Gerland to suggest in 1887 that the study of cultural phenomena should be separated from geography. He supported this view on the logical grounds that geography is the science of the earth, and that a science should be developed on the basis of natural scientific methods. Scientific methods, as defined, could not be used to study cultural phenomena.

Developments in physical geography were the main innovations in the discipline during the latter part of the nineteenth century. Gerland's proposal indicates how far the pendulum had swung in this direction, and his arguments may have led many to conclude that geography had lost its basic, theoretical balance.

ENVIRONMENTAL DETERMINISM AND POSSIBILISM

After Darwin, geographical research was primarily concerned with discovering the laws of nature. Nature was studied with open eyes: geographers sought as objectively as possible to identify the natural processes that governed the formation of valleys, uplands and coastlines. A more restricted view was taken of human activity; only the relationships between nature and humanity were considered to be of prime interest. Humanity's achievements were explained as consequences of the survival of the fittest under the pressure of natural conditions (see Box 2.6, p. 53–4).

Ratzel

Friedrich Ratzel, widely recognized as the founder of human geography, was greatly influenced by such ideas. The first volume of his chief work, published in 1882, was entitled *Anthropogeography, or Outline of the Influences of the Geographical Environment upon History*. In this volume (which sought to transfer the new methods of the natural science to studies in human geography), Ratzel stressed the extent to which humanity lives under nature's laws. He regarded cultural forms as having been adapted and determined by natural conditions. Although he may be criticized today for his determinism, we should acknowledge that Ratzel broke new ground in demonstrating that cultural, as well as natural, phenomena can be subjected to systematic study. Before his time human geography had largely confined itself to regional studies.

Environmental determinism is also evident in Ratzel's *Political Geography* (1897). In this book, the establishment of states is seen as an evolutionary necessity, and Ratzel explains the growth of political unities in terms of organic growth (Uhlig, 1967). These ideas quite clearly influenced his Swedish pupil Rudolf Kjellén, who was to become a propounder of **geopolitics**. Kjellén simplified and popularized Ratzel's ideas, maintaining that states follow the principle of the 'survival of the fittest' and have an independent existence over and above that of their citizens. These ideas were readily accepted and followed up by Karl Haushofer (1869–1946), who, as a geographer, tried to build up geographical arguments for a German right of domination over neighbouring peoples. Geopolitics became an important part of Nazi ideology. While it is unfair to hold Ratzel responsible for this much later development, we must be aware of the connections between environmental determinism, nationalism and racism (Peet, 1985). Somewhat the same, maintains Livingstone (1992, pp. 194–6), can be said of the founding father of British geography, Halford Mackinder. Based on his ideas of social evolution, Mackinder developed a political geography, that greatly influenced British foreign policies and military strategies. Thinking geographically was to him part of a strategy to secure the 'maintenance and progress of our Empire' (Mackinder, 1911).

In the second volume of **Anthropogeographie** (1891) Ratzel discussed the concentration and distribution of settlement forms, migrations and the diffusion of cultural characteristics. In this work he was influenced by his 'fatherly friend', the German evolutionary theorist Moritz Wagner, who argued that Darwin had failed to appreciate the significance of migration and geographical isolation for the process of evolution. For instance, Australia, which for many millions of years had been isolated from the other continents, have developed a quite distinctive animal and plant life that can be shattered when humans import new species. Ratzel realized that he could not solely explain phenomena in terms of natural conditions, but that the historical development and cultural background of local and migrant populations were also significant. At one point he even declared (as cited in Broek, 1965, p. 18): 'I could perhaps understand New England without knowing the land, but never without knowing the Puritan immigrants.'

The promotion of determinism

In scientific circles, however, the first volume of *Anthropogeographie* had a much greater impact than the second volume. Ratzel's American disciple, Ellen Churchill Semple (1863–1932), in particular, laid great significance on Ratzel's deterministic opinions in her teaching at American universities (Box 2.8). Semple and others of the same way of thinking, including the geomorphologist William Morris Davis, dominated American geography until the 1930s and exerted an influence over American school geography for much longer. In summing up the principles of 'geographical evolution' to the readers of a school magazine in 1900, Davis maintained that two great principles had been discovered, both of vast importance for geography. One was the evolution of landforms, contributed by geology; the other, the evolution of living forms, contributed by biology (Livingstone, 1992, p. 205).

Box 2.8	**Ellen Churchill Semple on environmental influences**

A major work by the American geographer Ellen Churchill Semple is entitled *Influences of Geographical Environment* (1911). It begins (p. 1) as follows:

> Man is a product of the earth's surface. This means not merely that he is a child of the earth, dust of her dust, but that the earth has mothered him, fed him, set him tasks, directed his thoughts, confronted him with difficulties that have strengthened his body and sharpened his wits, given him problems of navigation or irrigation, and at the same time whispered hints for their solution.

Semple believed that human temperament, culture and economic life could all be the result of environmental influences. She argued, for instance, that 'the northern peoples of Europe are energetic, provident, serious, thoughtful rather than emotional, cautious rather than impulsive. The southerners of the subtropical Mediterranean basin are easy-going, improvident except under pressing necessity, gay, emotional, imaginative, all qualities which among negroes of the equatorial belt degenerate into grave racial faults' (ibid., p. 620).

Davis, like Ratzel and Mackinder, was determined to keep the study of human and physical geography together under one explanatory umbrella. Given their educational background in the natural sciences and the scientific importance of evolutionary theory at that time, it seems inevitable that they would try to transfer evolutionary concepts to the study of the human world. Livingstone (1992, p. 210) has argued that the vocabulary best suited for their purposes was provided by the neo-**Lamarckian** version of evolutionary theory (see Box 2.6, p. 53–4).

Two influential geographers who continued the study of environmental effects until the middle of the twentieth century were Ellsworth Huntington, who related the rise of civilization in the mid-latitudes and the lack of development in the tropics to climatic conditions, and Griffith Taylor, 'whose determinist views so angered politicians interested in the settlement of outback Australia that he was virtually hounded out of his homeland' (Johnston, 1997, p. 43). Due to climatic conditions, Taylor insisted that possibilities for new settlements were limited. Taylor moved to the USA in 1928 and later to Canada. He insisted that he was not an old-fashioned determinist, but had based his views on scientific knowledge of the environment. In 1951, Taylor (p. 7) could state with satisfaction:

> **Thirty years ago I predicted the future settlement-pattern in Australia. At Canberra (in 1948) it was very gratifying to be assured by the various members of the scientific research groups there, that my deductions (based purely on the environment) were completely justified.**

At the age of 70, Taylor returned to Sydney, was welcomed as a national hero and was even commemorated with his picture on a stamp. This example shows that a scientifically based **environmental determinism** might have some merit.

Until the middle of the twentieth century, strong elements of crude environmental determinism played a major role in the selection of topics that were included in school textbooks in most countries. A 'commercial' type of geography, which laid considerable emphasis on raw material supplies and little on the distribution of entrepreneurial skills and institutions, was popular. The influence of physical geography on transport routes was greatly overstressed and oversimplified.

The advent of possibilism

Geographical research in Germany was soon to react against crude environmental determinism. Alfred Hettner (1859–1941) was the most significant contributor to this. Hettner was the first German to enter university with the declared aim of becoming a geographer. What intrigued him about geography was the idea of humanity's dependence upon nature (Beck, 1982, p. 215). Gradually, however, he modified his environmentalism and, in 1907, declared that as far as we restrict discussion to the influence of nature upon human beings, we are only dealing with possibilities, not certainties. In his monumental presentation of the history, content and methodology of geography, *Die Geographic, ihre Geschichte ihr Wesen und ihre Methoden* (1927), Hettner asserted that geographical synthesis is distorted when nature is regarded as dominant and humanity as subsidiary. Through this book and through his editorship of *Geographische Zeitschrifti*, Hettner became the most influential philosopher of geography. He maintained that the primary cultural task of geography is to build a bridge over the gap that had opened during the latter part of the nineteenth century between the natural sciences and the humanities.

Hettner reformulated Kant's concept of **chorography** (the description of phenomena that are found at the same place) to **chorology** – a scientific explanation of the total causal relationships of an assemblage of phenomena that are mutually coordinated, but not subordinated, in places. **Regional geography (*Länderkunde*)** was therefore the crucial part of geography. As Hettner moved away from environmentalism, he became more and more opposed to the development of **geopolitics** and particularly to the notion that there is some correlation between race and culture (Schültz, 1980).

The view that 'there are no necessities, only possibilities' was strongly urged by the French historian Lucien Febvre (1922), who termed this approach **possibilism** and contrasted it with environmental determinism. Febvre invented this term, but the development of the possibilist way of thinking had started earlier and is especially associated with the French geographers Paul Vidal de la Blache (1845–1918) and Jean Brunhes (1869–1930). Later, Isaiah Bowman (1878–1950) and Carl Sauer (1889–1975) became active advocates of possibilism in the USA. The possibilists did not deny that there were natural limits to the activities of humanity, but emphasized the significance of humanity's choices of activity, rather than the natural limitations to it.

THE FRENCH SCHOOL OF REGIONAL GEOGRAPHY

Paul Vidal de la Blache (see Box 2.9) is regarded as the founder of modern French geography. Vidal pointed out the weakness of deterministic arguments, the futility of setting humanity's natural surroundings in opposition to its social milieu and of regarding one as dominating the other. He considered it even less useful to tackle these relationships along systematic lines in the hope of discovering general laws that might govern the relationships between human beings and nature.

Box 2.9	**Paul Vidal de la Blache and the formative years of the french school of regional geography**

Paul Vidal de la Blache (1845–1918) started his academic career as a student of classics and history. It is not clear why he transferred his interests to geography, but the fact remains that, when he was appointed to a chair in history and geography at Nancy in 1873 (when only 28), he sought permission to teach geography alone. Andrews (1986) links this change of interest to the transformation of the French secondary school curriculum, which was inaugurated at this time. Alsace-Lorraine had been lost to Germany in 1871 and the establishment of the Third Republic led to much political rethinking and reform. The education in classics and religion was not suited for building a modern nation. The secretary of state for culture, Jules Ferry (1832–93), became the driving force in educational reforms that ended the influence of the Church in education. Ferry and secretary of state for education Jules Simon established in 1871 the 'Commission de l'Ensignement de la Géographie', which led to a reorganization of geographical education in the schools, with direct consequences for the universities. Education should concentrate on the local regions, but also strengthen the consciousness about France and its role in the world. As a consequence, better geography teachers were needed in French schools and it seems that Vidal grasped this opportunity at the right moment. He became *professeur* and holder of the chair in geography (alone) at Nancy in 1875, when he had attained the age of 30, which was the minimum age required for the title. Nancy, located on the border to the land lost to Germany, had its own geographical society, and local regional studies were promoted to strengthen national identity and the return of the lost region. Nancy set the example for the Ministry of Education, which became convinced of the desirability of naming chairs in geography alone rather than following the long-standing tradition of combined chairs in history and geography. In 1877, Vidal moved to Paris, where he was appointed senior amanuensis at École Normale Supérieure, a key position as it meant supervising students in the last part of their study, leading to an MA thesis. The candidates from this institution took positions in leading gymnasiums and universities all over France. In 1898 he became professor at Sorbonne with the task of supervising PhD students.

Geography attained an independent position in these years in France, but it is important to note that the connection between geography and history remained strong. This was also due to the important new trends in history which were later formalized through the **Annales School** of history. *Annales* is the name of a journal launched by Lucien Febvre and Marc Bloch in the early 1930s. Its aim was to reform the discipline of history by focusing on the history of ordinary people through such means as archaeological and other physical evidence and private archives, rather than through the traditional way of recounting history based on a study of written sources that stressed political events, military confrontations and the lives of kings, emperors and ministers. The 'new' history of the Annales School sought to discover the fate of the lower classes, the ways in which they were organized, and the techniques they used in farming or producing tools and other artifacts (Claval, 1996, p. 319). This was in line with, and inspired by, the *'méthode Vidalienne'* (Holt-Jensen, 2006).

According to Vidal, it is unreasonable to draw boundaries between natural and cultural phenomena; they should be regarded as united and inseparable. In an area of human settlement, nature changes significantly because of the presence of human beings, and these changes are greatest where the community's level of material culture is the highest. The animal and plant life of France during the nineteenth century, for example, was quite different from what it would have been had the country not been inhabited for centuries by human beings. Hence it is impossible to study the **natural landscape** as something separate from the **cultural landscape**. Each community adjusts to prevailing natural conditions in its own way, and the result of the adjustment may reflect centuries of development. Each single small community, therefore, has characteristics that will not be found in other places, even in places where the natural conditions are practically the same. In the course of time, humanity and nature adapt to each other like a snail to its shell. In fact, the relationship between humanity and nature becomes so intimate that it is not possible to distinguish the influence of humanity on nature from that of nature on humanity. The two influences fuse. Through time, local lifestyles (*genres de vie*) develop an integrated web of physical and social threads.

The area over which such an intimate relationship between human beings and nature has developed through the centuries constitutes a **region**. The study of such regions – each one of which is unique – should be the geographer's task. Vidal, therefore, argued for regional geography and against systematic geography as the discipline's core.

The *méthode Vidalienne*

Vidal de la Blache's method, which was **inductive** and **historical**, was best suited to regions that were 'local' in the sense of being somewhat isolated from the world around them and dominated by an agricultural way of life. These circumstances favoured the development of local traditions in architecture, agricultural practices and general way of life; these communities lived in such a close association with nature that they might be self-sufficient in the majority of goods. Vidal advised geographers to carry out research in folk museums and collections, and to investigate the agricultural equipment used in the past in order to study the region's individuality of development.

Vidal de la Blache (1903, p. 386) used the following illustration to underline the long associations between the major factors governing a community's development: while the surface of a shallow lake is being swept by a gust of wind, the water is disturbed and confused but after a few minutes the contours of the bottom of the lake can clearly be seen again. In the same way, war, pestilence and civil strife can interrupt the development of a region and bring chaos for a while, but when the crisis is over the region's fundamental developments reassert themselves. Changes can occur in such a community, and Vidal pointed out many developments that had taken place in the French regions during the centuries preceding the French Revolution, but these developments had taken place within a stable framework of interaction between human beings and nature.

Vidal's characterization fitted fairly well with those virtually unchanged communities in Europe with which he was most familiar. These had been agricultural societies throughout the Middle Ages and well into recent times, and had essentially local interests and interaction patterns resulting from a long interplay between humanity and nature. In certain circumstances, and for certain members of the small upper classes, the field of contact was national rather than local but, in general, Vidal's concepts were appropriate. Ironically, however, he was describing a rapidly disappearing phenomenon.

His method is still well suited to the study of the historical geography of Europe up to the Industrial Revolution, and also for the study of those parts of the world where society depends on subsistence economies. As Wrigley (1965, p. 9) pointed out, however, Vidal's method is not so well suited to the study of regions that experienced the Industrial Revolution of the nineteenth century. Towards the end of his career, Vidal was well aware of this situation. This is most evident in *La France de l'Est* (1917), in many ways his most original work, which studied the development of the landscapes and agricultural societies in Alsace and Lorraine over a period of 2,000 years. A considerable portion of the book, which is arranged chronologically, is devoted to changes that preceded the French Revolution of 1789. The Revolution produced a great ripple in the picture, but afterwards the main lines of development reasserted themselves. After a particular point in the nineteenth century, however (Vidal identified the year 1846 himself), the finely balanced interplay between humanity and nature was profoundly disturbed. The surface of the lake was, as it were, whipped up by something more significant and persistent than the earlier gusts. The visible contours at the bottom of the lake were reshaped. The building of canals and railways, together with the reformation of the Alsatian woollen industry through the introduction of cotton mills, initiated the decline of the traditional, local, self-sufficient economy. Industry was developed on the basis of new, cheap raw materials and rapid means of transport, and hence it could mass-produce goods for a wider market. And it was these developments that reduced the validity of the regional method in a growing number of areas.

Vidal regretted these developments, which he could not avoid observing. He considered that much of the best in French life was vanishing with the self-sufficient economy, but his stature as a scholar enabled him to suggest possible new approaches for further research. In the future, he suggested (1917, p. 163), we should study the economic interplay between a region and the city centre that dominates it, rather than the interplay of natural and cultural elements. Despite the breakdown of the self-sufficient regional economy, Vidal's work has been and still is a great inspiration to a vital tradition in geography – that of the **regional monograph**.

Regional monographs and the Annales School

Regional monographs (following the models of Vidal de la Blache) were concerned with the development of material culture. They were developed further by the Belgian geographer Pierre Gourou, among others. Gourou's first research (1936) was on the peasant culture in the Tonkin Delta of Vietnam. He was fascinated by the farming techniques which allowed an almost perfect control of water in a very difficult environment. He found that it was possible to understand peasant societies like the Tonkinese only through studying of their political and social organization, thus deepening the concept of *genre de vie*.

The French regional monographs acted as models for geographers around the world. At the Institute of Geography at Belgrade University, for instance, under the inspiring leadership of Jovan Cvijic, 25 monographs on the regions of Serbia were produced in the years before the First World War. These investigations made Serbia one of the best-studied countries of the world, and were also instrumental in the creation of the state of Yugoslavia at the Paris Peace Conference in 1919. In Britain, regional monographs were widely admired. They were studied and produced in the Oxford School of Geography and later introduced into the newer universities by Percy M. Roxby and others (Buttimer, 1983, p. 91).

LANDSCAPES AND REGIONS

Vidal de la Blache is only one, if the most significant, of the founders of regional geography. There are other directions and methods in regional geography, although their discussion and classification have been rather neglected by English-speaking geographers. In Germany and France (where regional geography has been regarded as the core of the subject until quite recently), contributions have been much more extensive in this field. Learning in Germany has a long tradition of classification and systematization, and we can turn to Fochler-Hauke's *Geographic* (1959, pp. 251–61) for a review of the different approaches to regional geography.

Before we do so, we must first clarify the concepts 'region' and 'landscape' and their German counterparts. The two German words *Land* and *Landschaft* may both be translated as 'region', but *Land* is a definite unit – a county or a country normally deemed by its administrative borders. *Länderkunde* is the art of describing such definite units, as in regional monographs such as Demangeon's *La Picardie* (1905) – regional geography in its traditional sense. The word *Landschaft* can be used, as in English, to refer to the *landscape* scenery of an area since there are many similarities in terms of the origins and the development of the German and English words. The German word, however, has a more explicit territorial meaning than the modern English word, in part because it has historically been used to refer to a small, often relatively independent, territory. German geographers have given this a more specifically scientific meaning: a small region that is defined, in part, by the character of its physical features. The difference between the English emphasis on landscape as scenery and the German emphasis on territoriality has led to differences of opinion regarding the appropriateness of using the German term in English (for a more thorough discussion, see Olwig, 1996). The German science *Landschaftskunde*, which concerns both the study of such small unique areas and the delimitation and classification of different types of region, straddles regional and systematic geography. Hannerberg (1968, pp. 132–3) considers that *Landschaftskunde* could be taken over by the systematic branches of geography, while *Länderkunde* remains as regional geography in its own right. With this in mind, we can now turn to the five approaches to *Landschaftskunde* as distinguished by Fochler-Hauke (1959): landscape chronology, landscape ecology, landscape morphology, regionalization and landscape classification (or systematization). The type of investigations included in the first three approaches we discuss somewhat more below. *Regionalization* simply means the delimitations of regions and is discussed with examples from Britain on pp. 75–7. *Landscape classification* denotes specification of different types of landscapes such as rural in contrast to urban landscapes. In most cases the classification is based on physical appearance; delimitations done particularly within landscape morphology are exemplified in Figure 2.2 (p. 76).

Landscape chronology

Through its concern with development over time as a device to present **regional synthesis**, landscape chronology might seem to include French regional geography. However, this approach must be regarded as a method of regional geography or *Länderkunde*, and not as an approach to *Landschaftskunde* (landscape geography) (see Figure 1.5, p. 15).

Landscape chronology concerns particularly the specific scientific work of reconstructing former landscape types – for example, on the basis of relict elements in the contemporary landscape. The use of aerial photographs to detect the ridge and furrow patterns of ancient fields, as first analysed by Mead (1954) and in the study of the lost villages of medieval England (Beresford, 1951), are examples of research used to reconstruct a chronology of shifting landscape types through history.

Landscape chronology might also include the type of geographical study described by Derwent Whittlesey (1929) as **sequent occupance**. Sequent occupance concerns the ways in which each culture uses a region in its own particular way. This can be demonstrated in America where most regions experienced a sudden change from Indian to European cultures, and also in many parts of Europe which progressed from agrarian to industrial cultures. Sequent occupance stresses the stages in the development of a region and not, as in the France of Vidal de la Blache, local differentiation as a result of the long-continued and largely undisturbed interplay over the centuries of humanity and nature.

Landscape ecology

Although particularly well developed in Germany, the concept of **landscape ecology** is less understood in the Anglo-American world. Carl Troll (1899–1975), who introduced the concept, defined landscape ecology as the complex of causal and reciprocal connections between biological communities (*Biozönoseni*) and their environment in a particular section of a landscape (according to Leser, 1980, p. 53). Troll did not consider this to be a systematic branch of geography, but rather as an approach to an integrating study of landscapes, for which he introduced and developed the art of aerial photography interpretation. This work placed biological and climatological conditions in a central position in German landscape research, the role of geomorphology hence being relatively reduced. Troll considered that landscape ecology was a unifying approach to the natural science aspect of geography, with **social geography** playing a similar role on the human geography side. Uhlig (1973; see also Figure 1.5, p. 15) similarly used social geography as a term for the integrated approach to geography, but employed a new concept, geoecology to represent Troll's landscape ecology. Uhlig and other German geographers reserve the term 'landscape ecology' for the study of humanity and nature at a higher integrative level, but even then this takes its inspiration mainly from the natural sciences, and particularly from ecology.

While in German the term 'landscape ecology' is fairly clearly defined, in the Anglo-American world it is often confused with such terms as **human ecology** and **ecological analysis**. In his textbook *Geography: A Global Synthesis* (2001), Haggett proposes ecological analysis as one of the three approaches to integrated geography (Figure 1.6, p. 17). The Anglo-American terms 'human ecology and 'ecological analysis' put a stronger emphasis on human geography than the German term 'landscape ecology'. This came about because the school of **urban ecology**, which was founded by the Chicago sociologists in the 1920s, concerned itself with the social and functional development and division in urban areas. In such a broad context, 'human ecology' and 'ecological analysis' could be considered as encompassing the functional approach in regional geography, which was developed to study the relationships between centres and their surrounding areas.

Landscape morphology

As a form of regional geography, **landscape morphology** was particularly well developed in Germany between the wars. Otto Schlüter, who played a central role in its development, asserted as early as 1906 that geographers should consider as their unifying theme the form and spatial structure created by visible phenomena on the earth's surface. From this point of view, mountains, rivers, pastures, forests, roads, canals, gardens, fields, villages and towns form a unity in the geographer's eyes: this visible picture is the geographer's object of study. Schlüter (1920), however, maintains that those who try to include too much in their field of vision cannot hope to cope with it all and he therefore argues against the all-encompassing chorological geography advocated by Hettner.

Schlüter regarded non-material geographical patterns (such as economic, racial, psychological and political conditions) as not being of primary geographical interest. These should be studied only as part of the explanation of material distributions. The French scholar Jean Brunhes illustrated this when he said that we should study the earth as if we were sitting in a hot–air balloon, looking down upon it. We should analyse the landscape and the characteristic interplay of observable phenomena from up there. The visible landscape is a result of both natural conditions and forces and a manifestation of humanity's work. The landscape itself creates a synthesis; there is no longer a gap between physical geography and the geography of humanity. Both geographies have the same object – the visible landscape – and there is also close contact between them in terms of methods. Because of this, says Leo Waibel (1933), the landscape morphological approach represents an advance for geography, even though the field of inquiry is thereby greatly narrowed.

Landscape morphologists have argued as to how much their field of inquiry should be limited. Should they consider, for example, travelling patterns and the transport of goods and services? Many landscape morphologists considered that these activities should not be objects of their study. They should only be considered as explanatory factors in so far as they contribute to an understanding of the landscape's evolution and character.

Alfred Hettner opposed Schlüter's limitation of geographical study to the visible landscape. He was (as described by Dickinson, 1969, p. 132): 'concerned with the uniqueness of areas, whether this uniqueness was evident in the visible landscape or not. He recognized the focal interest of landscape, but refused to recognize the limits set by it on the study of the human facts in space.'

Hettner maintained the universalistic character of geography on the basis of his evaluations of the philosophy of science. He considered landscapes to be very small *Länder* and, for this reason, regarded attempts to study only their visible parts as a restriction of the scope of regional geography. He argued (1929)

> that it is against the logic of science to permit the picture, i.e. the appearances, to be the decisive factor in defining the subject. ... They exclude thereby exactly those features which have been the pre-eminent concern of geography in the past (human life, nationality, state, partially even the economy) and ... still are.

Hettner presented his *Länderkundliches schema* as a guideline for a chorological regional presentation, starting with physical features and concluding with population. The presentation of thematic maps (juxtaposed 'on top of each other') makes some sort of integration possible, but it is quite clear that Hettner did not solve convincingly the problem of regional synthesis. Through his follower, Richard Hartshorne, Hettner's dominance of the geographical scene was perhaps greater abroad than at home in Germany. In Germany, the different types of landscape geography did not supersede regional geography – as Hettner had feared – but developed as a bridge between systematic and regional geography. Bobek and Schmithüsen (1949) suggested that landscape could be seen as the integrative product of the **geofactors** of the systematic branches (Figure 1.5, p. 15). Through this integration, only such features which appear in an orderly and regular fashion will be taken into account. Schmithüsen and others have developed methods to build up broader regional types through the delimitation of small units called *Fliese*, or 'mosaic tiles', of landscape (Uhlig, 1967 – see Figure 2.2, p. 76).

The methods employed in landscape morphology were widely adhered to in Europe and, in the USA, Carl Sauer provided a basic evaluation of the new direction in his 'Morphology of landscape' (1925), which was of great importance in the early development of his highly influential **Berkeley School** of geography (see Box 2.10). In 1939 Robert E. Dickinson described landscape geography as the most important new line of growth within the subject, but landscape morphology was, however, developed only by a limited number of British geographers even though it was an element in several courses in cartography and was an important component in the interpretation of aerial photographs.

Box 2.10	**Carl Sauer and the Berkeley School**

Throughout his lifetime, Carl Sauer (1889–1975) dominated North American cultural geography in a way that virtually made '**cultural geography**' synonymous with 'human geography' (Jackson, 1989, p. 10). He was appointed head of the Berkeley School of Geography at the age of 33 and held this position until three years before his retirement in 1957. During this time he supervised some 40 PhD students, of whom a great many were later to take up senior academic posts. Through these former students, Sauer's influence was assured on a second generation of geographers.

Sauer argued that the best training a geographer could receive came through **fieldwork** and through developing the skills of observation. A majority of his PhD students studied Latin American and Caribbean topics, and he imprinted on his students 'the need for first hand field experience and for learning the language of the people being studied' (Jackson, 1989, p. 10).

The research Sauer promoted focused on the material aspects of culture, as expressed in the 'cultural landscape', which is most clearly conveyed in his methodological paper 'The morphology of landscape' (1925). In this paper, he defined 'landscape' as 'the unit concept of geography', 'a peculiar geographic association of facts'. The landscape was perceived as describing 'a strictly geographic way of thinking of culture' (1925, p. 30): 'Culture is the agent, the natural area is the medium, the cultural landscape the result' (ibid., p. 46). For example, the USA–Mexico border runs through mountains, deserts and grasslands that are the same on both sides of the border. However, the cultural landscape is different as a result of differences between Mexican and US cultures.

In his early academic years Sauer focused on the morphology of the landscape – as inspired by the German and French regional and landscape studies of static societies that were shaped by centuries of traditional adaptations between humanity and nature. Having observed the dynamics at play in the cultural landscape transitions in America, Sauer shifted his primary research focus to 'a more active appreciation of the social transformation of landscape' (Jackson, 1989, p. 15). His analyses of human agency focused on a search for the origins of institutions and culture traits – for instance, the origin and spatial diffusion of agricultural techniques or the domestication of certain crops or animals. Concentrating on the material aspects of culture, he carved out a special field of study for cultural geography that linked humanity and nature (human and physical geography) and that was not contested by other academic disciplines.

In the tradition of the Berkeley School, cultural (and thus human) geography should not concern itself with individuals but with human institutions or cultures: 'The cultural geographer is not concerned with explaining the inner workings of culture or with describing fully patterns of human behavior, even where they affect the land, but rather with assessing the technical potential of human communities for using and modifying their habitats' (Wagner and Mikesell, 1962, p. 5).

This restriction has, in recent decades, been criticized strongly, from both a humanist and radical point of view. It 'fails to address the wider social context in which cultures are constituted and expressed' (Jackson, 1989, p. 18).

REGIONAL STUDIES IN BRITAIN

'There is fully as much confusion over the meaning of the words "regional studies" as there is over the German word *Landschafti*', states James (1972, p. 267), with special reference to British geography. **Regional studies** have at least three different connotations in Britain. First, there are regional studies that amount to descriptions of segments of the earth's surface, broadly synonymous with regional geography or *Länderkunde as* defined above. Secondly, there are regional studies that seek to divide the earth's surface into either homogeneous or functional areas of varying size, which we have termed **regionalization**. Thirdly, regional studies may denote regional specialization, when an individual geographer devotes a large part of his or her life to studying different aspects of some part of the world (a good example is Percy M. Roxby of Liverpool, who built up a formidable expertise on China).

Patrick Geddes

In Britain, regional studies were indebted to Vidal de la Blache and other French regional geographers and, to an even greater extent, to the French sociologist Frédéric Le Play (1806–82) through his influential Scottish follower, Patrick Geddes (1854–1932). As a starting point for the study of social phenomena in different parts of the world, Le Play carried out research

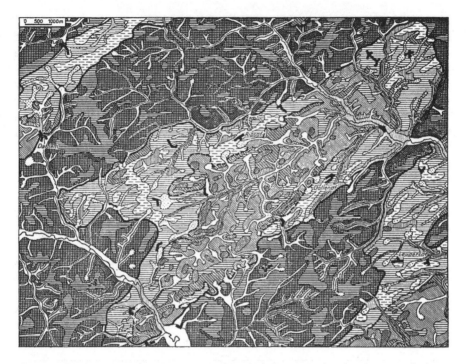

Figure 2.2 An example of cartographic techniques in landscape morphology, used by German geographers to build up broader landscape types from a mosaic of local types

Source: After Paffen, 1955

on family lifestyles and family budgets. He recognized that family life depended on the means of obtaining subsistence (that is, work), while the character of work is largely determined by the nature of the environment (that is, place). This leads to the basic Le Play formula – *place, work, family* – which Geddes transformed into the slogan *place, work, folk* as basic concepts in the study of cities and regions.

Although not a geographer himself, Geddes had a major influence on British geography, especially in the fields of regional survey, regionalization and applied geography. Field study – observation and recording in the field – was basic to Geddes' teaching. This led on to what he called '**regional survey**', embracing place, work and folk (alternatively described as geography, economics and anthropology, or as environment, function and organism – Dickinson, 1969, p. 204). Geddes and his followers established the Le Play Society (which grew out of the Sociological Society), to foster regional surveys. Geddes saw an important application of regional survey in **regional planning**. He compared the regional surveyor to an old family doctor who could interpret specialist knowledge and apply it to the actual condition of the individual patient, whom the doctor would know intimately. As a man of radical views, Geddes was rather impatient with geographers who defined their subject as a *descriptive* science – which tells us what *is*. He thought that geography should be an *applied* science that tells us what *ought to be* (Stevenson, 1978, p. 57).

Geddes also influenced the study of **regionalization**. Andrew J. Herbertson (1865–1915), who was an assistant to Geddes in Dundee and later taught geography at Oxford, presented a scheme for a division of the world into **natural regions**, based on an association of surface features, climate and vegetation. The main translator of Geddes' ideas into geography was Herbert J. Fleure (1877–1969) who, from his chair at the University College of Wales, Aberystwyth, rendered them accessible and acceptable to geography. In his paper on 'Human regions' (1919) Fleure, inspired by Vidal de la Blache, sought to reconceptualize the region by taking into account living experience – including the shifting relationships between people. A crucial role in Fleure's accounts of key moments in human history was played by contact zones between different cultures. Like Herbertson, Fleure also worked on the definition of global-scale regions.

A direct application of Geddes' ideas occurs in the work of Charles B. Fawcett (1883–1952), who translated the somewhat obscure ideas of Geddes into a workable form and made one of the first identifications of **functional regions**. In his book *The Provinces of England* (1919), which attracted considerable attention, he proposed for England a federal structure of 12 provinces. The six principles of the division were clearly inspired by Geddesian regionalism, particularly so in the organization of each province round a 'definite capital which should be the real focus of regional life', the drawing of provincial boundaries 'near watersheds, rather than across valleys', and paying 'regard to local patriotism and tradition in the grouping of areas' (Stevenson, 1978, p. 59).

Partly inspired by Geddes, a development of geography as an applied science started slowly in the 1930s, but took off after the Second World War with a growth in the job market outside the educational system and with the development of new methods of investigation. This is the focus of Chapter 3.

Questions for Discussion

1. Define and discuss the terms geography, cosmography, chorography, chorology and topography.
2. Why is it possible to call Erathostenes' measuring of the size of the earth as the first known geographic research project? What were the available methods to measure geographical latitude and longitude in antiquity and around 1850?

(Continued)

(Continued)

3. What role had Varenius in defining the scope of geography and what was the philosophical basis for Immanuel Kant giving geography a special position among sciences? *hist a geog = all knowledge*

4. What is understood by a teleological scientific stance? Ritter and Humboldt had a strong position in their lifetime, but created no breakthrough for geography as a university discipline. Why? *history*

5. Discuss the role of geographical societies and reasons for, and discussions about, the institutionalization of geography as a university discipline.

6. Discuss the arguments for and against a strong school of geography 100 years ago and today.

7. In which ways did Darwinism influence scientific development in general and geography in particular?

8. How was Darwinist evolution interpreted differently among 'social Darwinists' and 'social anarchists'? How can these different interpretations be said to have influenced later political trends up to today?

9. Define the concepts physiography and geomorphology. Give an account of the scientific achievements within physiography/geomorphology in the first period of geography's institutionalization.

10. Give a critical evaluation of Davis's theory of the cycle of erosion.

11. Give an account of the main ideas within environmental determinism. Has environmental determinism any merit at all?

12. What are the main differences between possibilism and environmental determinism?

13. What is meant with 'the *méthode vidalienne*'? Can this type of research programme have any relevance today?

14. Discuss the terms 'landscape chronology', landscape ecology' and 'landscape morphology'.

15. Discuss the role of Patrick Geddes in the development of regional studies in Britain.

3 GEOGRAPHY, 1950s–1980s: 30 YEARS OF PROGRESS

CHANGING JOB MARKET

Some disciplines have very clear career outlets for their candidates; when you study law, medicine, theology, architecture or even a discipline like geology, it is fairly clear which jobs you are qualified for. Many jobs require a specific degree, some even that you become an accredited or registered member of a certain professional organization protecting the profession and the interests of its members. Geography, as with most of the other 'open' university disciplines, does not have such a protected job market. True enough, for teaching at universities a PhD in the discipline is usually required, and geography was established, as mentioned in the previous chapter, to educate geography teachers for jobs in the high schools. The undergraduate curriculums at universities were organized to provide the needed qualifications for school teaching. Until the first decades after the Second World War school jobs were the outlet for the majority of geography candidates. Today the picture is very different. A survey undertaken in the USA in the 1990s (referred to by Haggett, 2001) showed that only 17 per cent of the surveyed geography candidates worked in educational institutions, including universities, but 40 per cent worked in private industry and business. Local, federal and state governments together employed 38 per cent of candidates. In the UK, teaching jobs in schools are probably still quite important and employment in public government is relatively stronger than in the USA. In recent decades school jobs have become rather marginal for Norwegian MA candidates in geography; the largest employers are municipal planning departments and other public institutions. Geography candidates seem to have fewer problems finding jobs than candidates from traditional social sciences, such as sociology and social anthropology. What are the reasons for this?

One obvious reason is the broad scope of geography. A candidate has a wide variety of topics to specialize in and it is relatively easy for geography departments to develop education in fields demanded by the market. It is more important, however, that the traditional key issues in the discipline have come to the forefront of public debate, such as the issue of sustainable development and global environmental protection, or the issue of economic globalization and how to meet the challenges this creates for regional policies and local responses. At the same time, geographical research has been able to develop new models which help us to understand geographical structures and also to utilize new instruments for mapping and analyses such as satellite photography and GIS (Geographical Information Systems). In this chapter we will give an account of the development that transformed geography to an applied science.

THE DEVELOPMENT OF APPLIED GEOGRAPHY

As pointed out in Chapter 2, Patrick Geddes inspired the development of **applied geography**. One concept derived from Geddes' work was that of the **regional survey** of potential land quality and land use as a basic input to plans for economic development. During the 1930s and on his own initiative, L. Dudley Stamp (1898–1966) organized and directed the first British Land Utilization Survey, employing some 22,000 school children in the mapping of **land use** on a scale of 1/2,500 in their home district under the supervision of school and university teachers. Eventually, the first **Land Use Survey** formed the basis for an official agricultural regionalization of Britain. When the Second World War began in 1939, the vital importance of the maps was quickly appreciated. They provided essential data for the extension of food production necessitated by the German blockade. At the International Geographical Congress in Lisbon (1949), Stamp suggested establishing a World Land Use Survey. The idea was adopted and an international commission under the International Geographical Union (IGU) was set up to supervise the work.

In the 1930s, economic depression accentuated the effects of longer-term economic changes that were creating marked divergences of economic prosperity and distress between British regions. Geographers contributed to national and local studies of these prosperous and 'depressed' areas – although description predominated analysis at this stage. During the 1940s, geographers were widely involved in planning the postwar reconstruction. And during the 1980s, several geographers claimed to have recognized a re-emergence of marked variations in prosperity between the regions of Britain. This latter work, which was obviously politically controversial, showed considerable advances in analytical techniques from that conducted earlier in the century.

An increasing interest also rose on the **cultural landscape** in connection with **regional planning** – partly as a reaction against the uniformity of modern buildings and other landscape features. The ease with which a landscape may be disfigured through technology awakened a concern to care for the landscape. Uncontrolled building has created so many eyesores that the need has arisen for an active policy of landscape protection – including both aesthetic and economic aspects. This was already pointed out by Steers in his book *The Coastline of England and Wales* (1946), which gave a clear indication of the major planning problems of coasts, including the notorious bungalow and campsite development which had been permitted during the interwar years (Freeman, 1980, p. 53).

J. H. Appleton (1975) and others have demonstrated the importance of an informed view of landscape if the attractiveness of long-settled countries like lowland Britain is to be preserved. The rapid development of industrial archaeology also illustrates a persistent general belief in the importance of preserving something of the past's visual culture, including derelict industrial buildings. Robert Newcomb (1979) called for a 'planning of the past' and gave suggestions for the active use of historic features so that the preservation of at least relics of historic landscapes and townscapes is possible. Important texts on the issues surrounding landscape heritage and protection are David Lowenthal's *The Past is a Foreign Country* (1985) and *Possessed by the Past: The Heritage Crusade and the Spoils of History* (1996).

Demand for area planning in districts, counties and regions has similarly increased interest in studies of the cultural landscape. In Norway, for instance, the book *Mountain Regions and Recreation* (*Fjellbygd og feriefjell*) (Sømme, 1965) – the result of research into the effects of the recreational use of upland areas – was a landscape study that attempted to provide a sound basis for a new national planning law.

A newer trend, connected to *humanism* and *postmodernism* (see Chapter 6), is work on the interpretation of landscape as text. Important contributions, for instance, are Denis Cosgrove's book *Social Formation and Symbolic Landscape* (1984) and Kenneth Olwig's *Nature's Ideological Landscape* (1984). Another important text is *The Iconography of Landscape* (1988), edited by Denis Cosgrove and Stephen Daniels.

Several **regionalization** projects have sought to delimit single-attribute regions – such as industrial, climatic, vegetational, morphological and social. While each project had links to the relevant systematic science – social regions with sociology, for example – geographers had a crucial role, focusing either on the **single-attribute region** of the specialist or the **multi-attribute region** of the synthesizer (Johnston, 1997, p. 47).

Whereas between the wars much effort was put into the development of methods to define multi-attribute regions, after the Second World War systematic studies in various specialisms gradually claimed the attention of the great majority of British geographers. Even those who regarded all forms of regional geography as blind alleys conceded that they would continue to exist within geography. E. A. Wrigley (1965, p. 13) put it this way:

> The regional period of geographic methodology, like the 'classical' (including determinism), has left many traces, some of which will perhaps prove permanent, on the methods used in organizing and presenting geographical material. Any discipline is both the product and the victim of its own past successes and these were two of the most important successes thrown up by geographical scholarship.

In the past, regional geography's widespread hold discouraged many geographers from seeking general relationships and theories, and led them to decry the formulation of geographical laws and models. Rejecting the general theories of the determinists, they sought refuge in regional methodologies where each area is unique and somewhat exceptional and must be studied as such. They upheld that geographers should continue with **idiographic** methods – that is, the description of unique phenomena and unique regions.

In the 1950s and 1960s the idiographic method and the humanistic way of thinking within the subject were strongly criticized. A new and dynamic school developed and new methods were brought into use. There was much talk of paradigm crises and revolution, a discussion we will come back to in Chapter 4. Here we continue the historical account of what happened.

A DISCIPLINE RIPE FOR CHANGE

After the Second World War theoretical considerations on the relativity of space (and also research issues such as the study of **diffusion** models and **location theory**) came to occupy a dominant position in geography. One factor in the adoption of the 'new' geography was the critical institutional situation many departments of geography found themselves in, particularly in the USA. In 1948, James Conant, president of Harvard University, had reportedly come to the conclusion that 'geography is not a university subject' (Livingstone, 1992, p. 311). The Department of Geography at Harvard was closed soon after, and the discipline was also gradually eased out of some of the other more prestigious, private Ivy League universities. Interestingly, however, since 2000 geography has been reintroduced at Harvard, due to the fact that theoretical economic geography now has acquired a considerable international recognition!

Among the practitioners of the ever more theoretical sciences, the claim that the regional synthesis constituted geography's essential identity lent the subject a dilettante image in the 1950s. After the Second World War the North American universities were expected to produce problem-solvers or social technologists to run ever-increasingly complex economies (Guelke, 1978, p. 45), and geographers were not slow in adopting theory building and modelling that might promote the status of their science and their own academic standing.

Gould (1979, p. 140) recalls how the new generation of geographers were sick and ashamed of 'the bumbling amateurism and antiquarianism that had spent nearly half a century of opportunity in the universities piling up a tip-heap of unstructured factual accounts'. Morrill (1984, p. 64) claimed that the young generation's vision, although it might seem radical to those satisfied with an inferior status for the discipline, was in fact conservative in the sense that 'we wanted to save geography as a field of study and join the mainstream of science'. Even though, or perhaps due to this, the 'new' geography of the 1950s and 1960s was spearheaded by the Americans. They were, however, inspired by earlier theoretical works in Europe that, so far, had been almost overlooked.

The situation was much less critical for the discipline in Britain because of the very strong and independent position geography held in both schools and universities. In many of the US states, geography was more or less absent from the curriculum as a discrete discipline at high school level, and less than 1 per cent of students entered universities to study geography. Geography graduates had to find career outlets in applied research and planning. The continual threat of departmental closure or staff reduction based on independent evaluations of research productivity also explains the frenetic search in American universities for new ideas and research programmes.

THE GROWTH OF SPATIAL SCIENCE

Location theory originates from economic theory. The classic location theories, including Johan Heinrich von Thünen's work on patterns of agricultural land use (1826) and Alfred Weber's study of industrial location (1909), are economic theories. Later economists and regional scientists, including Ohlin, Hoover, Lösch and Isard, developed theories of the areal and regional aspects of economic activity further. **Regional science** developed in some universities as a separate discipline; in yet others, this research came to be linked with economic geography or regional economics.

Walter Christaller (1893–1969) was the first geographer to make a major contribution to location theory with his famous thesis *Die Zentralen Orte in Süddeutschland* (1933), translated by Baskin as *Central Places in Southern Germany* (1966). Christaller, who had studied economics under Weber, declared in 1968 that his work was inspired by economic theory. When he was working on *Die Zentralen Orte* his supervisor was Robert Gradmann, a geographer who had himself made an outstanding regional study of southern Germany (1931) which, however, closely followed the current idiographic tradition in German **Länderkunde**. Although Christaller's thesis was accepted, his work was not appreciated during the 1930s, and when Carl Troll (1947) wrote a review of what had been going on in German geography between the wars, he did not even mention him. Christaller never held an official teaching position in geography (see Box 3.1 and Figures 3.1–3.3).

Box 3.1	Christaller's Central place theory

A theme in **landscape morphology** (see Chapter 2) – the morphological network of central places in southern Germany, as seen on the topographic map – was the starting point for Walter Christaller when he, as a 40-year-old PhD student, developed his central place theory. He started to 'play with the maps', connecting towns of the same size with straight lines until his map was filled with triangles (Figure 3.1). These triangles appeared to show some regularities. If the region had really been a flat plain with uniform rural population densities, it would seem that the morphological features could be idealized in a hexagonal, hierarchical structure of urban places (Figure 3.2). Christaller used economic theory to explain the rationality of this morphological pattern.

During the Second World War Christaller was asked to use his theoretical abilities in the planning of new German settlements in eastern Europe. But it was only after the war that central place theory had its first real application in the planning of the newly reclaimed Nord Oost Polder in The Netherlands (Figure 3.3).

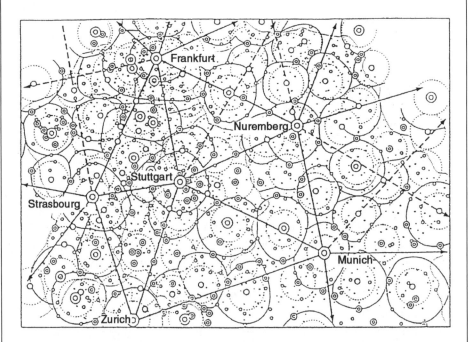

Figure 3.1 The geometrical hexagonal landscape of towns in southern Germany from Walter Christaller's classic study of central places made in the 1930s

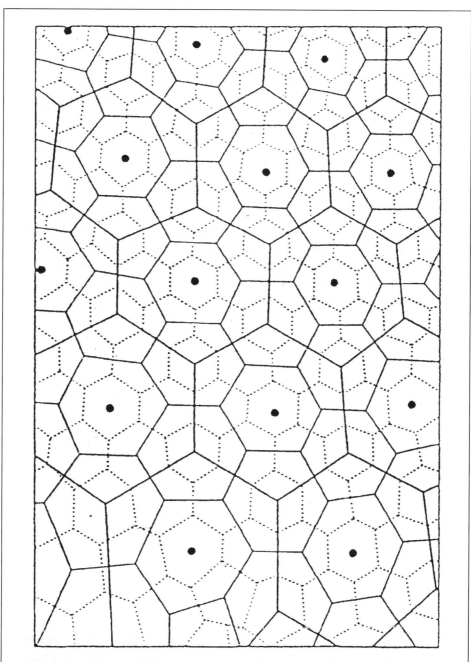

Figure 3.2   This figure shows the ideal pattern of settlements on a flat plain with relatively even distribution of agricultural settlements. When population densities are uneven, the lattice of central places adjusts to the changes, closing up in densely settled areas and opening out in sparsely settled areas

(Continued)

(Continued)

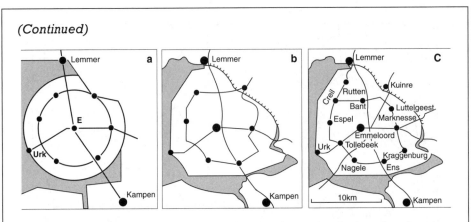

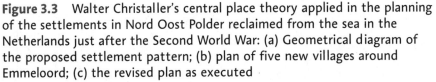

Figure 3.3   Walter Christaller's central place theory applied in the planning of the settlements in Nord Oost Polder reclaimed from the sea in the Netherlands just after the Second World War: (a) Geometrical diagram of the proposed settlement pattern; (b) plan of five new villages around Emmeloord; (c) the revised plan as executed

Source: After Meijer, 1981

Eventually Christaller gained a following, notably in North America and Sweden, when it was realized that his central place theory could be applied to the planning of new central places and service establishments (Figure 3.3) and also to the delimitation of administrative units. Edward Ullman (1941) was one of the first American geographers to draw attention to Christaller's work – American geographers were beginning to develop the theoretical models of urban structures and cities as central places that had been devised earlier by economists and urban sociologists (Harris and Ullman, 1945).

In an account of geography as a fundamental research discipline, the influential American geographer Ackerman (1958) encouraged students to concentrate their attention on systematic geography, cultural processes and quantification. A range of different statistical methods was gradually brought into use in several systematic branches of geography, enabling the development of more refined theories and models.

The acceleration of theoretical work was especially marked in institutions led by geographers who had studied the natural sciences, especially physics and statistics, and/or where there were good contacts with developments in theoretical economic literature. During the 1950s at several American universities, the frontier between economics and geography became very productive of new ideas and techniques.

A seminar for PhD students in the use of mathematical statistics conducted by William L. Garrison at the University of Washington, Seattle, from 1955 onwards was of particular significance. Garrison and his co-workers were mainly interested in urban and economic geography, into which they introduced **location theory** based on concepts from economics with associated mathematical methods and statistical procedures (Garrison, 1959–60). Many of the students from Seattle became leaders of the 'new' geography in the USA during the 1960s, including Brian J. L. Berry, William Bunge and Richard Morrill. Both Berry and Garrison later moved to work in the Chicago area. Through the inspiration of Berry, the geography department at the University of Chicago became a leading centre of theoretical geography. It attracted a large number of PhD students and published a well-known series of monographs. Berry and other leading professors later left the department (which was closed in 1986, demonstrating the vulnerability of geography on the American academic scene). In the 1950s there was a simultaneous development of theoretical geography at the universities of Iowa and Wisconsin.

It is possible, as Johnston (1997, pp. 62–73) maintains, to recognize in this period four schools of quantitative geography in the USA. Three were developed in the departments of geography at the Universities of Washington (Seattle), Wisconsin and Iowa, with Seattle as the most prominent centre of innovation. The fourth – the **social physics** school – developed independently, drawing its inspiration from physics rather than economics. Its leaders were John Q. Stewart, an astronomer at Princeton University, and William Warntz, a graduate in geography from the University of Pennsylvania (who was later employed as a research associate by the American Geographical Society).

Empirical studies indicated that the movement of persons between two urban centres was proportional to the product of their populations and inversely proportional to the square of the distance between them. Stewart pointed out the **isomorphic** (equal form or structure) relationship between this empirical generalization and Newton's law of gravitation. Thereafter, this concept became known as the **gravity model** (Box 3.2). Stewart's ideas about isomorphic relations between social behaviour and the laws of physics were introduced to geographers in a paper in the *Geographical Review* (Stewart, 1947). Here Stewart (ibid., p. 485) stated that human beings 'obey mathematical rules resembling in a general way some of the primitive "laws" of physics'. Warntz, working with Stewart, also borrowed analogy models from physics in his studies of population potentials (Warntz, 1959, 1964). He suggested that the mathematics of population potential is the same as that which describes a gravitational field, a magnetic potential field and an electrostatic potential field (James, 1972, p. 517).

The work of Christaller, August Lösch and others was introduced into Sweden by Edgar Kant (1902–78), an Estonian geographer who had tested their theories in his homeland before taking refuge in Lund after the Second World War (Kant, 1946, 1951). His research assistant in 1945–46 was Torsten Hägerstrand (1916–2004). Through his wife, Hägerstrand had contacts with the Swedish ethnologist Sigfrid Svensson, who had made a number of studies of the relations between innovation and tradition in rural areas using the currently

Box 3.2	The gravity model

Early in the nineteenth century, some scientists suggested that the laws of physics could be applied to the study of human relationships and that the laws of gravitation might explain patterns of travel and trade between places. By the mid-twentieth century gravity models were widely applied within the **spatial science** school of geography. In its simplest form, the **gravity model** can be expressed as follows:

$$I_{ij} = k \frac{(P_i P_j)}{(D_{ij})^2}$$

where I_{ij} represents the interaction between town i and town j; P_i and P_j are the populations of the two towns; D_{ij} is the distance between them; and k is a constant.

The equation indicates that the interaction between the two towns (for instance, numbers of telephone calls, flows of traffic) is proportionate to the *product* (.) of their populations, divided by the *square* – ( )² – of the distance between them.

accepted methodology. Hägerstrand became interested in the possibilities of investigating the process of **innovation** with the aid of mathematical and statistical methods. In focusing on the **process**, Hägerstrand made a clear break with the current regional tradition. His dissertation 'Innovations–förloppet ur korologisk synpunkt' (1953, later translated by Pred (1967) as 'Innovation diffusion as a spatial process') examined the diffusion (or spread) of several innovations among the population of a part of central Sweden. Some of these innovations concerned agricultural practices, such as bovine tuberculosis control and pasture improvement, and others were more general, such as car ownership. With the aid of the so-called 'Monte Carlo' **simulation**, which involves the use of random samples from a known probability distribution, he was able to construct a general **stochastic model** of the process of diffusion. Stochastic literally means at random; stochastic or **probability models** are based on mathematical probability theory and build random variables into their structure. Models may be classified as either stochastic or deterministic. In **deterministic models** the development of some system in time and space can be completely predicted, provided that a set of initial conditions and relationships is known.

The stochastic model enabled the spread of innovation to be simulated and later tested against empirical data. It was demonstrated that the form of distribution at one stage in the process would influence distribution forms at subsequent stages. Such a model *could* therefore be of use to planners in support of future innovations they wished to bring about. The department of geography at Lund University soon became renowned as a centre of theoretical geography, attracting scholars from many countries. Almost from the beginning, there were contacts between Lund and Seattle. Hägerstrand taught in Seattle in 1959 and Richard Morrill came from Seattle to study with him in Lund, where his work on migration and the growth of urban settlement was presented (Morrill, 1965).

In the years that followed, Hägerstrand's technical and statistical procedures attracted more attention than his theoretical analyses. He himself regarded his work as less important for its empirical findings than for its general analysis of the **diffusion** process. He stated in the first sentence of the dissertation that, although the material used to throw light on the process relates to a single area, this should be regarded as a regrettable necessity rather than a methodological subtlety (Hägerstrand, 1953/Pred, 1967, p. 1). This was, of course, meant as a deliberate provocation to the traditionally bound regional geographers. Hägerstrand regarded his (1953) analysis of individual fields of information and their change through time as his most important contribution to geographical thought, as the study of such information fields is basic to a deeper understanding of the processes of diffusion.

During the 1960s, Hägerstrand went on to make detailed studies of individual behaviour, using three-dimensional models to portray the movement of individuals in time and space. An important feature of **time–space geography** is that time and space are both regarded as resources that constrain activity. Individuals have different possibilities of movement in space, conditioned by their economic status and technical possessions, but time imposes limitations on everyone. Subsequent studies in time-space geography, which have been carried out actively at Lund and elsewhere throughout recent decades (see, for instance, Carlstein et al., 1978), have shed much new light on geographical aspects of human behaviour.

The 'new' geography spread over the world from the innovative centres, but it did not have the same impact in all countries. Christaller's work had aroused little interest in his home country, Germany. His theories had to take a detour into the English-speaking world – from whence they returned steeped in the 'new' geography – to be fully appreciated. Initial forms of quantification, such as the use of frequency distribution scattergrams, parameters and index numbers, were first applied around 1960. The introduction of **factor analysis**, notably in a classificatory study of Swiss cantons by Steiner (1965), was the real introduction to new quantitative approaches for most German-speaking geographers. The philosophical implications of the **spatial science** school were first presented by Dietrich Bartels in his book, *Zur wissenschaftstheoretischen Grundlegung einer Geographie des Menschen* (1968).

Another reason for the delayed impact of the 'new' geography in Germany was that geographers tended to follow Troll's appeal in *Erdkunde* (1947) in that they accepted the principle that worldwide research should be a normal component of an academic career. Virtually all established geographers were attracted to employing their talents abroad, leaving their graduate students to cultivate research at home. Research abroad undoubtedly contributed to

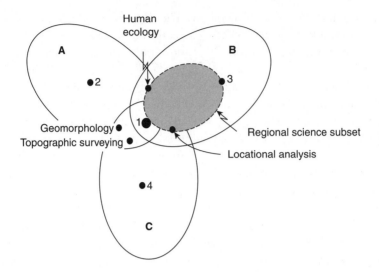

Figure 3.4   Geography and its associated subjects. A: Earth sciences, B: Social sciences, C: Geometrical sciences, 1: The core of geography, 2: Geology, 3: Demography and other social sciences, 4: Topology with other geometric sciences

Source: After Haggett, 1965

Germany's international reputation, particularly through the application of German methods of detailed landscape studies and cartographical work. German geographers also found that their existing techniques were well adapted to research abroad, particularly in the Third World where the statistical basis for quantitative analysis was sparse or unreliable.

Contributions to spatial science in the UK

Major advances in the spatial science school were made in the 1960s by British geographers, notably Peter Haggett, Richard Chorley and David Harvey. *Locational Analysis in Human Geography*, by Peter Haggett, was published in 1965. The importance of this book lay in its overview of much new theoretical work in the subject. Haggett (1965, pp. 14–15) used the diagram reproduced in Figure 3.4 to illustrate the argument that there are three traditional subject associations of geography: with the earth sciences (geology and biology), with the social sciences, and with the geometrical sciences. Haggett (ibid., pp. 15–16) maintained that:

> The geometrical tradition, the ancient basis of the subject, is now probably the weakest of the three. Much of the most exciting geographical work in the 1960s is emerging from applications of higher order geometries. ... Geometry not only offers a chance of welding aspects of human and physical geography into a new working partnership, but revives the central role of cartography in relation to the two.

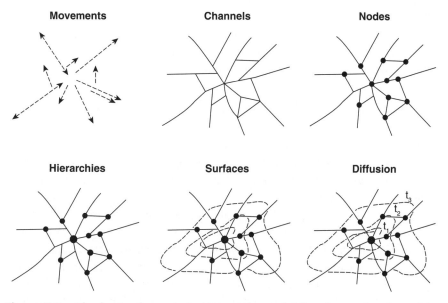

Figure 3.5   The basic elements in Haggett's model for the study of spatial systems, t_1, t_2 and t_3 representing stages in diffusion

Source: After Haggett et al., 1977, p. 7

At the heart of geography as a science is the distributional view: geography is a *discipline in distance*. When we discuss space, it is not the container space 'that frames the totality of a landscape; we prefer to think of space as a system of distance relationships between objects' (Hard, 1973, p. 184). The study of spatial arrangements may be summarized in Haggett's (1965) diagram (Figure 3.5) of spatial structures. The sketch may be seen as a disaggregation of **functional regions**, such as those established around central places in a Christaller model, into five geometrical elements (movements, channels, nodes, hierarchies and surfaces). A sixth element, diffusion, was added later reflecting the contributions by Hägerstrand (Haggett et al., 1977). In contrast to the traditional system of self-sustained regions, the primary element in a modern society is the need and desire for interaction between places which results in a pattern of *movements*. These might be studied as the geometric pattern of straight lines between points, but in fact most movements are channelled along particular route corridors, such as roads. So we can study the patterns of *channels* which, together with *nodes*, represent an organization *network*. The *hierarchy* represents the relative importance of the nodes and the *surfaces* represent the system of land use. Patterns of human occupance are, however, not static. The process of change in time therefore involves **spatial diffusion** as developed by Hägerstrand.

The rapid development of spatial model building and the use of quantitative techniques could not have taken place without computers, but computers did not determine the development of spatial science: 'Model building preceded the invention of the computer in many sciences, but in a discipline like geography, which handles such large quantities of data, it would hardly have been possible to develop operational models worthy of the name without computers' (Aase, 1970, p. 23). This technological development had given the subject new possibilities that young researchers had no hesitation in exploring.

CRITICS OF THE SPATIAL SCIENCE SCHOOL

The models of the spatial science schools inspired new research and opened the way for new work within applied geography. But critics also came early, particularly connected to the **positivism** debate, which we will return to in Chapter 5.

Other forms of critique also appeared. In Britain, Minshull (1970, p. 56) observed that the landscape was becoming a nuisance to some geographers, that many of the models could only be applied to a flat, featureless surface, and warned there was a real danger that these ideal generalizations about spatial relationships could be mistaken for statements about reality itself. In an article, Grigg (1965) had tried to argue that all parts of the earth's surface are unique. If it is held that geography includes the study of the location of its data and that 'locations are unique', then geography cannot fully employ the scientific method. In June 1966, however, Bunge published a short commentary to Grigg's paper, asserting that 'locations are not unique', but general. Locations are comparable, as witnessed by such terms as 'near', 'far', 'close', 'distant' and 'adjacent', which describe the relativity of locations. It is thus the relativity of spatial locations that can be analysed in a scientific way.

Fred Lukermann (1958) reacted especially to attempts by the social physics school to establish analogies with physics, maintaining that hypotheses derived by analogy cannot be tested: falsification is impossible. In a series of papers in the 1970s, Robert David Sack, a student of Lukermann, criticized the view put forward by Bunge (1962) and Haggett (1965) that geography is a **spatial science** and that geometry is the language of geography. Sack (1972) maintained that space, time and matter cannot be separated analytically in a science concerned with providing explanations. The geographical landscape is continuously changing. The processes which have left historical relics and which are creating new inroads all the time must be taken into account as important explanatory factors. The laws of geometry are, however, static – they have no reference to time. The laws of geometry are sufficient to explain and predict geometries; if geography aimed only at analysis of points and lines on maps, geometry would be sufficient as geographical language. But, 'We do not accept description of changes of its shape as an explanation of the growth of a city. ... Geometry alone, then, cannot answer geographic questions' (Sack, 1972, p. 72).

To exemplify why 'geometry alone' cannot answer geographic questions I might use the experiences I had in the work with my doctoral thesis (Holt-Jensen, 1986). It should be noted that this, fortunately, was the old type of doctoral thesis, on which you worked while having a full job as university lecturer; it took me almost 20 years to finish (Box 3.3).

Box 3.3	**Problems with explanation of changing settlement patterns**

The theme for my doctoral thesis was settlement and population changes in the Kristiansand area of southern Norway. Inspired by spatial science and new methods of quantitative mapping, I decided to locate the settlement and population in the grid of *c.* 4,000 square kilometres that constituted the area. Using the kilometre grid on the topographic maps as units of course involved a fieldwork that took a number of months, although many km^2 squares were uninhabited. When all cadastral units were located to squares in the grid, the next job was to link lists from five different population censuses (1900, 1930, 1960, 1970 and 1980) to the cadastral units and so to locations in the grid. In order to make the data available for computer mapping, the data for each square kilometre unit were set on punch cards (at that time). Finally, it was possible to produce nice maps that showed different features of dramatic population and settlement changes in the region. But the *maps* could not *explain* the settlement changes that had occurred through the time span of 80 years. Growth could only to a limited degree be explained by suburban development and decline by long distance or poor communication to major towns. Was the enormous empirical data collection of no use? After contemplating this over a couple of intensive years of teaching, I found that I had to do some extra investigations. I started new fieldwork investigating the present and former income basis in a number of selected settlements in the area, found data on the role of commuting and looked at the effects of master planning in each of the 17 municipalities from the 1960s to the 1980s. This gave the needed inputs to finish the thesis. But it became quite clear that good maps of the changing settlement patterns could not in themselves explain the same patterns. Somehow I felt trapped by the spatial science ideology, although the fault of course was my own. Fortunately, I was not required to deliver the thesis within a framework of three or four years!

Another problem with spatial science models, Broek pointed out (1965, p. 79), crops up if we project a model derived from our own surroundings over the whole world as a universal truth and measure different situations in other countries as 'deviations' from the 'ideal' construct. Models based on research within the western cultural world cannot be elevated into general truths. Brian Berry (1973b) came to the conclusion that a universal urban geography does not exist, and that urbanization cannot be dealt with as a universal process: 'we are dealing with several fundamentally different processes that have arisen out of differences in culture and time' (Berry, 1973b, p. xii). He divided the world into four universes: (1) North America and Australia, with their free-market economies; (2) western Europe, with its planned welfare economy; (3) the Third World, with its economy split between a traditional and modern sector; and (4) the socialist countries, with their rigidly planned economies. Each of these has its own urban geography, which again will change through time.

Haggett et al. (1977, p. 24) also noted that 'the Russian translation of the first edition of this book (Haggett, 1965) made clear how heavily the locational explanations were rooted in the classical economics of the capitalist world. Inevitably, the lopsidedness of the book will appeal to certain readers and condemn it to others.'

Students of **location theory** also got second thoughts as they came to realize that **'economic man'**, that decision-maker blessed with perfect predictive ability and knowledge of all cost factors, does not in fact exist. Locational decisions may be made on a rational basis, but this rationality relates 'to the environment as it is perceived by the decision-maker, which may be quite different from either "objective reality" or the world as seen by the researcher' (Johnston, 1997, p. 150). It was thus necessary to develop alternative theories to those based on 'economic man' and to investigate the decision-makers' behaviour and perceptions (see pp. 150–51).

THE ACHIEVEMENTS OF SPATIAL SCIENCE

It is commonly agreed that the spatial science school threw open the windows of a hitherto introverted discipline, which had had its major links with idiographic disciplines, such as history and geology. Disciplinary boundaries became much more open; methods and theories were openly borrowed from geometry, physics and social sciences as geographers became involved in multidisciplinary research projects. The 1960s and 1970s were optimistic decades for geographical innovators. Student numbers grew rapidly and career opportunities expanded considerably.

The redevelopment of geography as a social science raised the self-esteem of geographers and opened up a job market for candidates within planning and administration. Generalists (as geographers still were, but now with added technical and statistical knowledge) proved to be better adapted to the job market than candidates with narrower specializations.

Haggett (1990, p. 6) argued for practical and pragmatic approaches in geography: if 'science is the art of the soluble, then much geography is the art of the mappable'. 'Thinking geographically', liking maps and thinking by means of them is intrinsically linked with geography. More than any other natural or social science, geography is a *visual science* with similarities in this respect to architecture and the history of art. We like to climb a mountain in order to get an overview, a grand survey of the geographical patterns in front of us. We try to describe and explain the world as we perceive it.

Description and mapping were also central to the traditional schools of geography, but the spatial science school developed more refined methods that made spatial correlations and statistical tests possible. The most recognizable shift was, however, the downgrading of ordered description of what we know (**cognitive description**) and the development of sophisticated models and methods in **morphometric analysis**, such as are described in Figure 3.5 (p. 91). Most of the models created were simplifications of spatial morphological patterns based on empirical data. Christaller's central place theory is an example of this. When trying to achieve a general, theoretical explanation of patterns, theory was imported from other sciences. In many cases it was economic theory.

A major achievement of the spatial science school has been the development of sophisticated methods for the detection of spatial patterns. Many of the models, including such a simple one as the 'gravity model', are good devices to compare data and thus to describe geographical differences. These approaches have given valuable insights into the geographical patterns which form the bases of our analysis or are the results of our decisions. But it might be argued that spatial science research developed greater refinement of description than explanation. Many commentators within human geography have pointed out that spatial science research has been confined to the empirical level, and that we need a structuralistic approach to understand how 'real' or deep structures influence the empirical outcomes or events. (We will return to this in Chapter 5.)

But still, in the frenetic search for grand explanations, we often forget the value of descriptions that enlighten us. New descriptive models are certainly legitimate scientific endeavours as long as they create new knowledge. Spatial analysis provided better tools for descriptions, and new, intriguing developments have continued to be developed. Advanced **systems analysis** has proved its usefulness in **physical geography** and **ecogeography** – the study of humanity's role in changing the face of the earth. Gregory (1985), Goudie (1990) and Huggett (1993) provide many examples of these developments. Here we restrict the presentation to one example (see Box 3.4 and Figure 3.6 on the Sahel catastrophe), and agree with Unwin (1992, p. 129) that it is 'surprising that ecosystems are not more extensively used as a framework for empirical research by geographers'. One reason for this deplorable fact may be that biogeography has generally held a weak position in Anglo-American and Scandinavian geography, although the situation is much better in Germany and eastern Europe.

The potentialities of systems analysis in general, and ecosystems analysis in particular, have not been fully developed. Further, systems analysis could also be applied to human geography, as Mabogunje (1976) has demonstrated: it is well suited to give a conceptual understanding of the factors that influence for instance, rural–urban migration in developing countries.

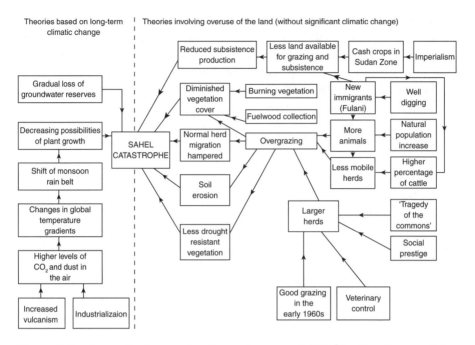

Figure 3.6 A practical example of a systems model illustrating the possible reasons for the desertification in Sahel

Source: After Reenberg, 1982

Box 3.4	The Sahel desertification explained with the aid of a systems model

Chorley (1973, p. 167) suggests that it is important that the challenge of environmental deterioration is *met* with new positive feedback in the form of better planning and control – a task for geographers. Let us consider the Sahel catastrophe, which is analysed in a *systems model* (Figure 3.6) by the Danish geographer Reenberg (1982). She uses the model to illustrate the great number of possible causes for the increasing **desertification** of the Sahel belt of Africa. One possible explanation is climatic change (on the left side of the figure). Climatic changes may be due to strictly natural factors that have prevailed many times in the earth's history. These changes may even have had specific causes, such as increased vulcanism. Alternatively, climatic change may also be induced by human activity, through increased industrialization and pollution. The assumption that increased desertification is the result of climatic change can be tested empirically by studying a series of meteorological observations taken over time.

Having studied the Sahel problem, however, geographers prefer the theories presented on the right side of the model. It is not possible to postulate a simple chain of causes and effects here since many of the elements intermingle and work on each other in complex ways. Some of these elements are associated with the region's traditional ways of life. For example, many tribes calculate their wealth in terms of heads of cattle, and so tend to overgraze. Other traditions include slash-and-burn methods of improving pasture and agricultural land, the collection of fuelwood and the production of charcoal.

When external influences (labelled 'imperialism' in the figure) were relatively small in earlier times, some sort of natural balance was struck, which was regulated by mortality in periods of drought. However, external influences have during the last century encouraged the population to use the more fertile parts of the region for cash-crop production for sale to industrialized countries. Consequently, areas of subsistence agriculture have been reduced and the pressures on these areas increased. Well meaning western initiatives, such as medical provision and veterinary control, have meant that the population of both people and cattle has increased, further exacerbating the problem of pressure on the land. Development aid in the form of well-drilling to provide supplies of clean water has also influenced the nomadic population's wandering routes, resulting in patchy overgrazing around watering places. Vegetation is destroyed and the desert expands day by day. A particular problem is the 'tragedy of the commons'. Although not continuously occupied in former times, most land was held in some sort of tribal ownership. Western administrators, however, often classified land that was not currently being used as 'common land', effectively removing local tribal responsibility for this land which resulted in a loss of ecological balance.

From this somewhat simplified example we can appreciate the complexity of the Sahel problem, which does not lend itself to mere cause-and-effect explanations or to general theories. In undertaking a research project we may not be able to analyse more than a few factors; hence the systems model remains conceptual but, as such, can help us to understand complex relationships. Such system modelling is increasingly needed to give some answers to the pressing environmental problems related to sustainable development of our world.

In retrospect, the 1960s could be characterized as an era of **'hard' science** whereas, in the 1970s, there was much questioning of the law-seeking approach. Michael Chisholm (1975, pp. 123–5) noted that geographical 'laws' in general would not meet the exacting specifications needed to qualify as laws, since they are not generally verifiable. In Chisholm's view, the essential characteristic of central place theory and other theories established by the spatial science school, is their **normative** character; the theoretical construct is not intended to show how the world is actually organized but to demonstrate the patterns that would occur if reality were rational.

Another problem was that many of the geographical models used in planning were static – for example, **central place theory** played a major role in many development programmes but little attention was given to the fact that functional space is dynamic and in more or less continual change.

An example from Sweden, discussed by Gunnar Olsson (1974), may clarify this point. In the 1960s Swedish geographers were engaged in a far-reaching reform of administrative districts, which was expressly intended to abolish spatial social and economic inequalities in the country. The new municipalities were to be large enough to sustain the considerable burden of the municipal welfare services. The methodology used was to observe how the majority of people interacted in space and then to translate the observations into a Christaller-type model:

> Unnoticed by spectators and performers, the play was changed in the middle of the act. The ought of justice disappeared into the wings, invisibly stabbed by the is of the methodology. Exit man with his precise visions, hopes and fears. Enter Thiessen polygons with crude distance minimisations and cost–benefit ratios. (Olsson, 1974, p. 355)

No one thought to ask whether people wanted to change their observed interaction patterns or whether the centralization led to disadvantages for some groups.

Another conclusion drawn by a number of geographers was that physical planning had not been as effective in fostering social change and equality as many people had hoped. For example, many of the land-use and transport plans that spread from North America to practically every large city in western and northern Europe, and in which many trained geographers had participated, seemed to have increased the segregation of social classes and to have sharpened differences in mobility between the car-owning and the car-less groups. In transport planning, the interaction pattern of the average family had been used as a guideline. Such 'deviant' travel patterns as those of old people with no access to a car had not been given much attention. The reason for this had been methodological; quantitative models were built to cope with aggregate and 'hard' data – that is, data easily expressed in numbers. 'Soft' data, which concern human attitudes and deviations in behaviour, could not be handled easily in such models. But even research workers involved in aggregate studies were bound to wonder about deviations from the 'normal', and this led to studies of the welfare of special groups of people, such as old people, and a growing concern for the position of the individual within a mass society.

Each new generation of geographers builds on what was earlier achieved in the discipline, but is also looking at the possibilities of using new research tools to work on the problems that are most important in the contemporary world. We are extremely lucky in that the most important global as well as local issues of recent times are of truly geographical character. And the new tools at our disposal, although posing some critical challenges, have the potential for further development and application.

This means that our discipline will develop and change in the future, but whether changes will be practical or have a fundamental philosophical character remains to be seen. This brings us to the discussion in science theory on **paradigms** and scientific revolutions. In the next chapter we will first discuss these concepts and then revisit the historic development of geography, which was presented in Chapters 2 and 3, to find out whether our discipline has developed in a paradigmatic way.

Questions for Discussion

1. Discuss the job market for geographers. Have there been distinct changes in your country since the Second World War? Try to find some statistics as a basis for the discussion.
2. What is meant by 'applied geography'? To what extent have geography graduates in your country been involved in planning and practical research projects in the last 50 years? What types of task have they been involved in? Are there some new and future tasks you think will be of importance?
3. Give an account of the different fields of investigation and central models within 'spatial science'.
4. Explain Christaller's central place theory and discuss its application in planning tasks.
5. What is the difference between stochastic/probability models and deterministic models? What are the main features of Hägerstrand's model of innovation?
6. Explain and discuss Figure 3.5, presenting the basic elements in Haggett's model for the study of spatial systems. Does this figure present the core of what geography is about?
7. Discuss the achievements of spatial science and the criticisms against it.
8. What is meant with systems analysis and ecosystems analysis? Explain and discuss the systems model for Sahel in Figure 3.6.

PARADIGMS AND REVOLUTIONS

Geography is concerned to provide accurate, orderly, and rational description and interpretation of the variable character of the earth's surface. (Hartshorne, 1959, p. 21)

A traditionally held view – that geography is concerned with giving man an orderly description of his world – makes clear the challenge faced by contemporary geographers. ... The contemporary stress is on geography as the study of spatial organisation expressed as patterns and processes. (Taaffe, 1970, pp. 5–6)

Geography can be regarded as a science concerned with the rational development, and testing, of theories that explain and predict the spatial distribution and location of various characteristics on the surface of the earth. (Yeates, 1968, p. 1)

While geographers would be in general agreement that major changes took place in every aspect of geographical thought during the 1950s and 1960s, there is no general consensus as to what degree the many innovations that took place during those decades fundamentally changed the discipline. The quotations above illustrate the divergent views expressed during this period.

Hartshorne and Yeates seem to differ widely in their prescription of methods but find more common ground in their definitions of the objectives of geographical research. While both are concerned with the variation of phenomena over the earth's surface, Hartshorne visualizes geography as an **idiographic** science, with its main emphasis on the description and elucidation of individual phenomena because these are unique. Yeates (1968, pp. 3–7) considers geography to be a **nomothetic** (law-giving) science that requires the development and testing of theories and models through **hypothetic–deductive methods** in order to develop **geographical laws**.

Taaffe suggests that geography had changed by 1970 – or was in the process of changing from an idiographic to a nomothetic science. Explanatory models that were once thought to be satisfactory for geographical work were discredited by a large number of geographers. John D. Adams (1968, p. 6) said that:

geography is currently in the throes of a paradigm crisis. Instead of asking the traditional question 'Is it geography?', or 'What is geography?', geographers are now asking 'What should geography be?' If a satisfactory answer is not found to the latter question the next question is likely to be 'Is geography relevant?'

It is clear from Chapter 2 that this was not the first crisis in geography's development: Ritter's teleological framework did not satisfy the determinists; and views that were scientifically acceptable to Ratzel and Semple were too deterministic for Vidal and Hartshorne.

KUHN'S PARADIGMS

Perhaps Thomas S. Kuhn (1962/1970a) was right when he claimed that science is not a well regulated activity where each generation automatically builds upon the results achieved by earlier workers. Instead, it is a process of varying tension in which tranquil periods, characterized by a steady accretion of knowledge, are separated by crises. These crises can lead to upheavals within disciplines and breaks in continuity. Even Hettner (1930, p. 356) had suggested:

> that a science does not always follow a straight line of development, but often zig-zags on its road to higher professionalization. This development often corresponds to changes in generations among its professional practitioners. It would be a bad thing if a new generation had no new thoughts ... [but] a science should not suddenly be changed into something quite different from what it has been before.

In his last remark, Hettner was upholding the importance of historical continuity. Kuhn rejected such veneration of the past, arguing instead that fundamental changes are often necessary to enable science to progress. While it is possible to determine objectively whether an explanatory framework is satisfactory and reasonable *within* a specific scientific tradition, we have to choose between different scientific traditions – and this choice is subjective. We must select what Kuhn calls **paradigms** (models or exemplars) for our science.

Kuhn defined paradigms (1962/1970a, p. viii) as 'universally recognised scientific achievements that for some time provide model problems and solutions to a community of practitioners'. Haggett (1983, p. 21) defines a paradigm as 'a kind of supermodel. It provides intuitive or inductive rules about the kinds of phenomena scientists should investigate and the best methods of investigation.' A paradigm is a theory of scientific tasks and methods that regulates the research of most geographers or, where there is a conflict between paradigms, of a group of geographers. The paradigm informs researchers what the object of their science should be, to which questions they should try to find 'acceptable' answers and which methods can be considered as 'geographical'.

Initially, Kuhn did not provide an altogether clear definition of the concept of paradigm. As Mair (1986) has pointed out, Kuhn later clarified some ambiguities and accepted that he had conflated two conceptually distinct, though empirically inseparable, types of paradigm. In the second edition of his book, Kuhn (1970a) argued that the most basic function of a paradigm is as an **exemplar**: a concrete problem solution within a discipline that serves as a model for successive scientists. Generally, such exemplars tie a scientific theory together, serving as an example of a successful and striking application. The most important paradigms are those that generate whole new fields of scientific endeavour. Paradigms (in the sense of 'exemplars') may not always have this all-embracing effect, but will guide research as they are presented to students as models the students should try to copy. An example from geography would be the **regional monographs** written by Vidal de la Blache and some of his contemporaries, which established examples that served a long-standing geographical tradition.

The other meaning of paradigm put forward by Kuhn is as a **disciplinary matrix** – 'the entire constellation of beliefs, values, techniques and so on shared by the members of a given community' (1970a, p. 175). A disciplinary matrix may be shared by a large group of members of a discipline while, at the same time, each member is working with different 'exemplars' in his or her everyday research (Mair, 1986, p. 352). It is in the sense of disciplinary matrix that the term paradigm has most commonly been applied to geography. The term 'paradigm' is used here in its disciplinary matrix sense as we attempt to interpret the history of geography in (simplified) Kuhnian terms. According to this Kuhnian model, scientific development consists of a series of phases (Figure 4.1; Box 4.1).

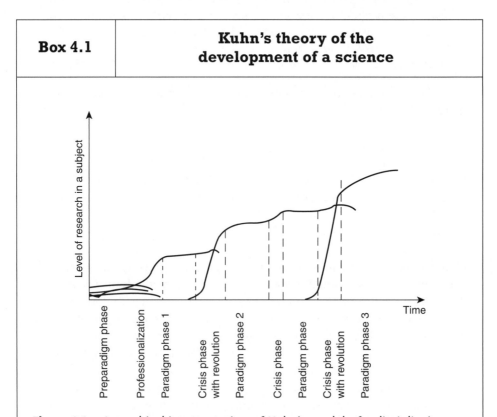

| **Box 4.1** | **Kuhn's theory of the development of a science** |

Figure 4.1 A graphical interpretation of Kuhn's model of a discipline's development. This figure indicates that paradigms and paradigm shifts dominate the whole discipline, whereas in his later work Kuhn pointed out that many scientific revolutions only impinge on the work of smaller groups of scientists within a discipline

Source: After Henriksen, 1973

In a branch of science that becomes the subject of thorough and systematic study, the **preparadigm period** is marked by conflicts between several distinct schools which centre around individual scientists. If we take paradigms to mean **exemplars** (that is, concrete examples of research to be followed), this phase could be labelled a multi-paradigmatic period, as each school of thought develops its own model solutions.

Professionalization (or the subject's development from the prepara-digm period to the stage of scientific maturity) has taken place at different times among the different sciences. Kuhn argues that mathematics and astronomy left the preparadigm phase in antiquity. The transition begins when the question as to what a specific science is about becomes acute. This happened in geography when a university degree in the discipline was needed to qualify as a high school geography teacher. A disciplinary matrix had to be defined for such a degree course, which would also secure and demarcate geography's domain from other university disciplines. One of the conflicting schools of thought will often dominate the others in that it seems the best suited to win the discipline academic esteem. A paradigm is established that leads to concentrated research within a clearly distin-guishable problem area – an activity described as **normal science**.

To bring a normal research problem to a conclusion is to achieve antic-ipated results from new empirical sources; Kuhn called this **puzzle-solving** because of its similarity to solving jigsaw or crossword puzzles. The research workers' perception is constrained by their paradigm; their observation of data is hence directed or attracted to the expected result; there is in-built opposition to unexpected discoveries. The paradigm can advance research and provide economy in the amount of research needed: research workers can go straight to the research frontier without having to define their philosophical bases and underlying concepts. Group identity among research workers is also a strong psychological advantage, which itself can stimulate scientific productivity.

Sooner or later a period of 'normal science' is replaced by a **crisis phase**. This happens when more problems are accumulated than can be solved within the framework of the ruling paradigm. The crisis phase is characterized by a reassessment of former observational data, new theoretical thinking and free speculation. This phase involves basic philo-sophical debates and a thoroughgoing discussion of methodological questions. The crisis phase may end when it seems that no significantly better theory can be developed to solve the problems and thus, conse-quently, research must continue using the old paradigm. Alternatively, the crisis phase ends when a new paradigm attracts a growing number of researchers away from the old paradigm.

The acceptance of a new disciplinary matrix inaugurates a **revolutionary phase**. This means a break in the continuity of research and a thoroughgo-ing reconstruction of the research field's theoretical structure, rather than steady development and the accumulation of knowledge. Accepting a new paradigm is also revolutionary because it attracts the allegiance of the younger research workers who are opposed to established scientists. The

(Continued)

(Continued)

new scientific 'reason' seldom triumphs by convincing its opponents; rather, it succeeds as they die and a new generation takes over. Younger workers who do not conform to the newly accepted paradigm are ignored by its followers, and researchers are continually forced to ask themselves whether the type of 'puzzle-solving' they are doing is the 'right' one.

Exchanging one paradigm for another is not a wholly rational process. The new paradigm will generally provide solutions for the problems the old one found difficult to resolve, but may not answer all the questions that were fairly easy to solve before. It is also seldom possible to argue logically that the new paradigm is better than the old. Even if a new paradigm can buttress itself with empirical and logical proofs, its original choice was basically subjective – an act of faith. Aesthetic considerations may influence the choice of a new paradigm – it may be regarded as simpler or more beautiful than the old one.

To many, Kuhn's picture of scientific activity is alarming: our faith in the objectivity of research is weakened when we consider how subjective the choice of paradigms can be and when we experience the often protracted opposition of some scientific workers to the establishment of new explanatory models. Few research workers welcome a general debate on the subjectivity of research – it may lead to the evaporation of respect and loss of financial support. On the other hand, as suggested by Peter Taylor (1976, p. 132), the youngest research workers who are at the bottom of the formal academic hierarchy have a clear vested interest in changing the existing scientific ideology, and thereby taking over from their elders.

The Kuhnian model has given the 'new prophet' a very effective weapon against the disciplinary matrix of a scientific 'establishment'. They do not need to justify their research as objective in itself; it is enough if they declare it to be objective within the subjective framework they have chosen. This can cause conflict among social scientists, as it is all too easy to equate the choice of a paradigm with the adoption of a particular value judgement. The ultimate conclusion may be that only those who affirm the same general outlook on the world and who have similar political beliefs are competent to evaluate a piece of scientific research.

CRITICS OF KUHN

Few geographers, said Bird (1977), have noticed that the concept of a paradigm ruling a community is akin to that of a dogma – which must be adhered to if a person is to be accounted orthodox. This is in line with the views of Karl Popper, the scientific methodologist who has most effectively criticized Kuhn. Popper (1970) maintained that an active and progressive science should be in a constant state of revolution. While acknowledging that Kuhn had demonstrated the existence of 'normal science' and 'paradigms', Popper deplored these periods as dangers to scientific progress. 'Normal science' becomes established when uncritical scientists accept the leading dogmas of their day and espouse some newly fashionable and formerly revolutionary theory. Popper feared that if scientists of this type were to dominate scientific thinking, this would herald the end of science. Dubbing 'normal science' the 'myth of the framework', Popper asserted that one of the scientist's most important roles is to break down myths. Given that we are always trapped within theoretical frameworks to some extent, we can break out of them at any moment if we act as true scientists. An active science will be in a state of **permanent revolution** (Bird, 1975). Most scientists have interpreted Popper's concept of a 'permanent revolution' as a prescription for what science should be rather than as a description of how it is actually practised. Kuhn (1970b), however, declared that Popper's demand for a 'permanent revolution' was built on assumptions that are just as unreal as are attempts to square the circle.

Paul Feyerabend rejected as historically false the Kuhnian model of alternating periods of 'normal science' and 'revolution'. He maintained that even in theoretical physics, which Kuhn (1962/1970a) used as his example, there have always been alternative basic theories that could act as 'exemplars'. Sciences do not show a chronological shift between periods of normal science and periods of pluralism. Hence, the historical development of a science might best be described by synthesizing the models of Popper and Kuhn.

This outline of Kuhn's ideas has largely been formulated within the context of a 'natural science', and a natural science does not question the basic implicit worldview that science is the study of the empirical world. A fundamentally different approach to the interpretation of the history of science was presented by the social theorist Michel Foucault (1972, 1980). Foucault's concern was to examine the political status of science and the ideological functions it could serve. Central to his argument is that there is a fundamental connection between power, knowledge and truth. Each society has its regime of truth, its 'general politics' of truth, that is the types of discourse it accepts and makes to function as true (Foucault, 1980, p. 131). Truth is therefore a relative concept, depending on the power relations within the society that produces it. To interpret changes in science throughout the course of modern history, Foucault focuses on the various worldviews (or structures of thought) people have held. These he calls **epistemes**. When epistemes change, then science will change as well. This implies that societies create relative truth in order to reinforce the power relations within that society. We will return to this value discussion in Chapter 5. The discussion between Kuhn, Popper, Feyerabend and Foucault depends on their different ideas as to how a scientist works and how scientific theories and laws are established. At this point, we therefore need to look briefly at models of scientific explanation.

INDUCTION, DEDUCTION AND ABDUCTION

Francis Bacon (1561–1626) defined the **inductive** route to scientific explanation (Figure 4.2). A scientist starts with a range of sense perceptions he or she works up conceptually and verbally into a number of loosely arranged concepts and descriptions that we like to call facts. Next, certain definitions are necessary to organize the data. Afterwards the facts are evaluated and arranged in relation to the definitions.

The ordering and classification of data are often the chief activity of a science in the early stages of its development. These first classifications may have only a weak explanatory function. Continuing study of the interaction between classes and groups of phenomena reveals a number of regularities; such regularities and laws may be called *inductive laws* since they are derived from the observations of a large number of single instances. The inductive route's weakness is, of course, the jump from a number of single instances to a general truth ('All swans I have seen are white: all swans are white').

Here we must clarify what a **scientific law** is. Braithwaite (1953, p. 12) defined a law as 'a generalization of unrestricted range in time and space', in other words, a generalization with universal validity. With this definition we can distinguish between **empirical generalizations** and laws. An empirical generalization is valid for a specific time and place but a law is universal. James (1972, p. 473) maintained that a law within Braithwaite's rigorous definition can hardly be formulated on the basis of geographical evidence. The only truly universal laws are those of physics and chemistry, although even in physics there are elements of uncertainty that make probability calculations necessary. Harvey (1969, p. 31) gave the concept of law a much wider significance and postulated a threefold hierarchy of scientific statements from factual statements or systematized descriptions, through a middle tier of empirical generalizations or laws, to **universal theoretical laws**.

Since the nineteenth century, inductive arguments have been increasingly replaced by **hypothetic-deductive methods** (Figure 4.2B). Research workers, starting from an inductive ordering of their observations or from intuitive insights, try to devise for themselves **a priori models** of the structure of reality. These are used to postulate a set of **hypotheses** that may be confirmed, modified or rejected by testing them with experiments using empirical data. A large number of confirmations are supposed to lead to the **verification** of a hypothesis, which is then, for the time being, established as a law and basis for theory construction.

Karl Popper pointed out, however, that the truth of a law does not depend on the number of times it is confirmed experimentally; it is easy enough to find empirical support for almost any theory. The criteria for its scientific **validity** are not the confirmatory evidence, but that those circumstances which may lead to the rejection of the theory are identified. It follows that a theory is scientific if it is possible to *falsify*. Kuhn criticized Popper for believing that a theory, or hypothesis, would be abandoned as soon as evidence is found which does not fit it. Kuhn maintains that all theories will eventually be confronted with some data which do not fit. A fundamental theory is not rejected if individual research data do not fit it, for if it were, then *all* theories would have to be rejected. Up to now the history of science does not record any theory that has not eventually been

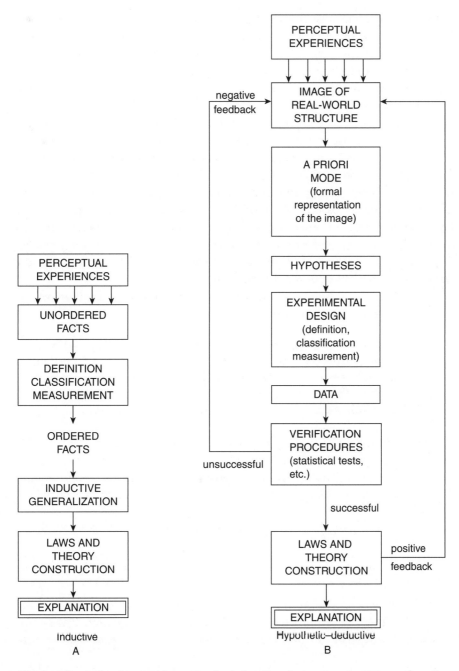

Figure 4.2 Inductive and hypothetic-deductive routes to scientific explanation

Source: From Harvey, 1969

confronted by contradictory circumstances (or instances of **falsification**). According to Kuhn, a fundamental theory is only rejected when a new theory is put forward that is *believed* to be superior (Johansson, 1973).

Feyerabend added that scientific development is much more *irrational* than Popper's scheme of falsification allows. As well as straightforward arguments, the proponents of new theories have also often used propaganda and psychological tricks. Feyerabend maintains that the development of scientific knowledge follows an irrational, almost anarchic path, along which almost anything goes, as far as methodology is concerned (Åquist, 1981, p. 11).

Kuhn did not accept Feyerabend's views on the irrationalities of scientific progress. He denied that he intended to present scientific theories as intuitive and mystical, more appropriate for psychological analysis than for logical and methodological codification. Kuhn asserted that every scientist must gather as much rational proof in support of a new theory as possible and to be precise and honest in his or her work. On the other hand, we need to realize that *data are dependent on theory*. All observations presuppose a certain conceptual apparatus by which the sense perceptions, or empirical verifications, can be arranged. Expectations and former ideas, that is, the hypotheses which have been set up, guide the interpretation of the data to a large extent.

Bird (1993, p. 2) points out that there is no agreed description of *the* scientific method, and continues:

> Just imagine the situation if it were. A totalitarian world of procedures would have to be learnt and obeyed. It is difficult to imagine such a universal framework lasting for very long. But that is not to say that there are no rules or tricks of the trade, although such as now seem useful are all on probation.

Bird (1993, in relation to human geography) and Haines–Young and Petch (1986, in relation to physical geography) find Popper's version of the hypothetic-deductive method and his **critical rationalism** most useful for scientific inquiry. The critical rationalist view of science can be said to build on three principles:

1) *The principle of falsification*: universal statements and theories can only be refuted, not verified.

2) *The principle of criticism*: scientific knowledge grows only when open to critics, trial and error.

3) *The principle of demarcation*: the characteristic of scientific statements are that they are empirically testable, capable of refutation if they are false. (Haines-Young and Petch, 1986, p. 44)

The starting point for any scientific project (see Figure 4.3) is **problem formulation**. This is often a difficult intellectual exercise. Having discovered a problem (P_1 in Figure 4.3) and formulated the restricted questions within the problem area you might be able to analyse in your research, the next step is to decide on how to proceed and then to follow the chosen procedures. In practice this means that, after the problem formulation, you will look at earlier research within your problem area and then discuss and evaluate tentative **theories** (TT) relevant to your research questions. Then you need

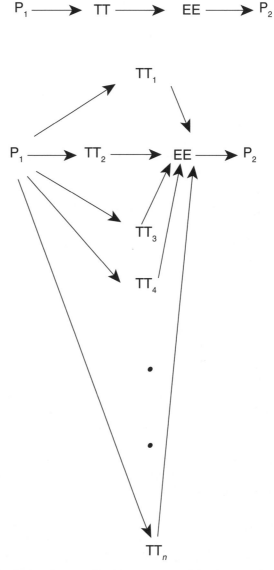

(a)

(b)

Figure 4.3   The hypothetic-deductive method as presented by Popper. P_1, initial problem, TT, $TT_1 - TT_n$: tentative theories, EL: error elimination, P_2 new set of problems. (a) sequence of scientific work with testing of one tentative theory; (b) sequence of scientific work with scientific examination of several competing tentative theories

Source: From Popper, 1972, pp. 119, 243; Haines-Young and Petch, 1986

to find relevant methods for empirical testing, or **error elimination** (EE) of the theories. This may lead on to a residual irreducible problem or problems (P_2), which may be different from the initial problem. P_2 may lead on to suggestions for further research.

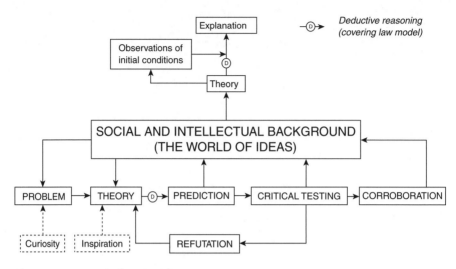

Figure 4.4   Critical rationalism

Source: Haines-Young and Petch, 1986, p. 45

In a scientific thesis it may only be possible to test one tentative theory (Figure 4.3(a)), but this often means a restricted choice between several hypotheses or tentative theories. Figure 4.3(b) presents an alternative procedure as prescribed by Popper (1972, p. 243):

> An excellent example of the method in operation is provided by the work of Batterbee et al. (1985) on the causes of lake acidification in Galloway, Scotland. They examine the hypothesis that acidification is due to acid precipitation against competing hypotheses that it is due to heathland regeneration, afforestation or long-term post-glacial natural acidification. (Haines-Young and Petch, 1986, p. 63)

Popper maintains that it is only through criticism that false ideas can be eliminated and theories gradually improved. Since the truth of an observation can never be established finally, neither can our theories. The best we can say is that our evidence **corroborates** (makes more certain) a theory (Figure 4.4).

Popper's **hypothetic–deductive method** is based on deduction from theories that have been created in the imaginative mind. Alvesson and Sköldberg (1994, p. 43) maintain that such imaginatively inspired theory seems to be a form of scientific virgin birth – probably as rare in science as in nature. Tentative theories, or hypotheses, are almost always based on previous reflections on facts – an inductive phase. **Induction** starts with facts and deduction with theory, but it is not necessary to choose one of them exclusively. **Abduction** is the third alternative, recommended by Alvesson and Sköldberg (1994).

Abduction, like induction, is based in empirical facts (Figure 4.5), but the real process starts with the 'lift' from empirical patterns to tentative theories. Then

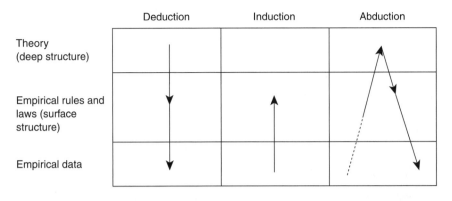

Figure 4.5 Deduction, induction and abduction. On abduction the first arrow from empirical data to empirical rules and laws is 'dashed' to indicate that the real abduction starts with the 'lift' from empirical patterns to tentative theory

Source: From Alvesson and Sköldberg, 1994, p. 45

follows the deductive process as proscribed by Popper – with critical testing leading on to corroboration or refutation, new problems and new testing, in a never-ending scientific process. Abduction may be likened to the process of medical diagnosis: the doctor observes the patient's symptoms and assumes they are caused by a particular disease. But his or her assumptions must be confirmed by tests and checked against other symptoms or comparison with data from other patients. In a scientific process there will be series of abductive 'jumps' between inductive and deductive reasoning, or between empirically loaded theory and theoretically loaded empiricism.

In this section we have discussed general theories of science that have mainly been developed with reference to theoretical natural sciences, such as physics. The transference of natural science methods into the social sciences has, however, brought about a vigorous debate among social scientists that will be discussed in more detail in Chapter 5. There may be similar problems in transferring the **paradigm** concept. Kuhn was trained as a physicist, and his theory derives largely from a study of the history of physics. How far is the history of physics relevant to the less theoretical and quantitative sciences? To answer this question we will now look at the history of geography in the light of Kuhn's model.

CHANGING PARADIGMS IN GEOGRAPHY?

Bird (1977) has argued that Kuhn has been the most influential scientific methodologist as far as geography is concerned. Mair (1986) suggests that geographers influenced by Kuhn fall into two groups. First, there are those who have used Kuhn to legitimize their propaganda for a 'paradigm change' within the discipline and as a weapon against the scientific 'establishment'. Secondly, several geographical historiographers have tried to apply a Kuhnian model to the

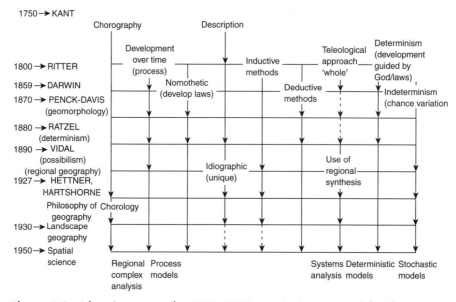

Figure 4.6   Ideas in geography 1750–1950 – two centuries of development

development of geographical thought (see, among others, Widberg, 1978; Schültz, 1980; Harvey and Holly, 1981; Stoddart, 1981; Martin, 1985; Johnston, 1997). The paradigm concept has taken on a life of its own beyond that originally envisaged by Kuhn, and as such has been regarded as a useful 'exemplar' (model or teaching framework) for histories of geography.

Figure 4.6 attempts to systematize the theoretical development of geography up to the 1950s, but it gives an incomplete and oversimplified picture as only the main concepts in the subject's development are shown. Over the course of time, these concepts have changed in significance and connotation. In Kuhn's terminology (Figure 4.1), until Darwin's time geography was in its preparadigm phase: Kant did not found a school of geography but indicated a role for the subject and suggested its position in relation to other sciences. Geography was, for him, a chorographic and mainly descriptive science, distinct from the systematic sciences and from history.

Ritter, on the other hand, and contrary to Kant and his school, did not emphasize the distinctive roles of geography and history but instead emphasized developments over time, linking history with geography. Ritter was, however, the first geographer to describe his method clearly, and his account conforms to Francis Bacon's classical model of how a scientist works (Figure 4.2(a)). However, because of Ritter's teleological outlook, this first apparently active school of geography did not lead the subject into its first phase of a paradigm: contemporary developments in Darwinism meant the rejection of those ideas that might have led to a paradigm.

It should be emphasized that Darwinism did not represent a complete break with the major ideas upon which Ritter's geography had been founded. The study of development over time was still regarded as very important and a deterministic explanatory framework was strengthened further. The break with Ritter was about the forces that shaped development. After Darwin, scientists looked for the laws which controlled nature (and for materially conditioned social laws) and so, to a considerable extent, they adopted a **nomothetic** (law-making) approach to science.

Neef (1982, p. 241) may be right when he suggests that it was at this time that the most important revolution took place in geography, when the universities subdivided their faculties into separate disciplines and a **cosmographic** way of thinking was replaced by the **causal explanations** characteristic of the developing natural sciences.

During the latter half of the nineteenth century, to make geography acceptable as a science, the newly appointed geography professors tried to recast the discipline as a nomothetic science. The hypothetic-deductive method was not, however, applied in a strict sense; we may agree here with Minshull (1970, p. 81) that determinists, as well as geomorphologists, stated generalizations first and then supplied a few highly selected examples as proof. Unlike physicists, geographers could not test hypotheses by verification procedures that involved a number of repeated experiments; statistical tests that might have played the same role as experiments were not as yet sufficiently developed to cope with complex geographical material.

Geomorphology and **determinism** may be said to represent geography's first paradigm phase. This paradigm was effective for geomorphology – it lasted for a good half-century and advanced the whole subject's scientific reputation through its accumulation of scientific information until alternative explanations could be put forward. While geomorphology expanded, other branches of geography experienced a series of crisis phases. For this reason, we can leave geomorphology to one side for the time being and concentrate on developments in human geography.

As the dominating paradigm in human geography, determinism had a short life, being challenged by the **possibilists** and the French school of regional geographers. These geographers stressed the idea that humans have free will, can evaluate different options and participates in the development of each landscape through unique historical processes. Methodologically, geographers were trained to concentrate their study on the unique single region. This inevitably limited the development of theory (as normally understood in science) and made the hypothetic-deductive method redundant. The appropriate methodology under this approach would be to try to *understand* a society and its habitat through field study of the ways of life and attitudes of mind of the inhabitants. Such methods (in the form of **participant observation**) characterize the work of many social anthropologists today.

Fieldwork was regarded as of the utmost importance in the French school of regional geography. Vidal de la Blache based his *Tableau de la Géographie de la France* (1903) on studies in each *departement*. Albert Demangeon walked every lane in Picardy before publishing his regional monograph on that *pays* in 1905. This fieldwork was, however, mainly concerned with presenting a picture of the material ways of life in the regions and had to be supplemented with the collection of factual material from statistical, historical and archaeological sources. In its handling of data – in the data's organization, classification and analysis – the regional approach to geography resembled the inductive method very closely. Regional geographers also sought general causal relationships but were rather unwilling to identify these as 'laws'. More explicitly **qualitative methods**, such as participant observation, were also only adopted directly in local studies much later.

Although possibilists reacted against the determinists' simple explanatory models, many of their ideas were derived from Darwinism. They took over Darwin's concepts about struggle and selection although they also considered that chance and human will played an important role in development. While possibilism could be said to constitute a new paradigm, it did not immediately replace determinism. Partly because of the strength of geomorphology and physical geography, the deterministic explanatory model continued to survive side by side with possibilism.

For a long time, however, geographers continued to stress the central position of **regional geography**. It is, however, fairly obvious that the greatest advances in geographical research during the twentieth century took place within **systematic geography**. In geomorphology, biogeography, economic geography, population geography and many other branches of the subject, a range of new theories and methods evolved. During the interwar period, landscape ecology and **landscape morphology** were subdivided, and many specialist studies were made on **urban morphology**. Research into the morphology of rural settlements was also separated from general studies of agrarian cultural landscapes.

Regional geography flourished in such countries as France, where in school and university teaching geography was closely associated with history and the educational system fostered a national self-image of sturdy peasantry and cultured townsfolk. Regional studies were also important to the academic leaders of the emergent nations in central and eastern Europe, who were seeking to establish and preserve the uniqueness of their national heritage. While the peace settlement of 1919–21 created many new European nation-states, arguments over boundaries between the 'winners' and 'losers' of the war continued to draw extensively on local historical and geographical relationships. In the USA, Edward A. Ackerman (1911–73) argued that 'taken as a whole, those geographers who had mastered some systematic field before the Second World War were notably more successful in wartime research than those with a regional background only' (1945, p. 129).

Another reason for the limited progress of regional geography was the basic philosophy for the subject held by Hettner and Hartshorne. While both regarded the regional geographical synthesis as central to geography, they discouraged historical methods of analysis, arguing (with reference to Kant) for geography to be regarded as a chorological science. Hartshorne was strongly criticized by, among others, Carl Sauer, who, within a year of the publication of *The Nature of Geography* in 1939, said: 'Hartshorne … directs his dialectics against historical geography, giving it tolerance only at the outer fringes of the subject. … Perhaps in future years the period from Barrows' 'Geography as human ecology' (1923) to Hartshorne's latest resumé will be remembered as that of the Great Retreat' (Sauer, 1963, p. 352).

The concept of the subject Hettner and Hartshorne had developed was, however, adopted by a large majority of human geographers from the 1930s until the 1960s. This, if anything, could be regarded as a **paradigm**. The disadvantage was that it did not lead to a universally accepted method of chorological regional description. Neither Hettner's *Länderkundliches Schema* nor Hartshorne's identification of regions through 'comparison of maps depicting the areal expressions of individual phenomena, or of interrelated phenomena' (1939, p. 462) solved convincingly the methodological problems of regional synthesis. Vidal and the French school of regional geography, on the other hand, produced scientific works that served as **exemplars** for a large group of students, and thus could be said to have functioned better as a paradigm.

Schlüter and his followers also provided a basis for the study of the cultural landscape by developing methods of **landscape morphology** (see pp. 72–3). However, the majority of geographers, including the influential Hettner, regarded these methods as being too restricted in scope for geography as a whole, since landscape morphology restricted its analysis to the visible landscape whereas a proper regional synthesis also includes the 'invisible' transactions of social and economic life.

Kuhn's model, so far, fits the development of geographical science only superficially. As we have followed the early progress of the subject, we have seen how new paradigms (in the sense of '**disciplinary matrixes**') have, to some extent, included ideas from older paradigms. New paradigms therefore lose clarity and value as a guide for research until, in the end, more and more people define geography as what geographers do. Despite the impressions we may get from simplified accounts (for instance, Wrigley, 1965), a closer look at the history of geography reveals that complete revolutions did not take place; paradigms, or what may be more appropriately termed schools of thought, continued to exist side by side.

AN IDIOGRAPHIC OR NOMOTHETIC SCIENCE?

Another reason why paradigm shifts can be regarded as more apparent than real is that each new generation of workers, or each individual trying to change the scientific tradition of the discipline, will tend to ascribe a more fundamental significance to their own findings and ideas than they really have. A number of times in the history of geography we have witnessed a characteristic oversimplification of the views held by the immediately previous generation or, rather, of those held by the leading personalities of the current tradition.

A rather good example is the vigorous criticism of Hartshorne presented by Fred Schaefer (1953) in 'Exceptionalism in geography'. Schaefer attacked the 'exceptionalist' view of the Kant–Hettner–Hartshorne tradition – the view that geography is quite different from all other sciences, methodologically unique because it studies unique phenomena (regions), and therefore is an **idiographic** rather than a **nomothetic** discipline:

> Hartshorne, like all vigorous thinkers, is quite consistent. With respect to uniqueness he says that 'While this margin is present in every field of science, to greater or lesser extent, the degree to which phenomena are unique is not only greater in geography than in many other sciences, but the unique is of very first practical importance'. Hence generalizations in the form of laws are useless, if not impossible, and any prediction in geography is of insignificant value. For Kant geography is description, for Hartshorne it is 'naive science' or, if we accept this meaning of science, naive description. (Schaefer, 1953, p. 239)

Schaefer maintained that objects in geography are not more unique than objects in other disciplines and that a science searches for laws. Having eliminated some of the arguments against the concept of a rigorous scientific geography, Schaefer sought to set down the kinds of laws geographers ought to seek. He also urged them to study systematic rather than regional geography.

Hartshorne (1955, p. 242) delivered a very strong counter-attack on Schaefer in which he maintained: 'The title and organization of the critique lead the reader to follow the theme of an apparent major issue, "exceptionalism", which proves to be non-existent. Several of the subordinate issues likewise are found to be unreal.' Hartshorne admitted to having used the words idiographic and nomothetic, but rejected the idea that different sciences can be distinguished as being either idiographic or nomothetic. These two aspects of the scientific approach are present in all branches of knowledge (ibid., p. 231).

Both Hettner and Hartshorne made a distinction between **systematic geography** (which seeks to formulate **empirical generalizations** or laws) and the study of the unique in **regional geography** (whereby generalizations are tested so that subsequent theories may be improved). Hartshorne (1959, p. 121) suggests that geographical studies show 'a gradational range along a continuum from those which analyse the most elementary complexes in areal variation over the world, to those which analyse the most complex integrations in areal variation within small areas'. It can hardly be denied, however, that the interwar generation of geographers were sceptical of the formulation of general and theoretical laws, partly as a reaction against the crudities of environmental determinism. Arguments for idiographic rather than nomothetic approaches seemed to justify the scientific character of studies of the individual case.

ABSOLUTE AND RELATIVE SPACE

Harvey (1969) argued that the concept of geography as a chorological science of the individual case was not tenable because it built on the assumption of **absolute space**. Space in this sense is only an intellectual framework of phenomena, an abstract concept which does not exist in itself independently of objects. In a practical, classificatory sense, absolute (Euclidian) space is, however, rather useful, but it may be argued that 'faced by the seductive utility of Euclidean space we have allowed an interest in maps to become an obsession' (Forer, 1978, p. 233). Space is in this way treated as a container; first, we delimit a spatial section of the earth, say the Newcastle region, and then start to examine its content. The notion of **vertical connections**, humanity's dependence upon local natural resources, was a conceptual basis for such studies. Let us reflect for a while on this and consider, using the **exemplar** presented from the French school of regional geography, how you probably would have presented the life and economy of an English village based on fieldwork in 1910. Contrast this to the current situation. In Box 4.2 we have presented Rothbury, a village in Northumberland, close to the Scottish border.

Box 4.2	The changing space relations of an English Village

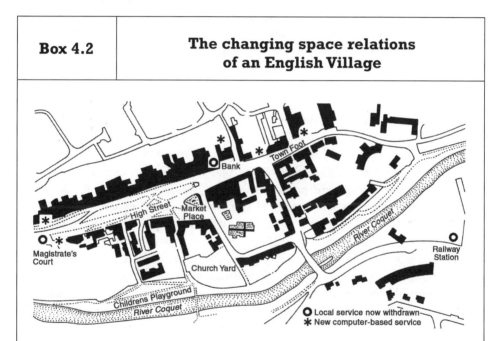

Figure 4.7 Rothbury

The rapid changes from **vertical** to **horizontal connections** during the second half of the twentieth century are illustrated from Rothbury (Figure 4.7), a small service centre of 2,000 inhabitants, 50 km north-west of Newcastle upon Tyne in an upland farming region. In 1950, Rothbury and its valley were substantially self-sufficient. Most people living in the village found work locally, all the nationally provided services were available in the village and most goods could be bought there. Now Rothbury is governed from Alnwick, 25 km away, and the high school is in Morpeth, also 25 km away. The courts and the railway station have closed and the future of the hospital is not certain. A recent survey showed that 38 per cent of the villagers did little or no shopping in Rothbury and 80 per cent of clothes and hardware shopping was

(Continued)

(Continued)

done outside the village. One third of the workforce now drive over 25 km to work and a further 10 per cent work from home, most using computer links. Five local businesses either design software, provide local computer facilities or sell their products nationally via the Internet. Village economy is now largely dependent on high levels of car ownership and on telecommunications.

By the end of the nineteenth century the traditional self-sufficient economies of Europe were giving way to an international market economy, and the value of this type of regional study was reduced. **Horizontal connections**, state and international policies, market forces, the interplay between regions, cities and countries, became more important for local development than the local connections between humanity and the land. This was (as noted earlier in Chapter 2) realized by Vidal de la Blache and it led to greater interest in horizontal, spatial structures.

By introducing the concept of **relative space**, horizontal, spatial relations and distance measured in different ways could be given explanatory power. Distance could be measured in terms of transport costs, travel time, mileage through a transport network and even as perceived distance:

Pip Forer (1978, p. 235) has observed that since distances in time, cost or even network mileage are partly artifacts of socioeconomic demands and technological progress, these types of spaces are naturally dynamic and truly relative. This leads him to the definition of **plastic space** – a space that is continuously changing its size and form. An illustration is given with his own time–space map of New Zealand (Figure 4.8) (ibid., p. 247).

These conceptual and empirical considerations were intrinsic to the development of the **spatial science** school that we discussed in Chapter 3. But did this school and the changes in geography (also called the '**quantitative revolution**') really represent a scientific revolution in the Kuhnian sense.

WHAT KIND OF REVOLUTION?

Throughout the world there was marked opposition among established geographers in the 1950s and 1960s to the learning and teaching of the new spatial science methods, and a reluctance to open professional journals to contributions the editors did not understand. 'There was something electrifying about tilting with the dragons of the establishment', says Morrill (1984, p. 59), and for this reason the young generation of geographers had the feeling of being revolutionaries. In the USA the lack of publication outlets led to the establishment of a theoretically orientated journal, *Geographical Analysis* (ibid., p. 65).

In 1963, a Canadian geographer, Ian Burton, arguing that what he labelled the 'quantitative revolution' was over and had been for some time, cited the rate at which schools of geography in North America were adding courses in

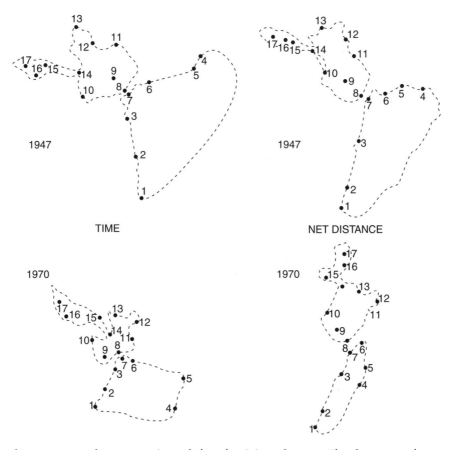

Figure 4.8 A demonstration of the plasticity of space. The four maps have been constructed from data on the New Zealand airline system and its changes from 1947 to 1970. The two maps on the left show how distance measured in time had changed as the airline network had grown and the speed of travel was increased. The maps on the right show how the net distance travel changed with the network

Source: From Forer, 1978

quantitative methods to their requirements for graduate degrees. It must be stated, however, that most geographers did not consider the theoretical developments within the subject as a revolution, and that many 'revolutionaries' were at pains to emphasize continuity in the ultimate objectives of human geography. The use of statistics for the making of relatively precise statements was generally accepted, although the related use of mathematics in modelling received much less attention (Johnston, 1978).

Most research workers regarded advanced statistical methods as being useful in some branches of the discipline; other branches, notably historical and cultural geography, felt less need for new techniques. Leonard Guelke (1977, p. 3) claimed that 'To an extent that is not widely recognised, the move to quantification took place within the basic framework of geography put forward by Hartshorne in "The nature of geography" (1939)'. In many geography departments the works of both Hartshorne and Garrison were on the students' reading lists, but philosophical and methodological differences between them were not an issue in teaching up to the mid-1960s; Schaefer's criticisms (see pp. 115–16) had been forgotten.

Johnston (1997, pp. 74–5) points out that the leaders of the spatial science school did not study the philosophy they were adopting very deeply – apart, that is, from William Bunge's thesis *Theoretical Geography* (1962, 2nd edn, 1966). Bunge, who had worked at Iowa for a short period, extended the arguments of Schaefer to the effect that geography is the science of spatial relations and interrelations, geometry is the mathematics of space, and so geometry is the language of geography. The chorological viewpoint, emphasizing the character of and interrelationships within specific places or regions, was rejected in favour of a geography based on **spatial analysis**, which stressed the geometric arrangement and the patterns of phenomena. *Relative position in space* – distance measured in various ways – became the main explanatory factor.

Quantification as such does not lead to any scientific revolution in the Kuhnian sense. The change from **absolute** to **relative space** as the focus of geographical study had, however, basic philosophical implications and was in this sense revolutionary. The major advances towards a unifying methodological and philosophical basis for the spatial science school were made in the 1960s by British geographers, notably Peter Haggett, Richard Chorley and David Harvey. Their contributions led to a fundamental debate within the subject. The arguments presented by Kuhn (1962/1970a) on paradigm shifts within the world of science were applied to the debate. Chorley and Haggett (1967, p. 39) stated that they had looked at the traditional paradigmatic model of geography and had found that it was largely classificatory and under severe stress. They suggested that geography should adopt an alternative model-based paradigm, and so made it clear that the new development within the subject not only represented a wider range of methods, but also demanded a fundamental paradigm shift. Each geographer was given the choice between the traditional and the new model-based paradigms. Model building was set up as the aim of geographical investigation, a task to be performed with the aid of **quantitative methods** and the use of computers to handle data. A **model** was defined as an idealized or simplified representation of reality that seeks to illuminate particular characteristics. The concept is a wide one – for Chorley and Haggett (1967), a model could be a theory or a law or a hypothesis or a structured idea.

The 'new' geography definitely provided the discipline with notable research projects that could serve as '**exemplars**' for new students as, for instance, Hägerstrand's diffusion model. And the renewed discussion on the basic problems of the subject that followed in the wake of the quantification process may be regarded as a sign of a crisis phase. Individual research workers felt themselves more or less obliged to take a stand and to clarify their own research situation, so there was little opportunity for straightforward **puzzle-solving**. The transformation to a **spatial science** on the basis that locations are essentially relative may also indicate a paradigm shift. But the meaning of this transformation was not generally understood or appreciated by the geographical community. Old ideas continued to flourish and new ideas cropped up as results of criticisms of the spatial science school. Bird (1993, p. 13) has characterized the changes in geography as constant revisions; they may also be regarded as a multiparadigmatic development, since different schools of thought continued to live side by side.

It may, however, be a characteristic of social science that new paradigms do not become so well established to enable a relatively long period of normal science. Or rather, we may have reached a stage of mature science where we experience revolution in permanence, in the Popperian sense. Opposing the so-called 'revolution', Stamp (1966, p. 18) preferred to call it a 'civil war', and noted that quantification had many points in common with a political ideology; it was more or less a religion to its followers, 'its golden calf is the computer'.

A 'CRITICAL' REVOLUTION?

In 1972 Haggett appeared confident that the spatial science school had taken the lead: 'Today the general acceptance of [quantitative] techniques, the more complete mathematical training of a new generation and the widespread availability of standard computers on campus make the conflicts of a decade ago seem unreal' (1972, p. 460). He also pointed out that 'the first years of over-enthusiastic pressing of quantitative methods on a reluctant profession have given way to the present phase in which mathematical methods are just one of many tools for approaching geographic problems' (Ibid.).

In the meantime, a new type of criticism had been developing. Harvey (1973, pp. 128–9) had become a notable apostate, declaring that 'the quantitative revolution has run its course, and diminishing marginal returns are apparently setting in. ... Our paradigm is not coping well. ... It is ripe for overthrow.'

Based on the arguments that many of the models used in spatial science and applied in social planning did not account for the situation of groups that deviated from the average (see p. 151), a **welfare geography**, working within the framework of the existing economic and social system, was promoted. Harvey, however, advocated **radical geography**, calling for both revolutionary theory and revolutionary practice. Its aim was clearly voiced in *Social Justice and the City* (Harvey, 1973, p. 137): 'Our objective is to eliminate ghettos. Therefore, the only valid policy with respect to this objective is to eliminate the conditions which give rise to the truth of the theory. In other words, we wish the von Thünen theory of the urban land market to become not true'.

Harvey maintained this could only be done if the market economy was eliminated. The task, therefore, was the self-conscious construction of a new paradigm for social geographic thought, which might stimulate a political awakening and start a social movement with the ultimate goal of bringing about a social revolution.

Berry (1974) commented that Harvey relied too much on economic explanations; in our postindustrial society, control is no longer economic but political, making a Marxist analysis more or less passé. Morrill (1974), however, in reviewing Harvey's *Social Justice and the City* (1973), confessed that he was pulled most of the way by the revolutionary analysis, but that he could not make the final leap in accepting that our task is no longer to find truth but to create and accept a particular truth.

REVOLUTION OR EVOLUTION?

Just as Harvey favoured revolution in society, so he supported the **paradigm** concept and the simplified Kuhnian model of the development of science through revolutions: 'A quick survey of the history of thought in social science shows that revolutions do indeed occur' (Harvey, 1973, p. 122). Harvey assumed that the motivation for the construction of a paradigm in social science is the desire to manipulate and control human activity and social phenomena. The spatial science paradigm, according to this view, came into existence as a response to pressures from the material, or economic, base of society, which suggested the desirability of discovering ways of manipulation and control, particularly within the planning sector (Quaini, 1982, p. 155).

Harvey (1973, p. 121) did not regard Kuhn as a revolutionary because of 'his abstraction of scientific knowledge from its materialistic base'. According to Jan Widberg (1978, p. 9), Kuhn provides a dialectic–idealistic interpretation of scientific advancement. Widberg maintained that it is possible to describe the history of scientific thought within a discipline on the basis of four fundamentally different views. These are categorized through two sets of dichotomies:

	Mechanical	Dialectical
Idealistic	I	II
Materialistic	III	IV

A **mechanical viewpoint** implies that the development of science is linear, with each new generation continuing from the point where the old generation left off. There are no revolutions, only growing specialization, professionalization and the advancement of better methods and understanding. Kuhn expresses the **dialectical** view when he maintains that a science develops through contradictions and revolutions with changes of paradigms (II above).

An **idealistic viewpoint** implies that ideas are the driving force behind scientific development and change. Each individual makes his or her own choice, and it is the genius of scientists that counts. A **materialistic viewpoint** implies that the material base governs the advancement of scientific knowledge. Scientific activity reflects the special interests of those who are in control of the means of production (Widberg, 1978, pp. 2–3). In Harvey and Widberg's telling, the story of geography has been the tale of the geographical legitimation of the social conditions that produced it. This locates their argumentation in IV above.

But it is also possible to argue that in geography paradigms (or, rather, schools of thought) have not succeeded each other but, to a greater extent, continue to exist in parallel. New schools slowly absorb the older ones, leaving some former contradictions to linger on within the new structure. Figures 4.6 (p. 112) and 4.9

suggest that concepts and lines of thought survive after basic shifts have taken place in the discipline, and may crop up again in new clothing.

Anne Buttimer (1981, p. 82) maintains that the idea of a 'paradigm' has proved appropriate for describing developments within the physical sciences; it fits less comfortably in the story of biological sciences and finds itself on rough ground when applied to any field that aims at a comprehensive understanding of humanity and environment. Buttimer maintains that everyone who has studied in some depth the life, work and experiences of those individuals who have taken a leading role in the shaping of our science will appreciate that the paradigm model gives a distorted picture of actual developments.

Figure 4.9 illustrates the existence of parallel schools of thought within geography since the Second World War. This is in line with Johnston (1997, p. 389),

'TRADITIONAL'	'QUANTITATIVE'	'CRITICAL'
Historical geography ――――――――――――――――――――――――――――→		
Cultural geography ―――――――――――――――――――――――――――――→		
		Humanistic geography ―――→
Landscape studies ――――――――――――――――――――――――――――→		
Regionalization ――――― Computer mapping – GIS ―――――――→		
Population and settlement ―――――――――――――――――――――――→ studies		
	Central place theory ―――――――――――→	
Economic geography ―――――――――――――――――――――――――――→		
	Location theory ―――――――――――――――→	
		Behavioural geography ―――→
	Social physics ―――――――――――――――→	
	Innovation studies ――――――――――――→	
		Time–space geography ―――→
	Systems analysis ――――――――――――――→	
		Ecogeography ―――――→
		Welfare geography ―――→
		Radical geography ―――→
	In current practice ――――――――――――――――→	

Figure 4.9 Schools of human geography 1950–1980. It must be stressed that this classification should be treated with caution, for the criteria for the classification are not consistent throughout the scheme. While 'traditional' schools are mainly classified on the basis of their themes, most, but not all, of the 'quantitative' schools are classified in terms of their type of theory. The 'critical' schools are a real mixture: some are classified on the basis of their special methodology, while others owe their position to a particular political approach. Systems analysis is better regarded as a general method which might be useful to a number of schools rather than as a school in itself. The expressions 'traditional', 'quantitative' and 'critical' are in inverted commas because the use of these terms as labels is highly debatable – as is the grouping of schools under each label

who concludes that 'human geography is currently characterized by a multi-paradigm situation at the world-view level – and by a wealth of exemplars on which research is based'.

From this we may draw the conclusion that the dichotomy between a dialectical and mechanical understanding of the history of our subject is an interesting academic study, but the truth as we see it lies somewhere between the contradictions. Shifts of major importance do occur, but they seldom encompass the whole scientific community – old ideas and concepts remain with us to a large extent; new discoveries may sometimes have the character of mutations – and usually they look more like the rephrasing of old truths.

To analyse the dichotomy between an idealistic and a materialistic view, we have to discuss social research and values more closely. Initially, this means we need to get a better understanding of the debate on **positivism** and **critical theory** (Chapter 5). And from there it will be possible to discuss branches of 'critical geography' and the other new trends of the discipline which have developed in the last decades (Chapter 6).

Questions for Discussion

1. What is the difference between a nomothetic and an idiographic science? Give some examples of nomothetic and idiograph approaches used within geographical research.
2. Define 'paradigm' and 'normal science'. What is the difference between understanding a paradigm as a disciplinary matrix and as an 'exemplary model'? Give examples from geography.
3. Explain Kuhn's paradigm model for the development of a science and discuss criticisms of the model.
4. Discuss, on the basis of Figures 4.2, 4.3 and 4.4, inductive, hypothetic-deductive and critical rationalist routes to scientific explanation. How can we understand abduction?
5. Discuss the changing ideas within geography in the period 1750–1950. Can we find some clear paradigm periods with 'normal science' during these 200 years?
6. What was at the core in the discussions between Harthorne and Schaefer in the 1950s?
7. Discuss the binaries vertical/horizontal connections and absolute/relative space. Consider a local community you know well and discuss to what extent these binaries are of value in an investigation of this community.
8. Did the spatial science school/'the quantitative revolution' represent a revolution in the Kuhnian sense? Give arguments for and against?

POSITIVISM AND ITS CRITICS

The prestige and support that aid research stem from the general belief that research is an almost objective, value-free activity. There has been a widespread tendency to think of research as an uncompromising search for truth, an activity unaffected by the emotions, beliefs, attitudes and desires of either the researcher or of the society in which the research takes place. When research workers discuss scientific results in the same way as politicians discuss political issues, many people will conclude that there must be something wrong with the research, thus putting its prestige at risk. Social scientists who work with less exact or less clearly definable data are particular targets for such attitudes.

Natural scientists, as a rule, work with discrete materials which lend themselves to experiment and objective analysis. Their conclusions are widely received as truths. Social scientists have a weaker database, are often personally involved in the research issue and can seldom experiment with their material. The question of objectivity is therefore most acute for social scientists. The results of social science research are often regarded by the public as if they were merely points of view. A discussion on the role of values in the social sciences is therefore important – not only for the viability of research activity but also for relationships between scientists and the general population, and for public attitudes towards science.

POSITIVISM AND CRITICAL THEORY

Scientific and philosophical discussion has produced two chief trends of meta-theory (theories about theories or theories about theory-making) for scientific research: **positivism** and **critical theory**. 'Both trends are in a sense more "climates of opinion" than definite schools of thought. There is far more discussion within the trends than between them', says Skjervheim (1974, p. 213). There are a number of different versions and definitions for each of these meta-theories. We cannot cover these here in philosophical stringent way, but will use the simplified **binary** positivism/critics of positivism as a starting point. From the very start we have to acknowledge that any binary is a simplification, a starting point in a learning project, but in the end a model that has to be criticized and eventually broken down.

Critical theory is associated with a group of scholars frequently known as the **Frankfurt School**, represented (particularly since 1950) by Jürgen Habermas. As we do not restrict the discussion below simply to the work of the

Frankfurt School, we will henceforth use the expression 'critics of positivism' rather than 'critical theory'. Positivism is usually identified with the school of **logical positivism**, as it was elaborated by the so-called **Vienna Circle** in the 1920s. Logical positivism was intended to be a renewal of two closely related traditions in the philosophy of science: the British **empiricism** of John Locke (1632–1704) and David Hume (1711–76), and the continental **positivism** of Auguste Comte (1798–1857). There are, however, other philosophers and scientists who belong to the empiricist and positivist traditions who do not accept the particular developments of the ideas adopted by the Vienna Circle of logical positivists. Karl Popper (1902–94), although associated with the Vienna Circle, was regarded by this circle as 'our official opponent' because he criticized their use of the **verification** principle as a central focus of positivist methodology, developing the alternative **falsification** principle. As we have discussed earlier (pp. 106–10), Popper has been considered as the founder of a new methodology of science called **critical rationalism**, which can be regarded as an alternative to logical positivism. Following Johnston (1986a), we will include critical rationalism in our discussion of positivism. Leaving the thorny semantics of philosophy of science, we will now try to give a simplified presentation of the development and leading principles of positivism.

THE DEVELOPMENT OF POSITIVISM

After the Renaissance, when a range of taboos against empirical research had been dispelled, science (notably in seventeenth-century England) developed as an independent school of thought, separate from religion. Locke formulated the empiricist principle that all knowledge is derived from the evidence of the senses; and what is not derived from the evidence of the senses is not knowledge. Reliable knowledge can only come from basic observations of actual conditions. To be scientific is to be objective, truthful and neutral.

Comte, who later defined **positivism** as a scientific ideal in line with Locke's principles, believed that alongside the natural sciences there should also be a science of social relationships (which he called sociology) that should be developed on the same principles as the natural sciences. As natural sciences uncovered the laws of nature, so scientific investigation of communities would uncover the laws of society. He admitted that social phenomena are more complex than natural phenomena but believed strongly that the laws governing society would eventually be discovered and hence subjective elements in research would be eradicated. This belief is central to Comte's proposition that social development takes place in three stages:

1) *theological,* when people explain everything as God's will;

2) *metaphysical* or free-based speculation (as a characteristic of the 'Enlightenment' movement – see below); and

3) *positive,* when causal connections are revealed between empirically observed phenomena.

Comte coined the term 'positivism' in 1830s France to counter what he regarded as 'negative' aspects of the pre-Revolutionary **Enlightenment movement**. The Enlightenment, associated with Voltaire, Rousseau and other French thinkers, had stressed the importance of universal education and the value of individual common sense. Through Enlightenment, the people were to be liberated from superstition and barbaric rule. This philosophical tradition also involved a romantic and speculative approach that sought to change society by considering **Utopian** alternatives to existing situations. Comte regarded this Utopian speculation as 'negative' since it was neither constructive nor practical; it demonstrated that philosophy was an 'immature' science. Philosophers, like other scientists, should not concern themselves with such speculative matter, but should study things they could get to grips with: material objects and given circumstances. This approach was to be recommended as the *positive approach*.

Comte himself wanted to change society's development but stated that the nature of positivism is not to destroy but to organize. He argued that organized, gradual development and change should replace the disorder created by the French Revolution. Comte identified free speculation, or *systematic doubt* – as defined by René Descartes (1596–1650) – as the *metaphysical principle*. **Metaphysics** was defined as that which lies outside our sense perceptions or is independent of them. Positivists should regard metaphysical questions as unscientific. Comte held the metaphysical principle (systematic doubt) responsible for the French Revolution, which, having begun to tear down the feudal structure of society in a state of emotional enthusiasm, had ended in despotism. In a positive society, scientific knowledge would replace both religious belief and free speculation. In this way positivism was progressive in that it strongly opposed the belief that the Bible was authoritative in scientific inquiry.

As was shown in Chapter 2, the publication of Darwin's *Origin of Species* (1859) was a major boost for positivism as a scientific ideal. The great stress laid by positivism on empirical data and replicable research methods enabled a marked development of science during the nineteenth century. Because metaphysical questions came to be regarded as unscientific, science developed its own objectives that were apparently free of belief and value postulates. Positivism tends to be *anti-authoritarian* in so far as it requires us not to believe in anything until there is empirical evidence for it, and it can be investigated by controlled methods. We should not therefore accept authority because it is authority, but only give credence to things for which there is scientific evidence. This sceptical attitude, and the consequential search for certainty, has naturally enough brought conflict for positivists and led them into confrontation with dictatorial regimes.

This was particularly the case with the Vienna Circle of logical positivism, founded in the 1920s. Its members were opposed to everything that smacked of metaphysics and unverifiable phenomena. They therefore became bitter opponents of Nazism, which they saw as a mixture of irrational prejudice and ideological dogma. 'Positivist' became a term of abuse in Nazi Germany and was applied to Alfred Hettner, among others (van Valkenburg, 1952, p. 110). The Nazis wanted research to be based on their own ideology. Moritz Schlick, the leader of the Vienna Circle, was murdered, and most of the Circle's other members were driven abroad. As long as science is uncompromising in its search for the truth it will threaten regimes that are based on systematic lies and ideological postulates.

In defining the rigorous principles that science must follow in order for it to be called science, the Vienna Circle added the adjective 'logical' to positivism. The methods of **formal logic** had to be used to define the elementary statements or **axioms** that would constitute fundamental empirical knowledge and to derive further statements of knowledge from those axioms. Euclidian geometry (geometry as you learnt it in school) provides a classical example of this process. A few fundamental axioms provide the basis for a system of geometrical knowledge proved through a formal scientific verification procedure. New, verifiable statements or hypotheses can be formulated from fundamental propositions and from formerly proven statements or laws. These new hypotheses must be tested in turn against reality to establish their veracity (Johannessen, 1985, p. 59).

PRINCIPLES IN POSITIVISM

A major aspect of logical positivism is its emphasis on the unity of science. Scientific status is guaranteed by a common experience of reality. A common scientific language and method ensure that observations can be repeated. Since science has a unified method, there can only be one comprehensive science. The common method is the hypothetic-deductive method (see p. 107) and the model discipline is physics. The language that will make a unification of science possible is the language of theoretical physics or **thing language**. The ultimate aim is, in the words of Rudolf Carnap, to construct 'all of science, including psychology, on the basis of physics, so that all theoretical terms are definable by those of physics and all laws derivable from those of physics' (cited in Skjervheim, 1974, p. 222). The poles and the system of latitude and longitude are the only special definitions that must be made before pursuing geographical research. It follows from this that disciplines are to be distinguished from each other by their object of study, and not by their method (Gregory, 1978, p. 27).

From empiricism, positivism derived the central thesis that science can only concern itself with **empirical questions** (those with a factual content), and not with **normative questions** (questions about values and intentions). Disregarding the question as to whether what we can sense as objects comprises the whole of reality, it could be said that empirical questions are about what a thing *is* as based on our sense perceptions and scientific investigations. Normative questions are about what a thing *ought* to be: 'How are the available food resources distributed between the inhabitants of the world?' is an empirical question. The corresponding normative question would be: 'How ought the available food resources be distributed between the inhabitants of the world?'

Positivism holds that, since we cannot investigate such things as moral norms with our senses, science should keep away from normative questions; we cannot justify our tastes scientifically. Science can describe how things are and, experimentally or by some other means recognized by scientists, discover the association of causes that explain why things are as they are. The research worker can, given his or her knowledge of contemporary associations of causes, forecast possible future developments from given propositions. But science cannot from 'is' statements draw conclusions about 'ought' statements. Ideally, science is value-free, neutral and impartial. When the scientist evaluates things, using 'ought' statements, he or she is no longer a scientist but becomes a moralist or a political campaigner. In this way it can be said that positivism also displays the characteristics of an ideology, in so far as it claims that its particular mode of inquiry is the sole valid approach to scientific knowledge and that other modes are metaphysical and non-scientific (Johnston, 1986a, p. 18).

CRITICISMS OF POSITIVISM

Because positivism seeks authority from the methods of natural science, it is not so anti-authoritarian as it claims to be. This may lead positivists into thinking that there are technical solutions to all problems – an essentially conservative standpoint. The wish to be free from value judgements may lead scientists to build ivory towers for themselves, wherein research takes place without much discussion of its objectives and implications. Positivist research workers might restrict themselves to describing how things are and how they will develop if they continue on the same track as now. Critics maintain that the prestige modern science has acquired creates an aura of inevitability around these 'are' statements and tendencies.

Others go further in arguing that value-free research is impossible. Subjective elements will intrude in many stages of the research process, especially at the stage when research workers choose a topic for study from the many available. We can, for example, imagine that research workers, starting from their own well established and strong opinions as to what the distribution of the world's food supply ought to be, will choose to investigate the empirical question as to *how* the food supply is distributed. Even if the researchers do not deliberately consider *what* the distribution ought to be, it would be difficult for them to exclude their own views wholly at the stages of problem formation and the interpretation of results. It is also obvious that once results are available, the description of the existing distribution will influence the views of decision-makers as to what the distribution ought to be. In this process we can say that scientific activity is itself shaping reality. In such a case the scientist is no longer a passive observer.

Other critics maintain that the positivists' belief in the unity of science is wholly unrealistic; positivism allows its view of the logic of science to influence its conception of the content of science. We should not oversimplify things by laying down rules as to how science should function without taking account of what actually happens within the livelier research traditions. The fact is that several main lines of scientific inquiry (including important schools in psychology and social science) do not show any sign of developing towards the ideal of a unified science: ideas about unified systems of concepts belong on the drawing boards of scientific theoreticians; the inner drift in science itself is to give each area of investigation its own form of expression.

It is even possible to argue that each and every scientific school of thought is a form of cognition, an agreed approach to the analysis of the world. Teaching a discipline consists of teaching its current forms of cognition. When, for example, one learns to see things geographically, it is not reality itself one learns about but a perspective on reality (see the 'cone' in Figure 1.8, p. 20). What the positivists are trying to do is to base all knowledge on methods that have been carried over from the natural sciences into the human sciences. They have developed a specifically technical conception of science, and try to exclude scientific traditions that do not adapt to their recommended technical language and methods. A typical example is Schaefer's rebuttal of the chorological viewpoint and his efforts to make geography into a **spatial science** (see pp. 115–16).

Wilhelm Dilthey (1833–1911) considered that while we *explain* nature, we *understand* social life and human intentions. This appreciation lies at the root of the **hermeneutic** (Greek *hermeneuin* = to 'interpret') tradition within social science that, by putting oneself into another person's shoes, tries to reveal, for instance, human intentionality by **verstehen** (a German word which means something between understanding and empathy).

We should note here that the English-speaking peoples use the term 'science' in the context of a positivist approach following the model of the natural sciences rather than those of arts and humanities. The German expression **Wissenschaft** is much wider and comprises all forms of methodological study carried out in a systematic way and based on defined theoretical assumptions about the nature of research objects (Johannessen, 1985, p. 153). There are at least two main types of *Wissenschaft* that are separate from and not inferior to each other. Wilhelm Windelband (1848–1915) agreed with Dilthey in rejecting the positivist concept of a unified science, preferring to distinguish between the **nomothetic** (law-seeking) sciences and the **idiographic** (descriptive) or historical sciences. As we have seen, this distinction has had a considerable impact on the debate on geographical methodology (see, for instance pp. 115–16 and Figure 4.6, p. 112).

Empirical methods are well suited for most research within the natural sciences, but the positivist stance that the social/cultural sciences should copy the methods of natural science is not acceptable. When social scientists borrow models of system building from natural sciences they must treat all their elements as objects. When the mind is treated in this way it is materialized either directly (by being conceived as the 'thing that thinks') or indirectly (by being considered as a relation between objects in the world). At the extreme, we might talk about brain processes instead of ideas or images, but we cannot study human behaviour in the same way as we study animal behaviour. The difference is that humans have intentions. Intentional expressions such as 'to imagine something', 'to believe something', 'to love somebody' cannot be translated into the **thing language** of the natural sciences: they cannot be understood as objects as seen from the outside. If you study your fellow human beings as physical objects you will not get to grips with their intentions. It is better to build bridges to other people by breaking down the barriers between the observer and the observed and creating an intersubjective understanding. This is the principle of **subjectivity** in social science, which says that behaviour has to be studied and described in terms of the acting individual's orientation towards the situation.

Immanuel Kant criticized empiricism as a philosophy because, as a man of deep religious belief, he was concerned about what he saw as empiricism's **nihilistic** implications. Neither empiricism nor positivism leave room for a God, nothing is a priori certain. Kant's need to ordain certain main features of truth was satisfied by his doctrine of 'categories', in which he claimed that if there is no prime cause for the content of reality, the form of reality must be primarily a given. What the well of consciousness is filled with is an empirical question but, regardless of what is put into it, the content of the consciousness is shaped by the form of the well. Human beings cannot know how things are in themselves; we only recognize things as they take shape through our senses and by our conceptualizing them. The reason why pure chaos does not reign within the field of scientific activity is that human perception and reflection are built upon common categories within which impulses are classified (space, time, **cause**) and, as was explained in Chapter 2 (p. 41), Kant classified the branches of science into three corresponding categories.

DIALECTICS, HEGEL AND MARX: BREAKING DOWN BINARIES

Georg Wilhelm Friedrich Hegel (1770–1831) made scientific inquiry appear even more subtle and complex by arguing that the categories we use for classification and thought (structure of concepts, speech) are not fixed for all time but are historically and socially conditioned. Often we cannot gain a full understanding of a thing by merely studying it on its own. We must also consider its antithesis – its opposite. In fact, continual consideration of the antithesis may well throw new light on the current thesis. The development of knowledge in the Hegelian model is described as **dialectic**. Increased insight into the new thesis, gained through contrasting it with its antithesis, may lead to a synthesis. This in its turn enables us to set up new binaries – theses and antitheses. This process does not achieve a permanent form of knowledge, correct for all time. Knowledge and science are not like a steadily growing ant-hill of pine needles but are defined better as continually changing and deepening processes. This method of setting up binaries has in fact been used in Chapter 4 and in this chapter as an educational principle. In Chapter 4 we asked whether geography had developed as a science through gradual evolution or through paradigm shifts and revolutions. The conclusion came as neither–nor, but. ... This chapter sets up positivism against its supposed antithesis and discusses to what extent geographers have followed one or the other.

Gunnar Olsson (1975, p. 29) suggests that the crucial point about dialectics is that understanding and creation themselves are moved by dialectical transitions; truths are relative; and statements can be designated as 'true' only at a given point in time and, in any case, they can be contradicted by other 'true' statements:

> While conventional reasoning knows only the either-or distinctions of the excluded middle, reality knows the both-this-and-that relation of dialectics and many-valued logics. Since contradiction is not external to reality but built into its structure, the language in which reality is discussed should itself have the same characteristics of internal negation. It is in this sense that reality is dialectical, for both reality and dialectics are governed by perpetual processes of internal tensions and not by stultifying juxtapositions of opposites. As a consequence, both the empirical and the logical bases of our theories should be open to conceptual change. It is rather to falsify for the sake of creative understanding. This is possible, because dialectic movement is not inference but deepening of concepts.
>
> (Ibid., pp. 28–9)

Hegel (1975, pp. 153–4) discussed dialectics with special reference to geography. He differed from Kant but agreed with his contemporary, Ritter, in defining geography as a historical rather than as a naturalistic discipline, 'a study of the possible modes of living offered by the environment to people settled in various regions of the Earth' (Quaini, 1982, p. 19). As the historical development of civilization gradually frees people from the constraints of the natural conditions under which they live, a dialectic relationship develops between the geographical environment and its population's way of life. It has been maintained that Karl Marx (1818–83), who developed the dialectical method further, was also influenced by Ritter – we know he attended Ritter's lectures – as he turned his thoughts from Hegelian **idealism** to **historical materialism** (Cornu, 1955). In so far as Marx's most important methodological texts are primarily devoted to a critique of Hegel, idealism and the mysteries of speculative construction, they naturally include rather important elements of **positivism**. Marx believed it was necessary to turn from the abstract to the concrete (Quaini, 1982, p. 29). The consciousness was for him more a product of material conditions than their foundation. The material world and humanity's behaviour therein were the **base** upon which thoughts and ideologies formed a **superstructure**.

An aspect common to Marxism and positivism is the *theory of realistic knowledge* as this was developed in early or 'naive' **realism**. Knowledge means cognizance of an objective truth: it regards the world as concrete. **Marxism** also proclaims the unity of science, but the basis for this unity is not so clear-cut as in positivism. Engels leaned to the natural sciences when he maintained that the gradually increasing similarity between theories of social science and those of natural science would lead to the accommodation of nature and society within a unified philosophical perspective. In his youth, Marx also wrote about a unified science which comprised nature, society and human psychology. However, while positivists maintained that a unified science should be based upon the methods of the natural sciences, Marx considered the philosophy of the social sciences to be potentially far superior to that of the natural sciences. Therefore the eventual fusion of the two fields of study would come about through the socialization of the natural sciences (Harvey, 1973, p. 128).

Marx asserted that we know only one science, the science of history (Quaini, 1982, p. 35). It also follows from the grand Marxist theory that society develops in stages in accordance with developments in the factors of production. Marx refused to accept that the scientific laws governing society were eternal. This view contrasts sharply with the claim of positivist science that scientific laws are universal in space and time. Engels pointed out that 'to us, so-called economic laws are not eternal laws of nature but historical laws which appear and disappear' (cited in Gregory, 1978, p. 73). Marx was particularly critical to the work of the economists Adam Smith and David Ricardo; he considered their outlook on reality to be ahistoric and non-dialectic. Society has inbuilt conflicts which will resolve themselves by change, both in practice and in theory.

SCIENCE AS A FORCE TRANSFORMING SOCIETY

Critics of positivism maintain that metaphysical assumptions cannot be excluded from science. Facts are not facts in themselves: they represent those parts of reality that can be appreciated with the concept apparatus available. Facts are facts only in relation to a given scientific aim which is itself structured by the values intrinsic in society. The scientific process is therefore restricted by the environment in which it takes place and is constrained within the limits of the research workers' perception. Foucault (see p. 105), for instance, argues that scientific truth is a relative concept, dependent on power relations within societies. Within particular societies and during periods of time power relations create particular **epistemes** (conditions for acquiring knowledge). In his insistence on the relativity of truth, Foucault rejects any form of absolutism or any perspective that will seek to provide a definitive view of society (Poster, 1984, p. 39).

The power regime of the present capitalist society is, however, problematic for scientists as natural science is applied by society in such a way that science becomes a tremendous force that transforms the community (Ackerman, 1963, p. 430). Value judgements are implicit in the application of scientific results – in nuclear physics, for example – and, consequently, natural scientists cannot avoid making up their minds about them. Even the priorities given to different types of research are connected with values; it is not irrelevant whether the priority we give to research funding is in nuclear physics or ecology.

In social science the problem of values is deeply involved in both theory and practice. Concepts in social science are related to human evaluation. A typical example is the concept of natural resources. A natural scientist might study coal as a thing in nature, but in social relationships coal is a resource which must be translated as 'something of value to humanity'. Coal is interesting to social scientists because it is a resource and forms the basis for coal-mining districts. But coal has not always been a resource, and not all coals found in nature are resources. The market situation and the cost of extraction may lead to closure of a coal-mine even if there is a lot of coal remaining. The human evaluation that creeps in makes the use of the 'thing' language difficult in social science.

Another problem is that ordinary language must be used widely in the social sciences because it is spoken by those who are investigated and also because there is a close affinity between daily speech and technical language. When, for example, we ask a commuter for his or her opinions about his or her own travel to work, we must take account of the concepts as understood by the interviewee. A problem arises when we define our concepts 'scientifi-cally' before embarking on a research project and later use these definitions to interpret our results without evaluating critically what happened during the investigation. The person who has been interviewed may have a wholly differ-ent understanding of the concepts. In the social sciences, a dialectic relation takes place between subject and object. It is impossible for the research worker who is investigating social phenomena to regard these as objects wholly exter-nal to him or herself. The subject is him or herself part of the object: the social scientist acts as a part of the society he or she studies.

The dialectic between the subject and the object leads on to what has been termed **double hermeneutics**. In their writings, social scientists explain whatever they have understood about the beliefs and attitudes of their fellow citizens, but the people they write for are more or less identical to the people they are writing about. If readers understand what the writer has understood, they may be led to change their attitudes or actions. These new attitudes can then be investigated again by the social scientist, explained and understood *ad infini-tum*. The meaning ascribed to the one constantly mediates the meaning ascribed to the other through double hermeneutics (Skjervheim, 1974, pp. 298–9; Gregory, 1978, p. 61).

Since our knowledge of the world is established through scientific presen-tations, reality and knowledge can be changed through human reflection and practice. 'Reality', as constituted by scientists, can therefore be transformed into something else. **Critical theory** suggests that science should take an interest in these possibilities of change. For this reason, the **Frankfurt School** developed *Ideologiekritik*, which aims to enlighten agents about their true interests. A distinction is made between ideology in the *pejorative* sense and ideology in the *positive* sense. Ideology in the pejorative sense is a system of **pseudo-constraints** or 'systems of beliefs and attitudes accepted by the agents for reasons or motives which those agents could not acknowledge' (Guess, 1981, p. 20). In general, such an ideology makes it possible for a minority group to impose surplus repression on their society – that is, more repression than is needed to maintain that society. The other members of society accept the minority ideology, unaware that the underlying motive of the minority is 'surplus repression'. Positive ideology, on the other hand, represents the desiderata for a particular society, which reflect the true interests of its members. This is something to be constructed, created or invented through discussion and reflection within the social sciences: 'A critical theory, then, is a reflective theory which gives agents a kind of knowledge inherently productive of enlightenment and emancipation' (ibid., p. 2).

However, although there are certain rules for *Ideologiekritik*, it is difficult to define an ideology objectively in the positive sense in so far as the 'agents' do not understand their true 'interests'. This is the point made by Lenin when he argued that 'the correct proletarian world-view must be introduced into the proletariat from the outside by members of the vanguard party' (ibid., p. 23).

Positivists argue that adherents of critical theory confuse scientific problems with others of a predominantly human interest. It is possible to describe ideologies and their *raison d'être* scientifically. It may well be possible to unmask the real motives behind an ideology in the pejorative sense. But it is not possible to construct positive ideologies scientifically. This is a task for political resolution.

PRACTICAL CONSEQUENCES FOR RESEARCH

The chief effect of the positivism debate on practical social research has been to enliven discussion about the influence of value judgements on research activity. The thorough-going positivist standpoint stresses the importance of reducing the value element as far as is possible. Research workers would be wise to refrain from problems on which they hold strong opinions that might influence the research process or cause faults that would reduce the value of the findings. Ultimately, we should avoid totally research themes where strongly divergent views are held so as to escape being implicated in political conflicts.

Others consider we should not avoid contentious questions or even questions in which we have a strong interest; in these circumstances we should be on the alert for outbreaks of subjectivity. This can be achieved by maintaining careful accuracy in description and by carefully describing our methods so that other research workers can confirm our results. Some scientists would not regard this as sufficient. As well as taking care to avoid subjectivity, research workers should express their personal viewpoints clearly so that their significance can be evaluated and accounted for in the overall consideration of the research results.

A contrary view is that research workers should take up exactly those questions in which they feel deeply involved. The influence of value judgements can be positive when it motivates us to greater efforts. Research workers should declare rather than try to eliminate the influence of values on their work, so that these influences, being observed, will enable different views within the research environment to correct each other.

Some would go as far as to say that research workers should use science to fight for their values. If the 'value' is a political viewpoint of the research worker, he or she may set the problem and publish the results of research in order to support his or her political viewpoint. People who think this way argue that research, according to the positivist ideal, does not consider how things could have been, only what they are. Such research supports the existence of, and consequently provides subliminal evidence for, the predominant values in society. The research worker who does not share these values must therefore be free to pursue research with the intention of changing basic values, and therefore the nature of society.

There will undoubtedly be different views as to how we should tackle the practical research problems created by value elements. We may agree that neither research ethics nor objectivism demand freedom from values: the influence of values must be accepted as an inescapable element in research. Research ethics therefore become closely associated with the degree to which value judgements are clarified. Gunnar Myrdal (1953, p. 242) claimed that 'We need viewpoints and they presume valuations. A "disinterested" social science is from this viewpoint pure nonsense. It never existed and it never will exist.'

The practical consequence of such an appreciation is that the research worker must be free to choose research projects he or she regards as critical. This implies that scientists themselves, by and large, should have the power to decide how the funds for research should be distributed. Certainly, each community will have a research policy but this should not be carried so far that politicians and those assigning tasks at the administrative level outside the scientific environment actually determine research tasks in detail. This approach to the freedom of research is widely shared among scientists, although in many countries the reality does not conform to this ideal.

Politicians and people in general are, however, just as qualified to make value judgements as are scientists. If science is admitted as a force that transforms society, and the ivory tower of science becomes a governing structure of society, clearly it must be brought under democratic control. It is impossible for science to maintain both privileged autonomy and a commanding position. Until now, scientists have generally regarded their autonomy as more important than their power, and have consequently tried to separate their political from their scientific activities. As both a scientist and a local politician, the author appreciates that he has been in a privileged position in his political activity, since scientists are generally better trained to formulate problems and to sift out the essential elements from voluminous official documents than is the ordinary citizen. For this reason, the influence of science and scientists may be a problem for democracy; the able academic has a stronger voice than the ordinary citizen.

The freedom of science is, however, threatened today by the way research is increasingly financed by private capital. When research assignments are funded by private firms, these firms will to a large extent decide the agenda for researchers. Governmental funding should, in principle, be more balanced, but here also the political agenda of the day will lead to a focus of some tasks and forget others of possibly greater importance. My role as coordinator of a large EU-funded research project (Neighbourhood Houring Models/NEHOM, 2000–04) somehow underlines this. We had initially formed a cross-national/cross-disciplinary group of housing researchers interested in **social exclusion** and stigmatization in European housing neighbourhoods and were looking at initiatives to counter-act this social problem. But it was difficult to find a programme section in the EU bid to researchers that suited our aims. The focuses in the EU framework programmes were on economic development and the physical environment. Social policies were stated as primarily being an issue of subsidiarity or responsi-bility of the single member states. After two unsuccessful bids we finally struck lucky the third time and received ample funding from the programme for 'Energy, Environment and Sustainable Development' in the fifth framework programme. We were required to deliver practical results – a handbook and an interactive CD-ROM that could be used as practical guidance for city planners and politicians – which we duly did (Holt-Jensen et al., 2004), but as scientists it was strange that we were not required to provide basic theoretical background analyses, and not even an elucidation of the methods we applied in the 29 case studies we undertook. Both were, of course, very important and were the basis for lengthy discussion within the team. This example shows a general trend in research assignments: the funding asks for practical results which can be used directly. To some extent this lack of focus on basic theoretical research is, however, balanced by requirements in academia to demonstrate theoretical abili-ties in PhD theses and to acquire promotion to professorships.

In most research projects value elements are most significant in the first phases of the process when research problems are chosen, set and defined; and also in the concluding phases of research when the results are interpreted and presented. In the intervening data-handling phase, value elements do not play such a large role – they concern primarily the classification of data. When interpreting and presenting research, the problem arises as to how far to carry the conclusions and where to cut it short. Is the assignment completed when the relationships shown by the data have been described, or should we also use our imagination and theoretical insight to add something about the circum-stances under which these relationships will change or disappear? This problem is particularly acute for social scientists, where the possibility of changing direction depends on human attitudes and intentions.

GEOGRAPHY AND EMPIRICISM

The intermediate position of geography between the natural and social sciences is one reason for the relatively late start of the debate on positivism within the discipline. Another reason is the **idiographic** tradition in geography, which has been supported by strong links with other idiographic disciplines, such as geology, biology and history.

Geology is the natural science that has traditionally been closest to geography. The research methods of geology were described *inter alia* by Simpson (1963, p. 46) as different in nature from those of physics. He associated geology with what he called historical sciences. Geology refrains from the formulation, verification or rejection of hypotheses through experiments and the establishment of universal scientific laws. Its approach is **empiricist**, but does not follow the strict scientific rules of **logical positivism**. It describes and clarifies 'concrete' simple phenomena and puts them into a geological chronology and classification.

Similar comments have been made concerning traditional views on history as a discipline. Dray (1966, p. 45), for instance, argued that 'History ... seeks to describe and explain what actually happened in all its concrete detail. ... Since ... historical events are unique, it is not possible for the historian to explain his subject matter by means of covering laws.' In physics, individual phenomena and their combinations cannot be presented as really new objects, but historical phenomena, either singly or in combination, can hardly ever be subjected to a uniform form of measurement; they exist as truly new phenomena. The laws of the natural sciences may be regarded as having unrestricted universal validity but historical generalizations are not valid for all times and places.

The majority idiographic view (based on the significance of individual occurrences) which has dominated these neighbouring sciences has, as we have seen in the historical account in Chapters 2 and 3, also been important in geography. The **determinism** of the nineteenth century proved to be rather an unfortunate attempt to establish laws, but its failure to do so led to *scepticism towards nomothetic approaches*. Geographers therefore turned their backs on that major element of positivism, that is the unity of science with one methodology whose results are not modified by time and space.

Since Darwin's time, however, other elements of positivism have dominated traditional geography. Geography was clearly defined as an empirical science. Its data were regarded as concrete – things experienced by the senses exist as facts. The question as to what reality could or ought to consist of was regarded as not scientific, being instead political or metaphysical in nature. This view may well present fewer problems for geography than it does for sociology and other social sciences. That part of the database of geography which concerns natural conditions is concrete, and may be defined by natural science terminology and methods of measurement.

Many data in human geography are similar to data in physical geography in that objects which appear on a map or aerial photograph (including patterns of settlement, lines of communication and elements of land use) are as concrete as are the data used by agronomists, geologists and biologists.

Although other material in human geography is not so clearly manifest in the **cultural landscape**, part of it is concrete and measurable. We may consider, for example, the numbers settled or employed at a particular place;

transport as measured in quantities of goods carried, or numbers of vehicles or persons; the use of raw materials and energy in production and the amount of material available, and so on. These are data that are, in principle, as easy to handle as those the 'concrete' natural scientists study but, in practice, human geographers must depend on data collected by others, such as maps and statistical material. This implies that the data are already interpreted before our investigation starts. In an investigation, interpretations crop up at many levels and can create much confusion and insecurity in the minds of research students. As pointed out by Biilmann (1981), all research includes both empirical and hermeneutic (or interpretative) methods (see Box 5.1).

| **Box 5.1** | **Interpretation and reflection** |

Whereas **quantitative methods** are well suited to analyse physical systems in which data are well defined, they have to be supplemented or replaced by other methods in the scientific analysis of human activity systems that are poorly structured and in which data are difficult to quantify. Alvesson and Sköldberg (1994, pp. 10–11) point out that a polarized debate on the merits of quantitative versus **qualitative methods** is not fruitful. This question cannot be solved in an abstract discussion, but has to be related to the actual research problem and its objectives. Some cases, even in social science, demand a purely quantitative approach; others require a purely qualitative approach; and often a combination of the two is more satisfactory. The main point is that the scientific problem has to be defined first. Then we might choose the most appropriate methods of solving it (Bourdieu and Wacquant, 1992).

Qualitative methods are concerned with interpretation and reflection and on this basis Alvesson and Sköldberg (1994) suggest four types of reflective research:

1) *Empirical approach* (particularly as exemplified by **grounded theory**), which gives weight to systematics and research techniques. Qualitative methods ought to follow a closely considered logical approach in relation to the empirical material and should also use well defined techniques for data handling. The result is an empirical descriptive study in which empirical induction plays a major role, but in which hermeneutic interpretation, critical theory and poststructuralism are also of some importance.

2) *Hermeneutic approach*, in which research is primarily seen as an interpretative activity. It is important to realize that all research includes and is done by an interpreter, who acts together with and studies other interpreters (see double hermeneutics, p. 134). Methods cannot be separated from theory, as preconceived concepts and suppositions guide the interpretations and the

(Continued)

(Continued)

results of the study. Here hermeneutics is a predominant form of research thinking, but in a research project other approaches will also play a role.

3) *Critical theory* stresses that the scientist needs to be aware of the political-ideological character of research. Social science is a social phenomenon which cannot be separated from its political and ethical context. Research and the modes of research will have difficulty in avoiding either the acceptance or challenge of existing social conditions. Interpretations and the theoretical assumptions upon which these are based are not neutral but are embedded in and support the construction of political and ideological preconceptions. A research project based on critical theory cannot, however, completely avoid the other approaches.

4) *Poststructuralism* suggests that texts may be seen as having an independent life: a scientific author's text is, in great measure, a reflection of the discourses that provide the context for the text. There is nothing chaotic or anarchistic about the way discourses emerge in particular settings (e.g. institutional), but this mode of thought does, of course, raise questions about the ability of individual geniuses to create wholly new texts (how could we understand such a text?). One important conclusion is that **self-reflection** is crucial for researchers: What role am I playing? How am I perceived by the subjects of my research? An important aspect is the importance of reflection on the power of language and concepts, since these are interpreted differently by different people. We need, therefore, some understanding of **semiotics**, which deals with symbols, signs and meanings as objects of research.

When it comes to practical research, the different types of research that have been described will employ and mix different approaches to interpretation and reflection. In each type of research, however, some elements are more dominant than others. It is also possible to argue that the four types of scientific reflection and approach are present and have different relevance in the different stages of a research project. In the initial stages of, say, a PhD project, the focus should be a critical evaluation of the empirical collection of data, either by quantitative or qualitative investigations, so a basic empirical approach is needed. In the next stage, when data are collected, they have to be interpreted, and you need a critical evaluation of your way of using this form of hermeneutic approach. Throughout your investigation, maybe in particular when you sum up the results, you need to have a critical understanding of the extent to which they are embedded in the contemporary episteme of the society in which you live. And finally, of course, you need to reflection how your text will be interpreted by others. Will the text have a life of its own that you did not intend?

Source: Based on Alvesson and Sköldberg, 1994, pp. 14–15

A concrete representation of 'reality', such as a map, is the result of a number of transformations that involve interpretation and human evaluation. The cartographer has to interpret data and transform them for the purpose of the map. The map's scale and symbols may well be decided by someone else, depending on the purpose the map is intended to serve. Axelsen and Jones (1987) even question whether all maps are not, in fact, **mental maps**. The map users, of course, will make their own interpretations depending on their ability to read maps and their level of critical appreciation.

We must often be content with data we have collected through interviews, which may be affected by the perceptions of both interviewers and interviewees. We may use data drawn from statistical publications which may have been collated from a number of sources. In both cases subjective elements can introduce flaws. The definitions of science may be different from those of daily speech. Another problem may arise when officials who prepare the statistical material for publication do not understand or do not use definitions in a proper manner. A third problem is that the definitions change from one census to another (for example, the concept 'household' had quite a different meaning in a census held in 2000 than in one held in 1900).

Geography is similar to social anthropology and sociology in its concentration on contemporary data. Geographers, however, usually work with more concrete or quantitative data, while sociologists and social anthropologists, to a greater extent, use 'interpreted' data – data about people's values. Sociologists are often concerned with the interviewee's subjective understanding of a value-loaded question. They must make certain the interviewee understands the question exactly so there are no misconceptions. Geographers have this problem too, but many geographical questions are easier to define precisely. Sociologists must decide whether the interviewee's answer expresses his or her subjective meaning in a true manner. This problem has also been recognized by geographers who have worked with 'soft' interview data. We often interview people who have not thought previously about our question, and who either give the answer they believe will be most acceptable to us or the answer that is in accordance with what they believe to be the general understanding of the question, even if this does not coincide with their own point of view. A young lad who was asked why he had moved from mid-Wales to Birmingham answered the question the easy way by saying there were no jobs in mid-Wales (which was an acceptable answer). He concealed his personal reasons for moving: 'Things are more exciting in Birmingham and there are more girls around.' Gradually, geography has become more involved in this type of data which, in the traditional, regional school, was regarded as sociological data geographers did not need to address.

The traditional, regional school of geography may be labelled empiricist and its methodology could, as pointed out by Hansen (1994, p. 46), be described as descriptive **induction**, or presentation of experienced facts. Bird (1993, p. 45), in a tabular simplification, characterizes the empiricist approach as follows:

- Things experienced by the senses exist as facts. These represent its **ontology**, its theory of existence.

- Knowledge can be achieved by sense experience. This is its **epistemology**, its theory of knowledge.

THE POSITIVISM OF SPATIAL SCIENCE

Quantitative methods may be employed by both critical and positivist schools of thought. However, when geography began to draw on economics to articulate more formal location theories, its own somewhat fuzzy empiricism, observes Derek Gregory (1978, p. 40), was considerably strengthened and sharpened. **Spatial science** involved accepting elements of positivism that had previously been disregarded – namely, the concept that there is one science and one methodology which extends from the natural into the human sciences. By rejecting the notion that geographical phenomena are singular, the spatial science school discarded the discipline's idiographic traditions and set out to discover universals: to build models and establish theoretical structures into which geographical reality might be fitted.

The more distinguished proponents of spatial science, however, made the essential reservation that their models and laws cannot be understood as if they were laws as in natural science. They are measuring rods – tools used to test departures from them, as observed in the geographical 'reality'. Critics like Gregory (1978), however, argued that even if it had not been possible to show that geographical phenomena are subject to universal laws, there was still some value in regarding them as if they were. Some of the spatial science models and laws, he maintained, had been used as devices whose utility is measured by the success of their predictions and not by their implicit validity or truth. This approach to laws, which may be termed **instrumentalism**, was borrowed by geographers from neoclassical economics in which (according to Gregory, ibid., p. 41) it has played an important supporting role. Instrumentalism refers to the extent to which models and laws are seen as instruments of manipulation rather than explanatory devices. Chisholm (1975, p. 125) referred to the same idea as **normative theory** (see p. 97).

Johnston (1986a, p. 33) maintains that Harvey's book *Explanation in Geography* (1969) – which gave the most thorough representation of the philosophy and methodology of the spatial science school – also presented a basically positivist methodology with strong overtones of **logical positivism**. Johnston (ibid.) further associates the more important theories within spatial science (including central place theory, land-use theories derived from von Thünen, industrial location theory and spatial interaction theory) with positivism. Livingstone (1992, p. 324) maintains that 'the early history of quantification reveals that social and political interests evidently underlay the enterprise. This of course should not be taken to mean that quantification was *only* ideological crystallization.' Harvey (1984) explained the advance of quantification in American geography as a strategic move to escape the political suspicion falling on social science in the McCarthy era. A technocratic spatial science, crystallized in the application of control engineering to geographical systems, may even be said to have bolstered western capitalism and demoted value judgements.

The spatial science school laid greater emphasis on the unity of science, on hypothetic-deductive methods and on the use of 'hard' data. Few of its members, however, were willing to accept the strict methods prescribed by the logical positivists as the only road to scientific knowledge. As the theoretical work of the spatial science school encouraged geographers to become more involved in planning, it became clear, however, that geography as a science was involved in shaping reality by explaining how situations are and what they could be like. Most research workers were perfectly aware of the political implications of this. Additionally, there was no agreement among spatial scientists as to the degree of universality of laws and models. Among the most quantitatively inclined geographers, few have been ready to argue that the laws and models of human geography and of the social sciences in general are unchanging and universal. Societies change and so do the laws of society.

There was also no common agreement on the role of science in advocating change. After the 1960s, geographers became more involved in applied research. Quantitative methods and models were, to a large extent, developed because they were thought to have considerable predictive value. This raises the immediate problem as to whether, in forecasting, we should rely on the projection of current trends or try to envisage alternative scenarios. The research workers' political outlook is very likely to affect their answers to that question. The present author considers that we should analyse and state clearly those assumptions (or **pseudo-constraints**) that can change or may be changed, and also the consequences such changes may have on social development. It would be dishonest of research workers interested in the prediction of future changes not to do so.

Not all scientists will be able to attain such an ideal. Those who support, even subconsciously, the maintenance of existing social structure soon come to believe that the overturning of certain assumptions or pseudo-constraints is unrealistic or wrong. Those who favour the overthrow of the social order, on the other hand, will easily overestimate the possibility of converting the rules of society into pseudo-constraints.

Gregory (1978, p. 77) maintained that 'the function of social science is to problematize what we conventionally regard as self-evident'. Gregory's argument leads on to structuralist approaches to human geography, whereas other critics of positivist tendencies within human geography adopted humanistic approaches.

HUMANISTIC APPROACHES

The positivism debate led to a revitalization of some of the methods of the traditional schools in geography, including those of the French school of regional geography (see Figure 4.9, p. 123). This trend, which may be regarded as a new initiative by geographers who had not been involved in the models-orientated approach of the 1950s and 1960s, emphasizes the need to study unique events rather than the spuriously general. Anne Buttimer (1978, p. 73) argued along similar lines to Vidal de la Blache that historical and geographical studies belong together. She stressed the need to understand each region and its inhabitants from the 'inside' – that is, on the basis of the local perspective and not from the perspective of the researching 'outsider'. Leonard Guelke (1974, p. 193) advocated an idealist approach which 'is a method by which one can rethink the thoughts of those whose actions he seeks to explain'.

Guelke mainly based his arguments on the writings of R. G. Collingwood, the Oxford historian and philosopher, and especially on *The Idea of History* (1946). Guelke argued that these ideas are crucial to **historical geography**; it is important that historical geographers 'focus their attention on the meaning of human actions of geographical interest, not merely their geographical [physical] expressions' (Guelke, 1982, p. 12). 'Different people in making use of the Earth have, for example, created distinctive field and settlement patterns. These patterns are not arbitrary, but reflect the thinking of the people who created them' (Guelke, 1981, p. 132).

We must not be constrained by the view that geographers are always obliged to use the methods of natural science. A natural scientist is normally an outside observer: it is difficult for him or her to take an inside view. Although a historian, in Collingwood's sense, is unable to see directly into the minds of his or her subjects, he or she is able to understand their actions as being products of **rational** thought. The historian will therefore use the **hermeneutic** interpretative approach (see Box 5.1, pp. 139–40), involving *verstehen* or sympathetic understanding – trying to rethink the thoughts of historical characters, as far as his or her knowledge of their cultural background allows, but not trespassing into psychology. When we understand the beliefs which encouraged Columbus to sail west to reach India, we have explained the motives for the voyage (see Chapter 2). It is not necessary to discuss *why* Columbus held those beliefs for that would take us into the realm of historical psychology.

The idealist approach, as advocated by Guelke, thus restricts itself to beliefs that are in some way rational, and it leaves aside the emotional and psychological aspects of human behaviour. We cannot re-experience the emotional life of other people. The approach, however, does not let us know for sure whether we have really succeeded in finding the true explanation for historical events. The idealist philosophy has elements in common with **phenomenology**, which has also been suggested as a useful approach for geographers.

Phenomenologists do not, however, make sharp distinctions between intellectual and emotional life. The phenomenologist is more concerned with describing the life experience of the researcher. This description must inevitably be subjective because 'the approach fails to distinguish those elements of human

existence that are open to subjective understanding and those that are not'
(Guelke, 1981, p. 144). Phenomenologists are primarily concerned with our
(subjective) *knowledge* of the world around us: they attempt to create an objec-
tified knowledge of our experience of the phenomenal world. Our knowledge
proceeds from the world of experience and cannot be independent of that
world.

Yi-Fu Tuan, although not defining himself as a phenomenologist in the
strict sense, has written a number of inspiring essays and books introducing
geographers to phenomenological ideas (1974, 1976, 1977, 1980). Tuan has
stated (1971) that geography is *the mirror of humanity*: to know the world is to
know oneself. Such a study is clearly based in the humanities rather than in
social and physical sciences: 'The model for the regional geographers of
humanist leaning is ... the Victorian novelist who strives to achieve a synthesis of the subjective and the objective' (Tuan, 1978, p. 204). Tuan prefers to use
the term **humanistic geography** for such studies, which are regarded here
as including both idealism (in Guelke's terminology) and phenomenology.

In his book *Conceptions of Space in Social Thought* (1980), Robert David Sack
maintained that those conceptions of space that stem from the natural sciences
are highly unsufficient. He suggests that, in other modes of thought, such as
art, myth, magic and the child's view of life, space may have very different
meanings:'If people see and/or evaluate things and space differently and "non-
scientifically", then social science must somehow represent and capture those
meanings' (ibid., p. 8).

Such humanistic trends of thought can be related to significant traditions in
both French and German geography. Ewald Banse, whom Hettner described
as the *enfant terrible* of geography, attacked the ruling disciplinary matrix of the
subject as early as the 1920s, arguing that it 'only attempted to describe external reality. To understand the essence of things in depth, says Banse (1924, p.
58), the science of geography should be redefined as an art: 'Only the unified
perspective of both the visible outer appearance and the inner core of things
constitute real geography, which is a spiritual presentation of experienced
impressions.'

Nicholas Entrikin (1976, p. 616) made the point that the humanist approach
is best understood as a form of criticism. However, as Johnston (1997, p. 196)
points out, we may also hold the view that 'the human condition can only be
indicated by humanistic endeavour, for attitudes, impressions and subjective
relations to places (the "**sense of place**") cannot be revealed by positivist
research'.

It is also clear that we will always use and need **hermeneutic** or interpretative methods in geography. Dorling and Fairbairn (1997) point out that even
a map is an interpretation of reality and has to be reinterpreted according to
the purposes of each particular use.

Following Bird (1993, p. 45), the humanistic approaches may be characterized as follows (see also Box 5.2 and Figure 5.1):

- What exists is what people perceive to exist (its *ontological basis*).

- Knowledge is obtained subjectively in a world of meanings created by individuals (*its epistemological basis*).

- *Methodology* will then be interpretative, using methods which make it possible to investigate individual worlds and to emphasize individuality and subjectivity rather than replicability. Within humanistic approaches there are different opinions on methods, as there are various modifications of ontology and epistemology.

Box 5.2	**Ontology, epistemology and methodology**

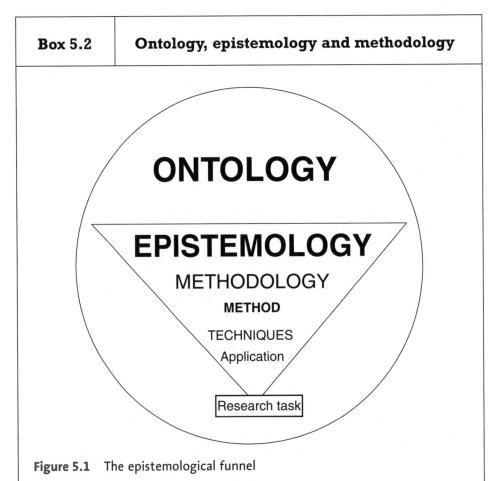

Figure 5.1   The epistemological funnel

Source: Translated from Löfgren, 1996, Figure 1.1

Ultimately any theoretical position (the outer frame of any research project) rests upon a basic philosophical position – an **ontology** (that is, a theory of existence, an understanding of what really exists as opposed to what does not). This general ontology is also the frame for a more restricted social ontology, which concerns the structure of a society, its elements and the basic mechanisms that link these. Marxism and humanism are examples of social ontologies.

Although we might have a basic conception of our theoretical position, and might adhere to an ontology of how the world of existence and the social world are constituted, most of this existence is unknown to us. So we need a theory about how to get knowledge about the world – an **episte-mology**, a theory of knowledge. Any research project or investigation is built upon a fundamental epistemological stance. It is the epistemology that guides the formulation of research problems, the evaluation of theory, the choice of appropriate techniques for empirical investigations and, above all, the interpretation of results. An ill-considered epistemological position can be an important cause of problems in a research project.

An epistemology is a general theory about how to look for knowledge as, for instance, exemplified in Sayer's (1984/1992) presentation of a realist epistemology (see Figure 6.2). To be applicable to research, an epistemology must be cast in a concrete form by way of models or programmes, that is *methodology*. The hypothetic-deductive approach is one such model. This gives certain rules about how research should, or ought to, be carried out if it is to be accepted as valid. If we stick to a specified methodology, the findings we present could be replicated by others. If we do not use a specified methodology, it is difficult for others to evaluate our results. Within each different methodology there is a host of different concrete *methods* we can apply. A method includes rules and recommendations (*shall, ought to* and *can*) on how to collect, work up, analyse and present data in relation to a given problem. A method is, in turn, built up from restricted and often interchangeable *techniques* on how to carry it out. For instance, collecting interview data can employ many different techniques, for example long interviews based on a semi-structured interview guide. Finally, any techniques and methods used have to be adapted to the special research problem and context that are being investigated. Often **method triangulation** is needed: even though we may be starting from the same ontological and epistemological basis, there will be many different methods to choose from. The approach to a particular research project will often need to be a combination of different methods. Figure 5.1 represents research work as a funnel – from the basic ontology to practical research techniques.

Source: Adapted from Löfgren, 1996

One important observation is that geography, more than any other natural or social science, is a *visual science,* with similarities in this respect to architecture and the history of art. We analyse landscapes and provide methods of visual presentation in our teaching of geography. The visual models and thematic maps that explain geographical patterns increase our knowledge and understanding of the world, partly because they activate modes of thought that words and numbers cannot reach.

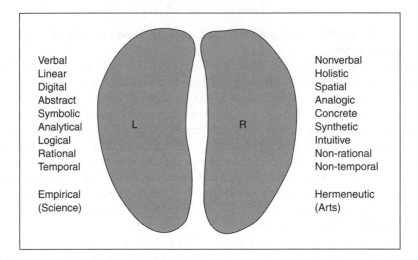

Verbal	Nonverbal
Linear	Holistic
Digital	Spatial
Abstract	Analogic
Symbolic	Concrete
Analytical	Synthetic
Logical	Intuitive
Rational	Non-rational
Temporal	Non-temporal
Empirical	Hermeneutic
(Science)	(Arts)

Figure 5.2 Comparison of left-hemisphere (L) and right-hemisphere (R) functional characteristics of the brain

Neurosurgeons have shown that analytic, objective and so-called scientific modes of thought are associated with the left half of the brain (Figure 5.2). These thought processes, however, will only function when they have been stimulated by impulses from the artistic, holistic, visual, intuitive and irrational thoughts which are based in the right half of the brain. Visualization helps us to exploit the full capacity of the brain but also implies that we must take into account those intuitive and less rational elements which contribute so much to our intellectual life. This goes to the core of humanistic approaches to geography in which, to a very large degree, research involves a personal approach employing both intuition and imaginative interpretation.

Granö (1981, p. 23) suggests that the focal point of geography as a holistic science lies in the reciprocity between the human mind and the environment – an attempt to explain land and nature in terms of humankind: 'Man's perceptions, experience, knowledge and action form, together with his environment, a totality, a unity which constitutes the basic premise of geographical enquiry.' We cannot appreciate how the world, the 'real' environment, actually is: we can only know how we interpret it on the basis of our experience and knowledge. In Figure 5.3 experience is isolated from knowledge. The immanent sensation of the environment, or **perceived environment**, is the same for everyone who is exposed to the sensation, but each person will have a different 'after-image', or **cognized environment,** based on his or her own experience, knowledge and/or memory. Our individually cognized environment constitutes our knowledge of the environment which forms the foundations of our actions, which, in turn, transform the real environment:

As knowledge has developed, so the cognized environment created by mystical, speculative and subsequently rational thinking has been subjected to an increasing number of influences from perception. The development of empirical

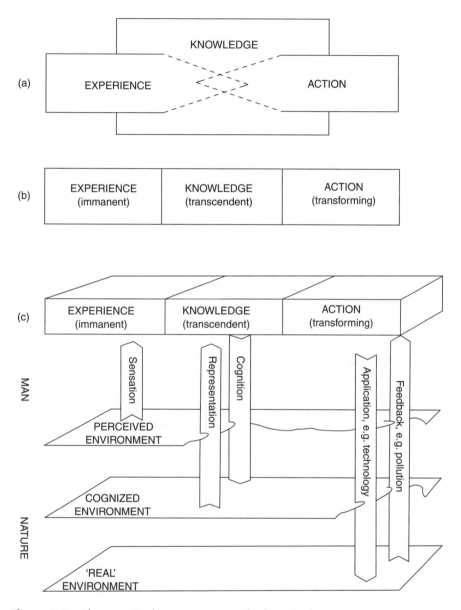

Figure 5.3   The cognized environment, which is the basis of our knowledge, is not identical to the 'real' environment in which our actions take place

Source: Granö, 1981, p. 24 (Figure 4.3 in 1999 edition)

science meant that attempts were made to identify the cognized environment as nearly as possible with the real environment. (Granö, 1981 p. 25) Humanists believe that such a conflation of cognized and real environment is impossible.

Humanistic approaches focus on the acting individual: the aim is to achieve an understanding of events, the thoughts underlying the actions that produced the world of experience: 'The role of the researcher is not that of a technician, one who promotes a certain solution, but rather that of a *provocateur*, one who promotes thought and reflection.' The goal is 'to increase *self-awareness* and *mutual awareness*' (Johnston, 1986b, p. 103).

Olsson (1978, p. 110) regards the spatial science and humanistic schools of geography as essentially opposites. The first aspires to formalized construction of knowledge, the latter to creative presentation. The humanistic approach cultivates the subjective interpretation of the world. Each one of us has his or her own subjective cognition of, for instance, the 'landscapes of fear'. Tuan's book *Landscapes of Fear* (1980) represented his personal creative presentation of this phenomenon. Reports of such personal cognitions give us an understanding of the relations between the actor and the environment, but if we follow a **phenomenological** philosophy (see pp. 144–5) we cannot claim to reach general truth.

Idealism may be seen as an alternative to phenomenology. Idealists use the method of sympathetic understanding (*verstehen*) and restrict themselves to thoughts that are in some ways rational in order to elucidate the reasons behind particular actions. The focus is on the actors, their intentions and meanings. This may be seen as an approach that supplements empirical research. Pickles (1985, pp. 52–3) points out that phenomenology is also not a type of irrational anti-science. **Phenomenology** provides the 'essential' basis for science, but does not replace it. In geography, humanistic aspects of the traditional schools, like the French regional school, have been clarified and developed further. There have also been some thought-provoking representations of, for instance, the feeling of home, identification with a place (Buttimer and Seamon, 1980), different conceptions of space (Sack, 1980), space, place and meaning (Jackson, 1989), the role of space and place in relation to gender (Harding, 1991, 2001; Duncan, 1996) and human territoriality (Malmberg, 1980; Sack, 1986). Sack's book *Homo Geographicus* (1997), which we commented upon in Chapter 1 (pp. 20–4) is also inspired by humanistic philosophies.

There are two main lines of criticism of humanistic approaches. The first – positivist criticism – has, however, lost ground as the number of convinced, clear-cut positivist geographers diminishes rapidly. The second, largely structural, critique 'presents the atomistic focus on the individual in humanistic work as a distortion of reality: it gives individuals freedom to act when in fact they are very much constrained, if not constricted, by external circumstances over which they have little control' (Johnston, 1986a, p. 95).

BEHAVIOURAL AND WELFARE GEOGRAPHY

In contrast to humanistic geography, **behavioural geography** may be seen as being based on criticism from within spatial science (see Figure 4.9, p. 123). This starts from a disillusion with **location theories** involving, for instance, the concept of **economic man**. However, the roots of behavioural geography are much older. In Europe, the Finnish geographer Johannes Gabriel Granö and his Estonian student Edgar Kant were attempting a behaviourist approach in the 1920s (Granö, 1929). Even in the USA, behavioural and quantitative approaches were contemporary developments: the behavioural approach was taken up in the late 1950s and the 1960s by Gilbert White, then at the University of Chicago, and his associates, who made a series of investigations into the human response to natural hazards, guided by theories of decision-making and influenced by methods used in psychology and sociology. It was regarded as more important to map the personal **perception** of the decision-maker than to describe the factual physical and economic conditions of the environment, since the decision-maker would act upon his or her own perceptions and not on the environmental factors themselves (White, 1973). Julian Wolpert introduced behavioural geography to many human geographers through a paper in 1964, which compared actual with potential labour productivity on farms in central Sweden. He found that the sample farm population did not achieve profit maximization and nor were its goals solely directed to that objective. The farmers were 'spatial satisfiers' rather than 'economic men'.

A further aspect of behavioural analysis is the concept of the **mental map** of the environment. Mental mapping has been taken up by a number of workers, among them Peter Gould and Rodney White (1974). A somewhat different approach to behavioural work is found in Allan Pred's two-volume work *Behaviour and Location* (1967, 1969), in which Pred tried to present an ambitious alternative to theory-building based on economic man. The **time–space geography** Hägerstrand and his associates (see p. 89) established may also be seen as a critique not so much of the spatial science school as of important aspects of social science research in general. In simple terms, it provides a method of mapping spatial behaviour while at the same time representing a reorientation of scale away from aggregate data towards studies of individual behaviour. More important, however, is its introduction of a new economic theory in which time and space are regarded as scarce resources, the allocation of which forms the basis of the social realities we study.

A corresponding concern for the individual within mass society is also basic to **welfare geography**, which developed as a special branch in the 1970s. Paul Knox (1975) stated that it was a fundamental objective for geography to map social and spatial variations in the quality of life. The study of such spatial inequalities was taken up by Coates and Rawstron (1971), Morrill and Wohlenberg (1971), Coates et al. (1977) and Smith (1979), and a number of others. While some of this work represented the geographer as a 'delver and dove-tailer', a provider of information, other examples, notably *The Geography of Poverty in the United States* (Morrill and Wohlenberg, 1971), also proposed both social and spatial policies for changing existing conditions. **Welfare geography** has become an important field of research and is particularly prevalent in urban social geography, for which a very good overview is provided by Knox and Pinch (2006). A particular focus has been on **social exclusion** and **diaspora** cultures in urban neighbourhoods (Box. 5.3).

Box 5.3	The geography of social exclusion

The indoor shopping centre has developed as a significant new mode of retail service provision which, at the same time, provides a new fantasy world of leisure and consumption. In the UK, the Meadowhall Shopping Centre in Sheffield 'recreates the romance of Paris and Florence under one roof' (Sibley, 1995, p. xi); the Metro Centre in Gateshead even includes an indoor amusement park. Such places have created a new form of holiday experience: pleasure combined with the 'needs' of shopping. In appearance these centres are 'classless' – a consumption paradise everybody can enjoy even if, in reality, they are not classless. They are located, in the main, out of town so that shoppers have to come by private car or pay for public transport. The centre's management will proudly announce that the centre is for all the family, preferably with a credit card, and that everything has been done to ensure the centre is a safe and clean environment the family can enjoy. The management may point out that the centre was located out of town so that idle youngsters, vagrants, etc., will not put in an appearance. If they do, the centre has guards to evict them. This suggests, says Sibley (ibid.), that shopping centres like these constitute a kind of ambiguity: seemingly public, but actually private space.

A society's degree of **spatial exclusion** practices seems to be inversely related to the degree to which that society may be regarded as egalitarian. In Scandinavian countries (in which historical tradition, welfare provision and job opportunities until recently tended to level off class distinctions), it is difficult to distinguish between upper middle-class, lower middle-class, working-class and social housing. Scandinavians who study housing provision in the UK and, even more so, in the USA, experience a shocking new world of difference. A simple explanation for this is, of course, the traditional role of class in the UK, and the ethnic diversity and the 'self-made man ideals' (by which poverty is your own fault) of the USA.

The white American suburb stands out as a prime example of exclusion in practice. Some of these suburbs have been described neatly as 'enclosed communities', socially purified and defended, fortress-like, against the supposed threat of the poor. North of Los Angeles, the author visited such a gated community – located on a hilltop around a golf club with no access other than a road for private cars. In the south of Los Angeles I encountered people living in cardboard boxes on the sidewalk, or as squatters in closed-down office buildings – a locality in which I did not even dare to stop the car. In Canada there is an ongoing discussion about planning regulations in areas designed for low-density housing – about whether extra apartments for rent should be allowed in houses in such neighbourhoods. The argument goes that allowing people to hire small apartments will devalue the neighbourhood's social standards, hence lowering the market value of adjoining houses (Poulton, 1995)!

In Europe, rising unemployment has led to increasing social problems, particularly in inner-city tenements and peripheral social housing estates. In the 1960s and 1970s in the UK, considerable 'brick-and-mortar subsidies' were provided by the government to build public housing estates, which accommodated some 31 per cent of households by 1971. By the 1980s and 1990s general housing subsidies in the UK had, as in most other European countries, changed to personal subsidies for those in special need. Through the 'right to buy' and urban renewal, a large part of the UK public housing stock has been privatized. This has meant a spatial concentration of the remaining public housing, which now mainly caters for those who are unable to cope in the housing market.

In such social housing, there tends to be a concentration of lone parents, the long-term unemployed, socially disabled people, drug addicts, etc. This spatial concentration means that disadvantaged groups such as these are effectively excluded from relocating to other neighbourhoods. Recent research into housing conditions in the north of England has attempted to give voice to people living in these conditions, to explain how their basic routines of everyday life are carried out. Lone mothers explain how they have to navigate a route to local shops through streets that are controlled by gangs of young men and grown-ups who solve all conflicts physically; their children are sometimes found playing with discarded syringes. As a result, children are kept inside the home and can suffer from illnesses more than is usual for their age. A 'wrong' address means it is almost impossible to get a job. Social and spatial barriers conspire to make it almost impossible to attain the normal life expectations of acquiring a home and a worthwhile job; young people are kept in 'their place' (Speak et al., 1995).

Healey (1999) suggests that the meaning of **social exclusion** and the significance of place and neighbourhood can be discussed in terms of the following concepts, which are closely linked to newer trends in human geographical research: webs of social relations, structure and agency, socio-spatial relations, and everyday life and neighbourhoods as living places.

'A *relational view of social process* takes a view of individuals, not as autonomous subjects with individual preferences, but as formed within social contexts' or through social networks (ibid., p. 55, emphasis added). For the majority, place-based **Gemeinschaft** networks have, to a great extent, been replaced by placeless **Gesellschaft** connections. Social networks intersect and cluster in particular places, but these are not necessarily residential neighbourhoods. The main point here is that **relational space** is of crucial importance in the active processes of building relationships and meaning, in social exclusion and in cohesion, which are active social processes. Research indicates that neighbourhood relations (for good and bad) are more important for those who are outside 'mainstream society' than for those who are actively involved in the workforce and cultural and political life. Strong social cohesion in a disadvantaged neighbourhood might give people strength and identity, but this

(Continued)

(Continued)

is not necessarily a good thing: it might reinforce the inhabitants' social distance from the rest of the society.

Structuring forces generate fractures and divisions which, in the UK, have their roots in the language of class and distribution. The division between the working class and capitalism is inherited, but in a postindustrial society this division has led to a situation where exclusion means exclusion from mainstream society: three-quarters of society belong to the 'mainstream'; one-quarter of the population are economically, socially and politically disconnected as this sector of society is outside the workforce, is not involved in social community work and, to a large extent, does not vote. In its most acute form, social exclusion appears to occur when factors of economic, political and cultural exclusion combine and dominate certain localities. Such combined concentrations of disadvantage are particularly apparent in inner-city tenements and peripheral social housing estates. In our research into deprived neighbourhoods, therefore, we have to look for other structural forces and relations between structure and agency than those based on traditional Marxist ideas. Society has changed, and so have the structuring forces, as we will discuss further in Chapter 6.

Socio-spatial relations are the main focus of human geographical research, and an understanding of how a **sense of place** is an important dimension in people's everyday life is essential if we are to deal with social exclusion. Certain living places are excluded from normal life as these are places of divergent behaviour – places with, for instance, high levels of crime. In building up a neighbourhood's organizing capacity – building up positive socio-spatial relations – it might be possible to draw people who are suffering from social exclusion back into mainstream society. In practice, this means creating jobs or empowerment through participation in community governance. To overcome the adverse effects of social exclusion, research would profit from looking at the following questions:

1) How social worlds of place affect people in terms of mobilizing for change: Where do people look for allies? Who are they mobilizing against? etc.
2) What brings outsiders to seek to engage in place-based mobilizing in someone else's place?
3) What conceptions of place and community are used by these insider/outsider mobilization processes? (Healey, 1998, p. 59)

The concept of everyday life helps us to focus on what living in places actually means. An everyday-life perspective focuses on the multiplicity of roles people play and the services they use each day. This is a bottom-up approach, in contrast to a top-down research approach that might study the efficiency of service deliveries in a particular area. This bottom-up approach takes its inspiration from the postmodernist scepticism about general models of explanation: humbly, one tries to let people speak for themselves, to elucidate the meanings, metaphors and ideas they follow in their day-to-day living practices.

Neighbourhoods are places of multiple motion, and the concept of *neighbourhoods as living places* focuses on this. Recent research (Holt-Jensen et al., 2004) has shown that, for good or bad, for people in deprived neighbourhoods these are the key places that define their social world. Structural relations are not as important for such people as individual, contingent relations and roles in the local living space. We can thus speak of 'my place', 'your place' and 'their place'. Cruddas Park in Newcastle upon Tyne was both 'the place I call home' for an **insider** and 'an appalling place' for an **outsider** (Wood et al., 1995): 'An important dimension of neighbourhood improvement work is to consider how people value their living places, how they compare them with others, and within what social context this valuing takes place' (Healey, 1998, p. 62).

Welfare geography has led to a **cultural trend** in human geographical research, which has developed since the late 1980s, focusing on difference within society and on such contingencies as ethnicity, gender, nationality, political persuasion, and so on. It also involves distrust of 'grand theory'. Different approaches to qualitative research have been tried out as geographers have started to investigate ordinary people's everyday lives, much in the same way as planners have advocated a bottom-up approach to the planning process to involve citizens in **social mobilization** (Friedmann, 1992).

Whereas, in principle, welfare geography works within the framework of the existing economic and social system, **radical geography** called for both revolutionary theory and revolutionary practice. This leads on to a discussion of structuralism, which provides a framework for the radical geography.

STRUCTURALISM

Positivism implies that if 'we are to explain processes we must discover the regularities or universal laws governing their behaviour. Hence the thrust of research must be towards the discovery of order' (Sayer 1985, p. 161). This strategy might work within the natural sciences, particularly in physics, but in human geography regularities tend to be approximate, temporally and spatially specific, and unique rather than repetitive. But as has been pointed out above, most models and theories put forward by the spatial science school are descriptive rather than explanatory. *Descriptive models*, such as the **gravity model**, are valuable and scientifically respectable in so far as they provide new knowledge as to how things are. But science should provide explanations of the observed regularities; causes are not associated with correlations and regularities – these are **surface appearances**. We need to look for the mechanisms within **deep structures**.

The shapes of the pieces in a jigsaw puzzle or the forms in a cultural landscape do not tell us much about the machine or mechanism that cut the pieces. So we need a **structuralist** approach to obtain an understanding of how the mechanisms or driving forces within these structures (often called the **real level)** form outcomes at the **empirical** level.

The French anthropologist Claude Lévi-Strauss presented the analogy of a camshaft machine cutting jigsaw puzzles. The machine is designed to make only a certain number of movements, but these can cut a large variety of pieces. So we cannot understand the nature of the mechanism (the machine) if we only study the outcomes (the puzzles). We must study the mechanism itself but we cannot do this by direct observation. We must try to establish a theory of the mechanisms and find out whether this theory is consistent with appearances at the empirical level (Johnston, 1997, p. 215).

A variety of structural approaches has been identified within the humanities and social sciences. Linguists have established a school of structural linguistics that teaches there are certain imprinted, fundamental characteristics in language systems. Language systems contain certain basic principles (such as those of binary opposition) which are used to create meaning. The structural principles of language are so readily absorbed by children that they appear to be transmitted genetically. Structural linguistics analyses speech to identify these deep structures, which may be common to all languages.

Lévi-Strauss (1969/1949) used structuralist analyses in order to comprehend the underlying structures of diverse human cultures, and maintained that human behaviour is preordained by structural forces of which we are, in most cases, unaware. The myths and rites of a particular society may be studied as transformations of deep structures at the real level. Lévi-Strauss argued, for example, that it is possible to identify certain basic elements within myths that may then be projected into a theory concerning the nature of these deep structures. Using the camshaft analogy, Lévi-Strauss maintained that we can understand the nature of its gear-box even if the only things we can actually observe are the characteristics of the jigsaw puzzles. Those types of structuralism that seek the universal, basic of the human mind have been called *structure as construct* types (Johnston, 1986a, p. 97). Lévi-Strauss's ideas have played a role in geographical research through the works of Tuan, Sack and other. One interesting example is concerned with children's perceptions of space and their acquisition of geographical knowledge (Sack, 1980).

What Johnston (1986a, p. 101) calls *structure as process* types of structuralism had a more direct impact on geography, particularly through **radical geography**. According to Murdoch (2006, p. 11), this was much inspired by the writings of the French Marxist theorist Louis Althusser: 'In keeping with mainstream structuralism, structuralist Marxism would look beyond the actions of individuals and social movements (operating in the context of class context) to the determining structures that lie "beneath" any social formation.'

Marxism, as a theoretical base for social sciences, tries to understand how the mechanisms of the economic base are gradually changed in dialectic processes that occur between society and individual agents. In general, it is the mechanisms of the economic base that form the determining element; hence this approach may be called **quasi-determinist** (Johnston, 1986b, p. 56). The individuals or agents are more or less puppets who are manipulated by the economic mechanisms. The **ideological base** (religion, culture, etc.) is generally relegated to occupying a position of dependence on the **economic base** – if not directly determined by it. Later Marxist-inspired researchers have, however, found that 'this "base and superstructure" model left far too much unaccounted for, and contradicted much of what is known about social and cultural history' (Henderson and Sheppard, 2006, p. 69). It is quite clear that this simple model did not find support in **Marxist geography**. Culture, laws, etc., are closely linked to the circulation of capital but, as made clear by Harvey (1982), capitalism varies in different times and places due to the intersection with, and even dependence on, local cultural and social variations.

Historical materialism is concerned with hidden structures, the 'theories' can never be finally demonstrated or empirically verified: 'The "test" of such theories is provided by the success or failure of actions founded upon them' (Johnston, 1986a, p. 109). So Marxism is as much a guide to political practice as a scientific method.

Harvey (1973, pp. 129–30) stated that the essential difference between positivism and Marxism is 'that positivism simply seeks to understand the world whereas Marxism seeks to change it'. The political aims of Marxist science are also expressed by Richard Peet (1977, p. 21):

> **Marxist science begins with a material analysis of society, proceeds through a critique of capitalist control of the material base of society, and proposes solutions in terms of social ownership of that material (economic) base ... the political aims of Marxism provide a common scientific purpose. As a holistic, revolutionary science, Marxism provides a firm theoretical base for the radical movement in geography.**

Geographical studies inspired by structural Marxism are mainly found within economic geography (see, for example, Harvey, 1982, 2006; Massey, 1984; Thrift, 1986) and social geography (Harvey, 1973, 1985a, 1985b). Bennett (1985, p. 221) criticized Marxist geography for regarding the effects on the physical environment as merely a product of the social system, with society the result of social control, and resource problems only seen as distributive problems deriving from class structure. Quaini (1982) demonstrates, however, some interesting relationships between Marxism and ecological questions, and Marxist-inspired social ecology has played an important role in some schools of geography (see, for instance Peet and Watts, 1996; Castree, 2003).

Whereas academics in general have distanced themselves from the orthodox Marxism (reading Marx as a Bible) that dominated a part of the student movements after 1968 (see p. x), Marxism has continued to inspire major science philosophers and academics, such as Foucault, Bourdieu and Harvey.

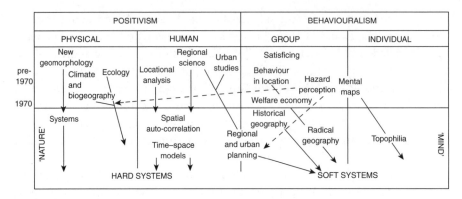

Figure 5.4   Geographical studies arranged according to relative 'hardness' or 'softness'

Source: This is an extract redrawn with permission from a diagram without a legend in Chorley, 1976, p. 31

Foundations has been laid for new scientific approaches in structuration theory, poststructuralism and postmodernism, which are presented in Chapter 6.

In Figure 5.4, Chorley (1976) shows a dichotomous classification of positivism and 'behaviouralism' (encompassing what we have presented as humanistic geography, behavioural geography and radical geography or structural Marxism). In the 1960s, as Bird (1993, p. 48) points out, there had been a movement from the right to the left across the dichotomous divide; human geography at that time adopted the positivist methodologies of 'hard science' and became spatial science.

Since the 1970s there was a drift away from **positivism**, but the purer forms of physical geography and parts of human geography, particularly within location studies, remained happily positivistic. This part of geography has, however, also increasingly become involved in debates on the philosophy of science, as has been neatly demonstrated by Haines–Young and Petch (1986). In physical geography they find, however, that a better understanding of research problems can be achieved within positivist traditions, but with Popper's **critical rationalism** (see pp. 108–10 and Figures 4.3, p. 109, and 4.4, p. 110) being particularly useful. On the other hand, in the 1980s and 1990s, the move to 'soft systems' led to new trends in human geography. Among these, we will consider in Chapter 6 **structuration theory**, **realism, poststructuralism, postmodernism** and **feminist geography**.

Questions for Discussion

1. Give an account of the historical development of positivism as an ideal guideline for scientific work. To what extent can positivism be said to be liberating and anti-authoritarian?
2. Contrast the principles of positivism with the critics of positivism. Why was positivism attacked by the radical philosophers and

student movement of 1968? Try to find out if this had any real influence, in practical terms, on educational programmes at your university.

3. How can we understand dialectics as an important part of academic discourse?

4. Define the term 'episteme'. Discuss whether there is a particular 'episteme' that rules the scientific community in your country/at your university. Does this need to be changed?

5. What kind of practical consequences would *ideologiekritik* have for geographical research? What kinds of research problems would be most important for geographers?

6. Define empirical approach, hermeneutic approach, critical theory approach and poststructuralism and discuss these in relation to the different phases of a research project.

7. What is meant with the idiographic tradition in geography and what impact has this had for the positivism debate within the discipline?

8. To what extent and why did spatial science lead on to a positivism debate in geography?

9. Discuss the relations between ontology, epistemology and methodolgy on the basis of Figure 5.1 (p. 146). Try to find some research examples that can illustrate the 'epistemological funnel'.

10. Give an account of, and the major arguments for, a new humanistic geography.

11. Why can behavioural and welfare geography be seen as a response to the models of the spatial science school?

12. Discuss the concept of spatial social exclusion. Is this a theme of interest in your community? Should geographers involve themselves in research and solutions for spatial social exclusion?

13. Structuralism can be seen as describing the major trend that developed on the basis of the positivism debate in geography. What became of the major fields for structuralist research within geography. Try to find some local projects that were developed at your university.

6 NEW TRENDS AND IDEAS

STRUCTURATION THEORY

In the 1980s, many observers regarded human geography as caught between the determinism of structural Marxism (which tries to read off the specifics of place from general laws of capitalism) and the voluntarism of most humanistic geography (in which events result from purely individual intentions). In the tensions between these positions some human geographers sought a resolution in 'a model which allows autonomy to social consciousness within a context determined, in final analysis, by social being, one in which history is neither willed nor fortuitous, and neither lawed nor illogical' (Peet, 1996, p. 873).

To achieve this resolution requires theories, and also analytic mediations. **Structuration theories**, as presented, among others, by Bourdieu (1977), Bhaskar (1979) and Giddens (1979, 1984), aimed at such a resolution. Among these authors it is the work of the British sociologist Anthony Giddens that has had the most profound influence on human geography. His theories were founded on a critique of the 'structural and interpretative sociologies that were connected to, but not synonymous with, the Marxist and humanist traditions that surfaced in the human geography of the early 1970s' (Cloke et al., 1991, p. 93).

We need to repeat here that any theoretical position rests ultimately upon two philosophical components: **ontology** and **epistemology** (see Box 5.2 p. 146–7). Epistemology gives guidance on how to work scientifically; ontology provides a basis for understanding the world. Giddens' structuration theory is largely ontological in its orientation. Giddens (1984) explains that he has tried to develop an ontology of human society (concentrating on how to theorize **human agency**) and to consider the implications of this theorizing for the analysis of social institutions. 'Human agency' refers to people's capabilities and their related activities or 'behaviour', but not to the agents themselves.

In **structural Marxism**, the activities of agents are ruled by structures. Giddens understands structures as being created and re-created through human agency; the actions of agents are the basis for structures. The individual agent has only an incomplete knowledge of either the empirical world or the 'mechanisms' (social rules) of society that set structural frameworks for his or her actions. If we are to make a scientific analysis, however, we must assume the agent's actions to be rational within the context of his or her incomplete knowledge. In Giddens' model, the **agents** are not puppets – they are conscious, but also very often unconscious interpreters between the real level

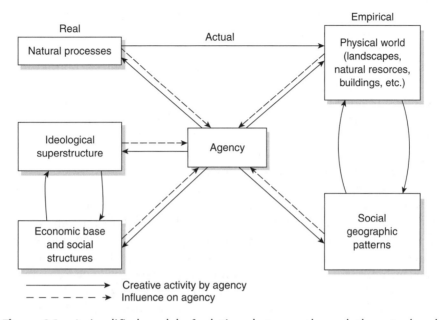

Figure 6.1   A simplified model of relations between the real, the actual and the empirical levels

(the level of social structures) and the empirical level. The agents interpret and transform the empirical world, but these interpretations and transformations are constrained and enabled by the structures at the real level. Even the structures of the economic and ideological base are interpreted and transformed by human agency (Figure 6.1).

Individuals are born into societies that entrap them within social structures, which both constrain and also enable them. While we live out our lives under the rules made by society, we are also reproducing these rules, but not necessarily in the same form. Since every individual is an interpreter, the rules are gradually changed. The gradual transformation of a language is a good example of this process. Religions and political ideologies are also gradually transformed through individual practice.

At the core of Giddens' theory lie the concepts of '**structure**', '*action*', '*social system*', '*social practice*', '*context*' and '**duality of structure**'. Structures are sets of rules (constraints) and resources (capacities or possibilities) which 'exist only as memory traces, the organic basis of human knowledgeability, and as instantiated in action' (Giddens, 1984, p. 377). Structures should be understood as rules and resources for action. There are rules for the constitution of meaning and rules for the sanctioning of social conduct. These rules can be either informal – as social norms – or formal – as laws and bureaucratic regulations.

Social rules are implemented through the interaction of people with each other. Social rules also structure interaction, and the rules which structure interaction are themselves reproduced by the process of interaction. We follow such rules consciously or unconsciously, depending on the degree to which they are self-evident to us. **Resources** may be regarded as either *allocative* or *authoritative*. Allocative resources control material relations (the economy) both in the private and public sphere. Authoritative resources control people both privately (domestic abuse) and in public (politics). It follows from this that 'the structural properties of social systems, as formulated in the rules and resources postulated by Giddens, are both a medium of social practices and an end result of social practices' (Cloke et al., 1991, p. 102).

For Giddens, the concept 'action' represents the routine actions of daily life. Action is regarded as a continuous process rather than as a series of isolated single actions with specific intentions or aims. Giddens does not deny that such isolated, intentional actions exist, but argues that most intentions and aims develop in a continuous, reflexive process, in which we think through our own actions or the actions of others. He calls this process 'the reflexive monitoring of action' (Giddens, 1984, p. 376). The knowledge upon which our actions are based includes both **discursive consciousness** (the types of knowledge we can explain and discuss in words) and **practical consciousness** (knowledge we see as more or less self-evident, which we use in our daily life, and which we cannot necessarily explain in words). Routine and repetitive tasks, which we do without thinking how or why, are based on this kind of knowledge.

However skilled and competent **agents** may be, their knowledge is limited. As a result, conditions of action may remain unacknowledged and the consequences of action may be unintended. Agents are just as much influenced by the actions of others as they are by the rules and limitations of structures.

Structuration theory thus takes account of both the acting subject and the social structures that exist independent of human consciousness, but not independent of human practice. Structures set the conditions for human actions, but they are also the results of human actions. Individuals are formed by society and its institutions, but they are also skilled agents who direct their own lives through actions (**agency**). This is called the **duality of structure**. Cloke et al. (1991, p. 98) point out that the notion of duality represents a key stage in Giddens' structuration journey. We need:

- to recognise the duality of structure: that is, the manner in which structures enable behaviour, but behaviour can eventually influence and reconstitute structure; and

- to recognise the duality of structure and agency: that is, to transcend the dualism of deterministic views of structure and voluntaristic views of agency.

Agency and structure are in real life knitted together by social practice. Repeated social practices, in the form of social relations and routines, create a social system. Well-established social systems create social institutions, such as schools and workplaces.

Giddens (1984) considers that social actions always take place within a framework – an empirical connection. From a geographical point of view,

Giddens suggests that links between structuration theory and Hägerstrand's **time–space geography** are important (see p. 89). Social systems are not only structured by rules and resources, they are also structured in time and space. Time and space are not passive frames for action but part of the action itself. Giddens uses the term '**locale**', which many geographers have (somewhat wrongly) understood as 'place'. Actions are imprinted by socialization in 'locales', which are created and re-created by people who use their intellectual capacities within the frames set by social rules and mechanisms. While empirical research may show us how this happens and describes what constitutes the mosaic of a geographical pattern, only theoretical research can answer the more fundamental 'why' questions about the relations between agents and what they regard as constraining mechanisms.

From a geographical point of view, Giddens' discussion of spaciality is fairly simple. He has been criticized for not knowing enough about the theoretical discussions among geographers concerning the continuous production and reproduction of space and on the different concepts of space and place. Geographers have, however, used structuration theory in their analyses. For instance, Pred (1984) has identified 'place' as having been produced in a 'historically contingent process', something which is changed continually as a result of the social actions of the people who have lived there, and which influences the same people and their activities at the same time. Sack (1997) (see pp 23–4) points to the reciprocal relations between place and 'self'. Place influences 'the self', but through human activity 'the self' also influences, sometimes transforms, place (this is illustrated in Figure 1.9, p. 23).

Structuration theory has been criticized for not giving direct guidance on how to proceed in scientific investigations, and for the absence of formal links between structuration theory and empirical studies. **Realism** may be seen as an attempt to achieve this linkage.

REALISM

The ontological basis for realism, as developed by Bhaskar (1975/1978), suggests that 'yes there is a *real* world', but that some of its most significant components are not immediately observable or obvious to human agency. There are two types of such structure. The first is in the form of capitalist or other structures and forces of power. We need theoretical analysis to elucidate how these work. The others are structures that are found in the form of experiences and conceptions 'in people's heads', which cannot be observed or measured directly but which are the basis for actions and, in this way, shape events in society. We may here see connections to both Giddens' structuration theory and humanism. It is recognized that knowledge about certain phenomena can only be achieved through the study of human conceptions. Human practices cannot be understood only as rational and functional, but must also *work meaningfully* for the people involved. This is neatly illustrated by Aase

(1999b) in Box 6.1 (pp. 172–4). Bhaskar (1975/1978, p. 56) recognizes three distinct domains in society which tend to be oversimplified and conflated in positivist (empiricist) approaches:

1) The *real* – mechanisms (which are often hidden and not easily observed).

2) The *actual* – events (which are observable phenomena).

3) The *empirical* – experiences of events.

Bhaskar (1979) questions whether nature and society can be studied in the same way, and he maintains that realism opens up a unity of scientific method in terms of the form taken by social and natural scientific knowledge, the reasoning by which it is produced, and the concepts which theoretize its production. In both cases, the objects of scientific inquiry are real structures, and the method of science implies moving from knowledge of manifest phenomena to the structures that generate them (Peet, 1998, p. 168).

So far, our discussion has broadly underpinned the ontological basis of realism. The real contribution to a realist **epistemology** for geographical research was provided by Andrew Sayer in his book *Method in Social Science: A Realist Approach* (1984/1992).

Positivism may suit the analysis of closed systems. As Sayer (ibid., p. 122) points out, in the objects of study in the natural sciences, 'closed systems may exist naturally (e.g. the solar system) or may be produced in experiments or machines'. For such systems it is possible to make universal statements and to conceptualize a constant mechanism that causes regularities. It is also possible to formulate a set of constant conditions in which the causal mechanism operates. An initial premise for Sayer (ibid., p. 123) is, however, that:

> the social sciences deal with open systems but lack the advantage of their equivalents in natural science of having relevant system sciences on which to draw. One of the main reasons for the openness of social systems is the fact that we can interpret the same material condition and statements in **different** ways and hence learn new ways of responding, so that effectively we become different kinds of people.

Open social systems are thus much more complex to analyse: more than one mechanism may explain an event, and mechanisms may change during our investigation, and even possibly because of it. In open systems, changing external conditions make it impossible to extract regularities and explanations from actual events. Theory can elucidate the **necessary conditions** that characterize the mechanisms acting to create specified actual events, but these are not **sufficient conditions** for an explanation.

Sayer (ibid., p. 92) points out the importance of asking qualitative questions about the nature of our objects with the aim of identifying social **structures**. We may, for instance, observe that some industries are more strike-prone than others.

Many social scientists will try to find causes for this through statistical analysis of possibly independent variables (such as size of establishment, union membership or gender composition of staff). We might find a correlation between size and strike-proneness, but is it size itself, or social relations, or forms of management systems associated with different sizes of firms that are important? New statistical tests cannot solve this problem. To answer the qualitative questions about the nature of our objects, science must *abstract* from the many conditions of an object to focus on those it is believed have a significant effect. To abstract means to isolate in thought a one-sided or partial aspect of a concrete research object, and to form abstract concepts about it before going back to the concrete armed with a host of theoretical understandings (Peet, 1998, p. 168). Sayer (1992, p. 92) maintains that there is a continuum rather than a dichotomy between abstract and concrete. However, abstraction is necessary to distinguish essential characteristics from the maze of incidental characteristics:

> Abstraction is particularly important for the identification of structures. These can be defined as sets of internally related objects or practices. A landlord–tenant relation presupposes the existence of private property, rent, the production of an economic surplus and so on; together they form a structure. Contrary to common assumption, structures include not only big social objects such as the international division of labor, but small ones at the interpersonal and personal levels (e.g. conceptual structures) and still smaller non-social ones at the neurological level and beyond. Within social structures there are particular 'positions' associated with certain roles. It is particularly important to distinguish the occupant of a position from the position itself.

It is often assumed that individuals have free will and must be held responsible for their actions. However, people are also constrained by rules and structures, even though such structures only exist where people reproduce them (see Giddens' structuration theory above). Structures are thereby seen as durable and sometimes capable of causing social change. However, they can also lock their occupants into particular role positions. Durable social structures have positions associated with roles independent of the persons occupying them. As Bhaskar (1979, p. 44) states: 'People do not marry to reproduce nuclear family or work to reproduce capitalist economy. Yet it is nevertheless the unintended consequence of, as it is also a necessary condition for, their activity.'

It is thus important to distinguish between necessary causal powers (or **necessary conditions**) and **contingent conditions**, and also between internal and external relations. Gunpowder possesses the necessary conditions to explode, but whether it will explode or not depends on an 'accidental' spark. In most cases an industrial workforce has the necessary power to go on strike; whether they strike or not depends upon particular contingent conditions, which may be highly local and on which generalization is impossible. As demonstrated by the miners' strike (Box 1.4, p. 13), necessary causal powers operate only at a high, general (in this case, national) level, whereas the local level is associated with external, contingent relations. Sayer (1991, p. 300) points out, however, that

> the 'general-causes-and-local-contingent-effects' model may sometimes be appropriate, but realism gives no special privilege to it, as many commentators on locality research (both advocates and opponents) have supposed. Other variants, such as local causes and local effects, or local causes and general or global effects, or global causes and global effects, are just as compatible with realism, and just as relevant for understanding society.

The relationship between landlord and tenant is *internal* and *necessary* since the existence of either presupposes the existence of the other. How the landlord treats the tenant is, however, **contingent** on the personalities of the persons, whether they are male or female, etc.

When striving to put realism into practice we need theoretical categories to understand theoretical relations. For this reason, it is one of Sayer's main intentions to clarify obscure theoretical concepts. The realist terminology for basic theoretical categories of necessary relations is called **abstract theory**. In this sense, 'abstract' does not mean 'vague', but refers to a particular relationship between causal powers and an object of study. Abstract theoretical research deals with structures and mechanisms. Events are only considered as possible outcomes: 'Abstract theory analyses objects in terms of their constitutive structures, as parts of wider structures and in terms of their causal power. Concrete research looks at what happens when these combine' (Sayer, 1984/1992; Figure 6.2).

Concrete research is the empirical study of events and not-necessary (contingent) relations. Such relations represent all the conditions relating to the individuals, firms, organizations or whatever we might study, which are not part of the actual internal relations. At the abstract level, we find a number of structures with causal power that can be activated through certain mechanisms. The results can be studied at the concrete level of events. The same mechanisms can produce different events, as indicated by the vertical lines in Figure 6.2, and the same event may have different causes. Concrete research focuses basically on the events, but Sayer recommends us to employ a combination of concrete and abstract research.

In Figure 6.2 'generalization (extensive research)' may illustrate the type of concrete research activity within spatial science that tries to find explanations by searching for regularities in extensive quantitative empirical investigations. Sayer recommends '**intensive concrete research**' that, on the basis of abstract considerations of some structures and mechanisms, analyses their possible effects in limited empirical **case studies** to achieve an understanding of the functions of necessary and contingent relations.

For instance, Bjørlykke (1996) compared the establishment of oil terminals in Shetland, UK, with Øygarden, Norway. She assumed that the oil companies would be embedded in the rationality (necessary relations) of the global market

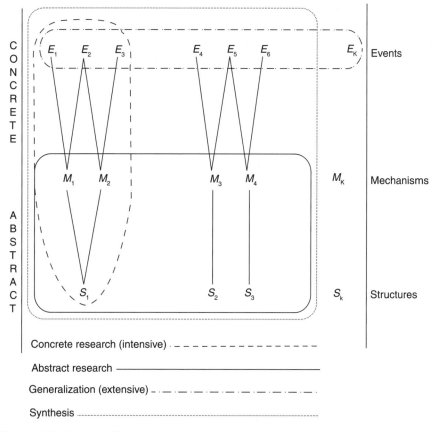

Figure 6.2 Types of research

Source: From Sayer, 1984, p. 215; Cloke et al., 1991, p. 153

economy and that the outcomes (events) in both locations would be very much alike. Intensive concrete research, based on qualitative methods, revealed, however, that contingent relations at the local level led to events that were rather different at the two locations. So with different contingent conditions, the same mechanism may invoke different events; on the other hand, the same kind of event may have different causes. It is important to note here that the form of contingent relations must always remain an empirical question, answered through observation of the actual cases. However, structural relations might be found at different geographical levels. The international relations of oil companies might be regarded as being at a structural level, but the local rules of the Shetland community could equally be regarded as structural. Depending on the level of the investigation, these might be seen as either necessary or contingent factors.

Some would like to include a fourth level in the vertical dimension of Figure 6.2 to cover **agency** (in the form of meanings, experiences, interpretations, actions, etc.). But as agency can form structures, can function as causes or be considered as events, Sayer (1992) maintains that this is already included. This means it is impossible to equate the concepts of structure and mechanism in Figure 6.2 with structure and agency in structuration theory. Realist discussions on structure and agency include, in general, a series of warnings about the complexity of these issues, particularly, of course, because realism concerns itself with establishing a guide to research. **Epistemology** – the theory of knowledge – is at the heart of realism, whereas structuration is mainly concerned with **ontology** – the theory of existence.

When geographers observe the geographical mosaic, they can, says Johnston (1985, p. 335), regard every place as *unique* but not as *singular*. General rules and societal structures exist, but they are adapted at each place in a unique combination of individual interpretations made by human agency at the specific 'locale'. The structural rules of society, like the capitalist mode of production, are given. Capitalism is not, however, a deterministic mechanism; its imperatives have been interpreted in many ways. Former interpretations are imprinted as a part of culture and create frames for new interpretations. Actions based upon these interpretations also result in distinct physical landscapes and social patterns, which in turn constrain and enable new interpretations and actions (see Figure 6.1).

It might also be possible to regard geography's traditional role as a bridge-builder between the natural and social sciences in these terms. While social scientists are primarily interested in the empirical results of interactions between human beings, geographers are additionally concerned with the natural environment and with the constraints and relations between this environment and humanity's activities. The limitations and possibilities of the physical environment are interpreted and changed through human agency in just the same way as the limits and possibilities set by both basic social structures and empirical social patterns. It is of crucial interest to society how and why environmental constraints are interpreted so variously by different actors at the same place, and how interpretations and intended actions *vis-á-vis* the physical environment can differ from place to place.

POSTSTRUCTURALISM

A revival of interest in anti-modernist philosophies (Nietzsche and Heidegger particularly) gradually grew within the radical, social-anarchist movement that was a product of the 1968 upheavals among students and working-class militants in Paris. Notions of a **postindustrial** society and critiques of modernist, western models for economic development in Third World countries merged with cultural critiques of modern architecture and aesthetics. Power relations in our postindustrial society have changed, making an orthodox Marxist theory of power obsolete. Power no longer resides in institutions or in the economy, but resides instead in codes, simulations and the media, and it becomes increasingly abstract, maintains Baudrillard (1987). As opposed to Marx's productivism, poststructural theory emphasizes consumption, in which (for instance) the broadcast media, particularly television, create a hyper-reality that is more than real (Peet, 1998, p. 213). Poststructuralism generally interprets modern society as a system of power, and it expresses a fundamental scepticism towards any form of totalitarian regime – capitalist as well as communist. This has led to new interest in **social anarchism** (see pp. 55–9).

> There is no sharp difference between poststructural and postmodern philosophies. Generally, however, *poststructural philosophy* criticizes the certainties of modern knowledge, as with its claim to coherence, neutrality and truth, while *postmodern philosophy* carries this further into an alternative discourse based on oppositional modes of understanding. Postmodernism proposes new ways of being a person which involve, on the one hand the liberation of desire, yet on the other, utter cynicism or nihilistic 'resistance' to the forces of modernity. (Peet, 1998, p. 208)

We may state, however, that poststructuralism basically rests upon a philosophical position that relates both to ontology (the theory of existence) and epistemology (the theory of knowledge). In short, poststructuralism comes after structuralism and confronts structuralism with a 'sceptic attitude towards determination by "underlying" structures and attempts to grasp the ultimate "truth" of language, culture, society and psyche' (Gibson-Graham, 2000, p. 96). There are no **deep structures** that can explain everything; actions are also based on relations that are found on the surface. However, as pointed out by Murdoch (2006), poststructuralism does not mean a clean break with structuralism, as many of the adherents retain an obvious debt to structuralism. Underlying structures exist, but meanings and actions cannot be seen as simple manifestations of these; there are often unexpected relations. In this way systems are 'open' rather than 'closed', but poststructuralism is concerned with 'systems', rather than individuals, and thus remains anti-humanist. Murdoch (2006), in analysing poststructuralism, finds it closely linked to **actor–network theory** (see pp. 194–6). He points out the

> actor-network view of agency begins not with fully formed agents/actants but with an already constituted social space (the network) and shows how agents/actants (both human and non-human) emerge from a series of trials in which they are continually striving to become actors with powers. (Murdoch, 2006, p. 68)

Power relations within geographical spaces, from local to global, represent one main theme within geographical studies that has benefited from poststructuralism. Much of this work has been carried out by scientists who were originally attracted to Marxist structuralism, like David Harvey, but who have gradually elaborated both a critique of structuralism and developed more refined approaches. Just like Michel Foucault (1926–84) and Pierre Bourdieu (1930–2002), Harvey is an advocate of social consciousness and a supporter of the weak in society, but he has applied more complicated system models to understand and analyse the power games in the present globalized postindustrial societies. Great inspiration for radical theory building in geography and planning has come from the work of Pierre Bourdieu in his development of the **habitus** concept and the understanding of **social capital** (see particularly Hillier and Rooksby, 2005). Bourdieu, according to Hillier and Roxby (2005: 21) defines habitus as 'a system of durable, transportable dispositions, structured structures predisposed to function as structuring structures, that is, as principles which generate and organize practices and representations'. Habitus is an embodied as well as a cognitive **sense of place**.

To understand this seemingly obscure definition we need to set it into a context. Habitus must be understood as social space; as a sense of one's place and sense of the other's place in the world. We can relate this to Sack's presentation of the relation between 'self' and place in Figure 1.9 (p. 23), in which 'place' can be seen as very concrete, like the home in which you grew up. Bourdieu's 'place' is *not* the same: it is the social place, or rather 'position', for instance your feeling of command in society. This is also related to his understanding of **social capital** as features of social organization, such as trust, norms and networks that can improve the efficiency of society by facilitating coordinated action. It consists of resources that are built into a collective by trust, shared norms and network relations. Social capital is not something that can be owned by the individual, but an individual can benefit from it as a partner in the collective. The benefits of social capital are of course very much related to power, class relations and the distribution of economic resources in society. In addition to social capital, we can talk about economic capital and cultural capital that you have access to and even physical (capital) strength and abilities. Social, economic and cultural capital make up **symbolic capital**. This is the basis for your **habitus** or sense of place as well as your understanding of the other's place.

These concepts have given geographers very good tools in analysing power games at the root of geographical differences; social differences in local communities as well as global conflicts and nation-building. Healey (2005) demonstrates how in a planning case elected representatives and officers of Newcastle City Council had little sense of the place of their inner-city residents. Habitus of local authority representatives are often supported by 'feeling important'. Subordinated people very often accept their habitus as something unavoidable, but which in reality can be changed. This provides a good basis for analysing gender, the sense of place of females and males in a society, and also how territoriality functions.

Another field within poststructuralist research in geography concerns man–land relations and planning. In one case study, Murdoch (2006) shows how 'nature' in the postwar decades was understood as one large category like 'the English countryside', which had to be demarcated into zones of protection.

Today the countryside may rather be regarded as 'rurban', a mixture of different lifestyles and economic activities (see Box 4.2 on Rothbury, pp. 117–18) and nature protection has both wider global (global warming) and local (pollution) connotations. To analyse man–land relations we need much more elaborate network approaches. This is also directly related to the development of planning theories, which initially were quite simple rationalist approaches focusing on the physical characteristics of places. Today we are concerned with social network building, governance and **collaborative planning** (Healey, 1997), just to mention a few key words. This means that geographers involved in applied research and planning have to make use of much more complex actor networks to analyse possible futures for even a small community.

Poststructuralism has thus a direct bearing on scientific models and methods. If we adopt a poststructuralist stance, we must also take the process of 'writing' geography – of representing our findings in words, sounds and pictures – far more seriously. This must involve a critical reconsideration of our research methods. Box 5.1 (pp. 139–40) shows how this leads on to **self-reflection**, that is reflection on your own place as a researcher. Geographers need better training in interpretation and reflection, and on the role of concepts and signs in the research process. '**Semiotics**' (a Greek word that means 'showing' or 'signifying') encourages research into **signs** and meanings, and has succeeded in expanding our understanding in many recent research projects. Semiotics attempts to uncover the underlying cultural codes that determine how people interpret the spoken word and other forms of human communications. The **semiotic triad** (Figure 6.3) provides a background for the analysis of the relations between an object and its interpreters. For instance, anyone investigating a proposal to build a nuclear power station in an area of outstanding natural beauty would have to communicate with both the officials of the energy company and the local inhabitants. These interest groups are called the **interpretants**. Interpretants interpret the symbols and other signs used, for instance, in the description of the area and the power project. In the communication between the different groups and the investigator, other signs might be conveyed, which are interpreted by the investigator. There are three main types of sign: symbols, icons and indexes. All words are symbols. An icon is a 'motivated' sign that looks like the object (for instance, a map of the site). An index is a motivated sign that links to the object in the same way as smoke is associated with fire (or nuclear power with radioactive waste). The concept of **metaphor** is often used to describe a kind of iconic sign by which, for instance, a new phenomenon is given meaning by comparing it as, or akin to, something already well known.

An approach based on semiotics is needed, in particular, when we carry out research into foreign cultures. It will often be impossible to understand factual events if we do not achieve an intersubjective understanding of the meaning embedded in a local culture or even in an individual creed. We have to get an understanding of the different habitus of local people. The study carried out by Aase (1999b) in the Sai Valley in northern Pakistan illustrates this point (see Box 6.1).

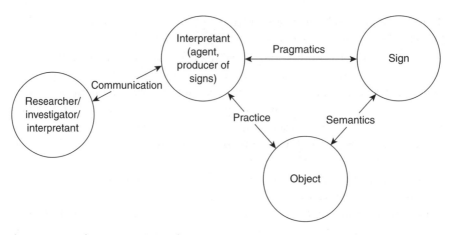

Figure 6.3   The semiotic triad

Source: Based on Personal information from T. H. Aase

Box 6.1	**The use of metaphor in Himalayan resource management**

In the Sai Valley in northern Pakistan, a hydroelectric power project created the administrative problem of adapting traditional practices in land and water rights to formal state rules. Adaptation is not only a question of finding the practices that seem objectively to function best, but it is also a matter of finding practices that *work* meaningfully for local people.

A hydroelectric power project is a rather dramatic example of modernization that could lead to the fragmentation of the local community if not handled wisely. In such a process, people may try to create a feeling of 'integrity' through their use of **metaphor**. A metaphor is a word or phrase that is applied to an object or concept it does not literally denote in order to suggest a comparison with the other object or concept (as in 'a mighty fortress is our God'). In this case, however, it implies that meanings from known realms of life are ascribed to new, modern phenomena in order to restore a notion of integrated reality.

In the case of the Sai Valley development, the inhabitants searched in their culture and history for meaning that could be ascribed – transferred, so to speak – to the new arrangements. The practices are loaded with local meaning based on former experiences. The cultural change that is usually read into events of modernization is exactly the result of such metaphorisation.

Precipitation in the region's valleys is insufficient for agriculture, but glacial meltwater from the mountains and cultivable land is plentiful. For centuries, the construction of long irrigation channels in the steep mountain sides provided the necessary extensions to agricultural land, and increased animal husbandry provided manure to fertilize the extra

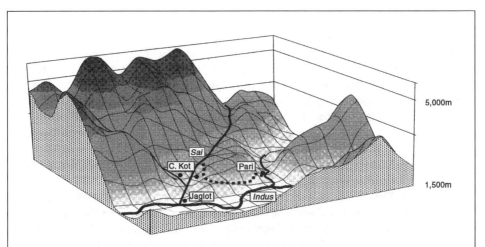

Figure 6.4 Three-dimensional diagram of the region. The dotted line shows the diversion channel for water from the Sai River to Pari

Source: From Aase 1999b

growing areas. Land and water rights depended on a local balance of power between the villages, and conflicts were solved in traditional ways. Today, vital resources are managed formally by the Pakistani state. In the case of the new power station, the authorities, wisely, tried to reach a consensus with the local villages about the ownership of the land that became available for irrigation.

To utilize the height difference for the production of power, it was proposed that the bulk of the water from the Sai River should be diverted to the village of Pari in the deeper Gilgit River valley (see Figure 6.4). A new agricultural area, Pari Das, could thus be established close to Pari. This, combined with the fact that the villages along the Sai Valley are divided from Pari Das by a high mountain ridge, would make it a natural choice to give the new land to the villagers of Pari. But, astonishingly, Chakker Kot village in the Sai Valley acquired the new land, and this was readily accepted by the villagers of Pari. The new owners have to climb the mountain ridge to reach their land, which is in an area that was previously hardly ever used by the villagers for either pasturing or forestry!

What arguments were applied to come to this decision, and how was consensus reached? The answer relates to a division between the villages in portering duties (the duty to carry goods for the Kashmiri garrison, which was located further upstream above Pari at Gilgit) from the period between the 1880s and 1947. Even though Chakker Kot is not located in the Indus–Gilgit Valleys (which the porter route followed), its inhabitants were obliged to carry goods between the confluence of the Gilgit and Indus Rivers to Pari. As the new land was located a little downstream from Pari, Chakker Kot argued that the land was theirs since it was situated in the

(Continued)

(Continued)

area of their old portering duty. This was accepted by the neighbouring villages. Since the Pari villagers also accepted this, we must assume that the episode was the result of a common meaning or shared understanding among the villagers. However, this common meaning must, notes Aase, be related to another field of experience, where a similar constellation of meanings is accepted and practised. We cannot follow the arguments further here, but we do need to point out that Aase documents that the land-rights claims were accepted because of their metaphorical resemblance to traditional arrangements.

Chakker Kot villagers, who gained ownership of the new land, eagerly supported the power scheme, whereas villages further down the Sai River strongly opposed it. In this discourse, the upstream and downstream settlements refer to differing systems of meaning – namely, to traditional understandings. So modernization is not just the assimilation of traditional society into a universalistic state. Rather, people try to make sense of the changes by searching for meaning in traditional practices. Out of this innovative, cultural process, new practices emerge, combining traditional 'meaning' with the challenges of modernity. Thus, the Sai case is an expressive example of 'local particularism in a globalizing world' (ibid.).

As was noted by Peet (1998) (see p. 169), there are no sharp differences between poststructural and postmodern philosophies, but a lot of confusion has emerged because both concepts are popular with researchers who have not gone back to the origins of these ideas in the theory of science and philosophy. These concepts, just like **paradigm** described earlier, have thus lost their original definition. They have been diluted to serve the purposes of other points of views. A simple understanding focuses on *post* as something that comes *after* structuralism or after modernism. Poststructuralism, therefore, is a creed of thoughts that responds to the ontology and epistemology of structuralism, or revises structuralism. This is an approach, partly based on Murdoch (2006), which provides many practical entry points to concrete research projects. On the other hand, this simple 'post-' interpretation is critiqued by those going back to the philosophical roots of poststructuralism, as exposed by Derrida and Foucault. This form of critique is voiced by Harrison (2006) and Wylie (2006). They point out that poststructuralism does not offer a 'how to' guide or a blueprint for how to do research that in magical ways will produce a new understanding; the main aim is for the researcher to get a deeper understanding of **deconstruction** and **discourse analysis**. Deconstruction is a method to analyse how language, meanings and messages conveyed by language work (the connection to semiotics is quite clear) in order to 'haunt, inhabit and contest claims to truth' (Wylie, 2006, p. 300). Discourse analysis is a method set out to 'deconstruct discourses' of race, gender, sexuality, the state, nature, landscape, and so on (Wylie, 2006, p. 303).

deconstruction and discourse analysis are *critical* methods – used in making critical assessments of social institutions, identities, cultural beliefs, political arrangements and so on. However, I have been concerned to stress that both are post-*structural* methods, in so far as they are concerned to go beyond 'top-down' structuralist conceptions of how power is exercised, of how identities are constructed. (Wylie, 2006, p. 307)

It is quite clear that discourses on 'how power is exercised and how identities are constructed' is of particular interest if we look into the **political geography** of contemporary regional and local conflicts such as in Yugoslavia, between Israelis and Palestinians, and the wars in Iraq and Afghanistan. An example of what discourse implies is given by Aase (1999a) in the background of a religious conflict in Gilgit, Pakistan (Box 6.2). This case study is set in a region that was a focus of world politics at the time of writing this fourth edition, as it is located on the border of Pakistan and Afghanistan. Without a deeper geographical understanding, which the case gives us a small glimpse of, it will be very difficult for the USA, NATO and the United Nations to promote peace and good government, as understood in the western world, in Afghanistan, Iraq or Pakistan. This is now also understood by some military leaders, most notably by Britain's distinguished military general Rupert Smith in his book *The Utility of Force: The Art of War in the Modern World* (2005). Using the term 'paradigm', he maintains that the politics of war is still based on an outmoded paradigm of interstate industrial war which clearly served its purpose up to the Second World War but 'it is now time to comprehend the paradigm of war *amongst* the people in the same way' (ibid., p. 3). The use of military force is useless if it is not based on political and humanitarian efforts that change the will of the people. If this is not properly understood and acted on, the interventions in Iraq and Afghanistan may end in the same disaster as the Vietnam war. One of the few examples of a successful 'war amongst the people' was the British encounter with the guerillas in Malayia in the 1950s, in which the will of the majority of Malayans was effectively won so that the guerilla support dwindled. We can thus reflect on how geographical investigations and understanding can aid political solutions on both the global and the local scene.

Box 6.2	**The advent of religious conflict in Gilgit, Pakistan**

Until 1988, the Sunni and the Shia Muslims in the Gilgit area of Pakistan (Figure 6.5) lived in harmony with each other, and intermarriages were frequent as people followed the tradition of *kaom* (a form of 'caste' division)

(Continued)

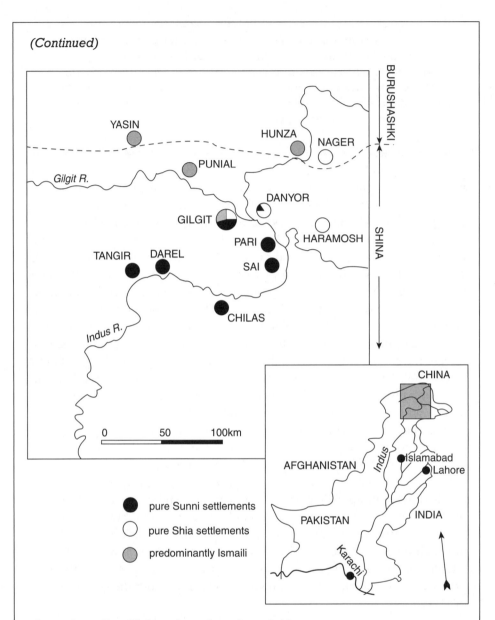

Figure 6.5   The Gilgit region of northern Pakistan

Source: Aase, 1999a

rather than basing their marriages on religious adherence. In 1988, however, fighting broke out between Sunnis and Shias as a result of a quarrel over the start of Ramadan. Anti-Shia graffiti smeared on the walls in Gilgit on the second day of Shia fasting, and which claimed that Shias were *kafir* (heathen), triggered a riot. This occasion has become a highly significant historical event in Gilgit; nothing was the same after the 'tension'.

Segregation among the groups is now a fact: intermarriages no longer happen. The puzzling thing is that the religious roots of this conflict date back to AD 660 and concern the rightful successor as the Fifth Caliph. If this strife did not cause serious trouble before, then why now?

'We have to go beyond religion in order to grasp the process of re-signification that has taken place in Gilgit. Symbolic processes are always contextual; likewise, the religious discourse in Gilgit yields no meaning unless it is situated in time and space' (Aase, 1999a). In earlier times, the different religions of the region were fragmented into various independent valleys and settlements. The area was called the 'unruled country' in British colonial times. Each of the three religious groups (Sunnis, Shia and Ismaili) lived in separate principalities, and 'reasonable' mixing as a result of *kaom*-based marriages was not a problem. Some of these principalities retained their semi-autonomous status until 1974, when the northern region of Pakistan was divided up into four districts to be governed more effectively from Pakistan's capital, Islamabad. The northerners, however, felt that they had lost local power and were being neglected by central government. This was especially the case with the Shias and the Ismailis, as the majority of Pakistani Muslims are Sunnis.

In addition, Gilgit has developed as the administrative capital of the region and, as is often the case in growing towns, there has been a mixing of different religious groups in the town (see Figure 6.5). Modernization and new forms of employment have led to a reduced importance of the *kaom* structure, and affiliation to a religious group has become a stronger means of identification. This has made Gilgit the most sensitive part of the region, and the town was the centre of the build-up of 'the tension'. The quarrel over the start of Ramadan was the 'straw that broke the camel's back' – the camel was already 'overloaded with goods from outside'.

While one factor in the conflict has been the change from local to central rule, another has been the opening up of the territory through the construction of the Karakoram Highway. This road has integrated the region into the national economy and has brought in new business as tourists and other foreigners have started to come into the area in growing numbers. However, this has not equally benefited all local groups: the Shias remain cultivators whereas the Ismailis are enterprising business-men who have profited as owners of shops, hotels and bazaar stands in Gilgit. The Ismailis, on the other hand, have to compete with the Sunni Pathans who have migrated from the lowlands and who now operate one-third of the bazaar in Gilgit.

Hence the Shias have been deprived of local political power and have benefited little from **modernization**. This deprivation, of course, has been worsening over a period of time, and to be called 'heathen' in graffiti was to add insult to injury. Religious affiliation has served as a symbol for this growing tension, and it has become the dominating factor in the distinction between 'us' and 'them' (Aase, 1999a). This example shows how stable,

(Continued)

(Continued)

local factors change when influenced by external structural forces, but in specified ways that make an understanding of local conditions crucial. This is what geography is all about. It also shows the importance of **political geography**, of power relations and of the concept of **territoriality**.

When power relations are dramatically changed, as when US and allied troops overturned the rule of Saddam Hussein in Iraq, it is very difficult to re-create stability. The Kurds in Northern Iraq have so far benefited from the weak central rule, whereas the Sunni and Shia Arabs and their different militias have had real problems in accepting the new power balance. The Kurds, the largest language group in the world that does not have a nation-state, dream of an embryo Kurdistan in Northern Iraq. But this is seen as a serious threat to NATO member Turkey, as the largest Kurdish population lives in eastern Turkey, where they also have an active guerilla movement and political parties. A substantial number of Kurds also live in Iran, and their minority status is also not accepted. Do you have a solution to this intricate situation?

The strictly philosophical understanding of poststructuralism, as promoted by Wylie (2006), is underlining the general aim of this book to explain to the reader that the purpose of science is not to find a special truth, but to set in train a discourse to question accepted positions and truths in order to create a deeper understanding. So far, so good, but there is a danger here that we ends up in **nihilism** (although Harrison (2006) contradicts this by saying that with Nietzsche, poststructuralism is dedicated to resisting nihilism). Nihilism, a denial of all real existence, does not bring us much further in practical research, if we become too obsessed with the philosophy of poststructuralism we may become too afraid to write as we know that all concepts and words can be interpreted in different ways. In a research project, poststructuralist considerations, as exposed in Boxes 6.1 and Box 6.2, are needed, but it should be blended with other forms of interpretation and reflection.

POSTMODERNISM

The simple understanding of **postmodernism** is that it comes *after* modernism and that it relates directly to factual changes in our societies, and actions and reactions to those changes. In this way postmodernism is seen in a periodizing sense, as an epoch coming after modernity. Clarke (2006), however, strongly attacks this simple understanding of postmodernism, presenting a devastating critique on geographers who use of the concept. Clarke builds his understanding mainly on Lyotard's exposition, particularly in *The Postmodern Condition* (1984), in which 'postmodern' is defined as an incredulity towards metanarratives; that is, a disbelief in any 'kind of "overarching principles" that *legitimated* a certain kind of *modern* discourse – a discourse which claimed to be capable of disclosing the *truth*, hence guaranteeing the value and utility of *knowledge*-based action to society at large' (Clarke, 2006, p. 110). Just as we lost faith in God, we have now lost faith in the grand narratives. The lasting value of postmodernism for geographical research is, maintains Clarke (ibid., p. 116), that it gives us new eyes with which to see spaces and places. It gives, in the same way as poststructuralism, some basic underpinnings of science as such without connecting this to a particular time or empirical research task.

Clarke (ibid., p. 109) maintains that geographers have contributed to the confusion over postmodernism more than most, adding that readers should *never* trust anyone's arguments about postmodernism, and that they should be particularly cautious when it comes to geographers. A direct attack is aimed at Harvey's book, *The Condition of Postmodernity* (1989), and to a somewhat lesser degree at Soja's *Postmodern Geographies* (1989). One reason is that Harvey, although willing to reassess and criticize grand narratives, is seriously concerned that, in practice, postmodernism delegitimates social critique and progressive politics rather more than it delegitimates venture capitalism and neo-conservatism. Whatmore (2002, p. 150) points out that this critique of postmodernism is based on a political and ethical understanding of the primacy of the individual as the ethical subject. Communitarian approaches, however,

> **re-assert the situatedness of the individual and point to the inter-subjective constitution of ethical agency. However, they tend to do so by invoking normative configurations of community, like the family, the neighbourhood and the nation, without examining the power relations they enact. Moreover, this 'situatedness' is defined (only) in terms of relations between people. (Whatmore, 2002, p. 151)**

Whatmore wants us to include both power relations and the nature/human issues and responsibilities.

The crucial question is whether we adhere to a strict definition based on the work of certain leading philosophers or follow the different meanings that the concept has been given among science practitioners. I find the latter position most fruitful as it makes many new inroads to geographic understanding, and I would like to start with the theoretical contributions by Foucault, rather than those by Lyotard.

Michel Foucault (1926–84), professor of the history of systems of thought at the College of France, has been regarded as the main proponent of *postmodernist philosophy*. Throughout his work he maintains a hostile position towards modernity, for what he finds to be its repressive, totalizing modes of thought. He favours 'difference, fragmentation, and discontinuity, multiple forms of analysis rather than single truths, microanalyses interwoven with macroanalyses, pure opinion mixed with exact historical studies' (Peet, 1998, p. 200). He argues against global, totalitarian theories such as Freud's theories of psychoanalysis and

Marxism, favouring instead a non-centralized, autonomous, local theoretical production whose validity does not depend on approval from established regimes of thought. In practical terms this endorses a 'bottom-up' approach to research – a focus on *everyday life* and local perceptions. A significant aspect of postmodernist thought is its focus on *difference* – an alertness to and appreciation of the many differences that exist among the people of the world.

The term 'postmodernist' has been applied to many cultural objects, including paintings, novels, plays and films. Postmodernist trends are also visible in architecture and town planning. The schools of modernist and **'placeless'** architecture represented by Le Corbusier and functionalism are no longer fashionable: grand planning designs are out of favour and strict spatial differentiations of functions (housing, parks, services, industry, etc.) are no longer countenanced. We now look for variety in townscapes – mixtures of functions and the rehabilitation of old buildings rather than the erection of new, modern, high-rise and functional blocks. Instead of expert, top-down planning, we now emphasize participation and the 'bottom-up' involvement of citizens and interest groups in the planning process.

Much of the geographical interest in postmodernism has been focused on the economies of western societies, where traditional capitalism is changing. Lash and Urry, in their book *The End of Organised Capitalism* (1987), analyse the restless and essentially 'disorganized' character of contemporary capitalism. Harvey (1989) sketches the impact of a new flexible capitalism on the revised experiences of time and space upon which postmodern cultural developments crucially depend. In societies where most people find employment in tertiary and quarternary activities and only a minority work in agriculture and manufacturing, postmodern developments have influenced the tastes and lifestyles of a new middle class which reflects the recent restructuring of the capitalist system. With Harvey analysis and theoretical understanding provide a map for radical political action as part of a liberatory politics but with important differences from orthodox Marxism (Peet, 1998, p. 221).

Foucault (1986) pointed out that 'the present epoch will perhaps be above all the epoch of space'. Soja (1989), partly basing his argument on Foucault, associates 'modern' with history and 'postmodern' with geography, and finds a new, postmodern, critical geography emerging 'which reasserts the significance of space or, rather, sees time and space together in a creative commingling as the vertical and horizontal dimensions of being' (Peet, 1998, p. 223).

Postmodernism warns us against grand theories and urges us to employ reflection and self-reflection at all stages of a research process. Sayer (1993) points out, however, that the postmodernist preoccupation with the problems of discourse and language, its suspicion of concepts of truth and falsity and of empirical testing, mean it is in danger of flipping over into an equally untenable position of cultural relativism: 'Moreover, to point out the irreducibly metaphorical and rhetorical character of knowledge does not mean that logic, protocols of reason, just disappear. They remain, indispensable as ever: no flip from reason to rhetoric is needed' (ibid.). Sayer argues that, instead of flipping from naïve positivism to postmodernist relativism, **realism** offers a third way between them. We may drop the idea of truth as absolute but we cannot ignore the relationship between discourse and the world.

Dear (1988) argues that postmodernism makes geography an offer it cannot afford to refuse because the positioning of space is the privileged realm of postmodernism. But as postmodernism holds there cannot be any grand theory of human geography, we might be concerned with the extremes of deconstructive relativism: 'It is from this paradoxical position, enticed by postmodernism, worried by its anarchy, remaining modern, that Dear wants to reconstruct human geography' (Peet, 1998, p. 218).

In addition, says Gregory (1989, p. 92), when reflecting on 'areal differentiation and postmodern human geography'

> we need in part, to go back to the question of areal differentiation: but armed with a new theoretical sensitivity towards the world in which we live and the ways in which we represent it. Whether we focus on 'order' or 'disorder' or on the tension between the two – and no matter how we choose to define these terms – we still have to 'look' – We are still making geography.

'New theoretical sensitivity' has to a large extent been contributed to by feminist approaches, a statement that we are now going to qualify.

GENDER AND FEMINIST GEOGRAPHY

> Feminist geography is concerned first and foremost with improving women's lives by understanding the sources, dynamics, and spatiality of women's oppression, and with documenting strategies of resistance. (Dixon and Jones, 2006, p. 42)

This sounds like a political programme of women's rights rather than an outline of academic contributions. The reason why feminist geography was not given a proper treatment in earlier editions of this book (Holt-Jensen, 1988/1999) was that a major part of feminist contributions could have been written in any discipline, focusing on the general unfair gender positions both in academia and society at large. However, during the last couple of decades feminist geography has provided very important contributions to new geographic understanding. Dixon and Jones (2006) point out three basic headings under which we may list these research contributions:

1) *Gender as difference*, which is addressing the different life experiences of women and men in a number of cultural, economic, political and environmental arenas. An example (based on Jarvis et al., 2001) is given below on how **social reproduction** and time-space analysis have brought a quite

new understanding of urban geography into focus. Another example is how gender differences regarding 'landscapes of fear' have brought a reassessment of neighbourhood planning: the traditional 'male' physical plan, separating roads and pedestrians by providing leafy pathways and underpasses, is now contested as physical and sexual assaults are more likely to happen on pedestrian pathways than along main roadways.

2) *Gender as social relation*, which analyses how the relationship between males and females differ from place to place, between different cultures and changes over time. In its most hierarchical form these relations are realized as patriarchy, a social structure with many different forms, spatially and historically, working to dominate women and children. Research within this field is crucial to understanding economic, social and political geography in any region of the world, but also in micro-level studies of neighbourhoods and home spaces. Major contributions have studied Third World economies and **diaspora** neighbourhoods in urban social geography. A pervasive example in fiction is given by Khaled Hosseini in his book *A Thousand Splendid Suns* (2007), which exposes the life of two females in Afghanistan during a period of 40 years.

3) *Gender as a social construction*, which is related to investigations of how concepts and metaphors are 'gendered', when concepts are related to traditional understanding of male or female characteristica. What gendered coding lies at the heart of the concept 'Mother Nature' and what do we think of when we talk about 'male tasks' and 'female obligations'. Many of the words and concepts we use daily are gendered and they are socializing children into gender relations which ought to have been changed.

Another contribution from feminist geography is that it has helped to revolutionize the methods used in geographic research (Dixon and Jones, 2006, p. 42). According to Cosgrove (1993), there has been a tradition that geography fieldwork is dominated by 'hairy-chested feats of scholarly endurance', and is not regarded as a place for female students. In texts and research in economic geography the focus has been on the location of industries, production by a paid workforce, transportation systems and financial transactions in global and local markets, but almost no focus on the production going on in homes and local community work. In their book *The Secret Life of Cities*, Jarvis et al. (2001), focusing on the concept of '**social reproduction**' as they understand it, present a perspective that for a long time was absent in urban geography and planning. Based on empirical studies of London, they demonstrate that the life and development of the city is based on millions of individual and family-based decisions on how to link work, home, transport and 'reproduction' in an acceptable way. Routinized mobility is strictly limited by transport availability, costs and the time-space agreements within a household. The daily routinized actions such as shopping habits, travel to work, by **human agency** are to a large extent conserving or changing structures of city life. More fundamental 'material household decisions', such as changing jobs, moving home, getting married, having children also have a profound impact. Work, home and the transport links between them have always been studied by geographers, but social reproduction encompassing all the other activities that have to be taken care of in addition to paid work – childcare, shopping, housework, foodmaking, organizing school and leisure time activities, etc. – have mainly come into focus through feminist contributions. At the core of this is the time–space arbitrations and compromises in family life: Who takes the children to school?' Can grandfather babysit if we go to cinema? Will father make dinner when mother is on the evening shift at McDonald's? To analyse this, Jarvis et al. (2001) make use of **time–space geography** (p. 89). They conducted long interviews with a selection of families in different parts of London. It can be argued that city life has become much more diversified and complex with the increasing participation of women in the paid workforce: a hundred years ago the home was defined as the feminine sphere of influence; the geographical focus was on the activity spaces of men, their work and transport networks.

Typically, through area planning, workplaces have been spatially separated from housing areas, including schools and kindergartens, supposedly because women stay at home and take care of the 'reproductive' part of family life. But things started to change when hospitals and other institutions with a high concentration of female workers had to build kindergartens to keep their workers. That kindergartens were not built close to men's workplaces still demonstrates the traditional gender obligations, noting here that the term **gender** or 'social sex' is theorized as 'the cultural or social elaboration of differences between women and men, and so mutable, variable and open to change' (McDowell, 2003, p. 607). When industries were noisy and polluting manufacturing plants, there were some reasons for the physical separation of workplace from housing, but presently most workplaces could very well be integrated in housing areas. This could bring back the situation in traditional farms where children learn the work of their parents from the very beginning, although farm work was strictly gender-defined and dominated in most cases by patriarchy.

The work of feminist geography has given us a very important new understanding of shifting regional characteristics, as demonstrated in Box 6.3 (pp. 185–7). Another significant contribution is a new understanding of how to conceptualize private and public space and territoriality. There is an old saying, 'My home is my castle'. The female critique is that this is a typical male understanding. Even though the home has been understood as the female sphere of influence, as a 'castle' it is a closed place in which women can be kept in isolation. In the worst cases it can feel like a prison. Nancy Duncan (1996), in formulating an ideal future geography, set as a primary aim the needs to reduce the different households **space** for the benefit of each family member's private **space**. She points out that the geographical differences of gender relations in the world, with some societies having very strict regulations of public interference with private life, in general means that the private house is male-dominated and involves the repression of women. A harem is, of course, the extreme example.

Duncan also discusses the concept 'public women', which has a double meaning. It can mean the women who break out of the private space and actively take part in politics, such as Hillary Clinton. On the other hand, it also denotes prostitutes – women who also take themselves into public spaces. In many societies these two understandings are conflated, a female politician has transgressed her gender obligations and is 'out of place'. To the student audience in western universities this might seem quite outdated. Female students often outnumber male students at all levels of geographical study. But when I attended my first geography excursion abroad in 1964 there was only one female attending and 40 male students! Today, by law, all Norwegian shareholding companies are required to have at least 40 per cent of each sex on their boards, which for a long time has been the rule in national government. But these changes have come quickly: the first Norwegian female secretary of state was appointed in 1945. She, however, was a member of the government without a special ministry to run!

Fieldwork is no longer a defined male type of work. This is demonstrated in physical geography by Heather Viles (1992) in her quite intriguing examination of the **fieldwork** difficulties she had in analysing sedimentation in salt marsh areas in Sussex, UK. In human geography, gender relations may often play a decisive role in fieldwork. In many situations female researchers are an asset compared to men. This is, of course, quite clear if you are investigating gender relations in, say, a Muslim society. But even in an open western community it seems less problematic for interviewees to let a female investigator into your home than a male one.

A quite interesting example is given by Overå (1998) in her exposition of her PhD fieldwork in three coastal communities in Ghana, West Africa. The investigation analysed the role of men and women in the fisheries. The dissertation demonstrated that gender relations differ greatly between places and that they can change a great deal over time, based on local, **contingent** processes. The general western understanding is that women in developing countries are oppressed and that their role focuses on reproduction, childrearing and homecare. But along the coast of Ghana women have become central actors in the fish trade. The men go out in the boats to catch the fish, but they will tell you that 'women know how to treat money' and so confine the sale of fish to them. Trade is a natural role for women; fishing is male work. But the modernization of the fisheries has led to transitions in gender power relations. Women who have earned good money in the fish trade have become important investors in fishing technology, in buying boats and equipment, and eventually hiring crews and controlling fishery companies. In this way, 'fishery mammies' have acquired a central position in the local communities.

In this type of fieldwork it was an asset to be a woman, and in hiring translators Overå had the good fortune to find three women older than herself who had command of the local languages and English. The translators were also 'insiders' in the local communities. During interviews they had authority and respect, whereas the young European researcher could not act with authority. The researcher was also invited to stay with the families of the translators. With hindsight, it was necessary to reflect on the field situation – would the results been different if the researcher had been a European male, or if she had hired three male translators?

Feminist geography emerged in the first place out of the women's liberation movement and was partly linked to radical geography. In 1998, Peet stated that feminist geography and thought is 'one of rapidly growing sophistication and enhanced political awareness, yet one of potentials only partly realised' (Peet, 1998, p. 291). However, in the last decade feminist geography has infused economic, political, urban and cultural geography with new perspectives and research approaches. The few examples above should document this. In recent times, the increasing migration and mixing of different ethnicities has made a focus on the geographical differences of gender relations more and more important.

One entry point here is the changing **habitus** of women brought about in **diaspora** cultures and in the transformation of traditional societies. An example is given by Friedmann (2005) in a discussion of habitus in an increasingly transnational metropolis, Frankfurt, in Germany, where large groups of migrants from Turkey, Morocco and other countries have settled. Migration and settlement in a quite different culture have particularly challenged the habitus of women in the diaspora where the patriarchial hegemony is generally much stronger than in the city in which they have settled. Their original habitus is challenged when individual women try to escape the habitus into which they are born, and this creates new political challenges.

Box 6.3	**A woman's place?**

Massey and McDowell (1994, pp. 191–210) point out that the growth of capitalist forms of production in the nineteenth century created a spatial division of labour in Britain, in which different regions played different roles. Capitalist relations in production were accompanied by other changes, particularly changes that disrupted the traditional relations between women and men. Capitalism presented patriarchy (male dominance) with different challenges in different parts of the country. These changing relations were studied in four areas:

- the coal-mining areas of northeast England
- the factory-working areas of the Lancashire cotton towns
- the sweated, homework-based sewing areas in inner London
- the agricultural gangwork areas of the Fenlands

(Continued)

(Continued)

Life in colliery villages could be described as being dominated by male solidarity and female oppression. The male was the breadwinner and did dangerous work, which created strong solidarity between workers. Women had few possibilities for paid work but had a hard time serving the men, who worked shifts and demanded hot meals at all times of the day and night. Dirty clothes had to be washed and the miners' backs scrubbed before the men could assemble at meetings or at the pub. This system of male dominance remained unchanged until the middle of the twentieth century.

On the other hand, factory life in cotton towns created many opportunities for women to obtain paid work outside the home. Spinning and weaving factories were a direct challenge to the traditional sexual division of labour, which made it more difficult for men to maintain their patriarchal domination. Spinning, however, had traditionally been women's domestic work but, in the factories, it was classified as 'heavy' work and was taken over by the men. In the weaving industry, on the other hand, women and children were mainly employed. As women received their own wages their self-confidence grew. As Engels (1969, p. 173) pointed out, in many cases family relations were turned 'upside down. The wife supports the family, the husband sits at home, tends the children, sweeps the rooms and cooks.' Because of this, Lancashire women workers joined trade unions more frequently than women in other parts of the country, which also created highly localized support for the middle-class-based suffragist movement.

The rag-trade industry in Hackney, inner London, also created jobs for women, but the workplace was the home. Sewing was something that was traditionally regarded as women's work. From a man's point of view, homework had its advantages: the womenfolk stayed at home and the sewing jobs had to be completed in between other domestic duties. Hence in the sweated trades of London, capitalism and patriarchy conjoined to produce a system that was less of a threat to male dominance.

In the large fenland farms of East Anglia, there was a need for a workforce that consisted of the rather large, landless, agricultural proletariat. Women were an integral part of this workforce, doing all kinds of heavy work. In nineteenth-century England this provoked moral indignation, as did the cotton-mill employment of women: it was often necessary for the workforce to travel in working gangs from farm to farm, which engendered an independent attitude of mind that was condemned by the Victorian establishment. However, women's waged labour seemed not to present any threat to male supremacy. One reason was the seasonality of the work; another that men, too, were predominantly agricultural workers: 'Women served their menfolk, and both men and women served the local landowner, nobody rocked the boat politically' (Massey and McDowell, 1994, p. 201).

It might be thought that these local differences would disappear with the advent of a postindustrial society: with all parts of the country linked by mass communications (TV, radio and the national press), which imprint a national culture that is believed to wipe out regional differences. Massey and McDowell maintain, however, that regional differences remain, although they are not as pronounced and appear in a different manner. A great deal has changed since the nineteenth century, since over 40 per cent of the national paid labour force in the UK is now female. However, the gender division of labour has changed in different ways in different areas. One reason for this seems to be the particular social and economic history of women in each of the places Massey and McDowell studied.

In the coal-mining districts of the northeast, pits have closed down while new jobs, particularly for women, have been created in service industries and light manufacturing. It seems that such industries are attracted to this region as women here have no tradition of waged labour and little union experience. The jobs are classified as semi-skilled and unskilled and so are low paid. Male outrage over the new gender division of labour has been vociferous, with male pleas for 'proper jobs'. The dominant male working-class culture is still evident in pubs and clubs, but even here male exclusivity is threatened. It might also be noted here that the same type of story is told humorously for the 'steel town' of Sheffield in the film *The Full Monty*. A career as a male stripper is both a desperate solution and symbol of new gender relations!

In the fenlands, there seems to be continuity rather than change in gender relations: agricultural work still dominates the area and attitudes to domestic responsibilities remain traditional. In the Lancashire cotton towns, women's employment has been declining for decades. With its pool of skilled, female industrial workers, Lancashire would seem a good place to establish new light industries and yet the new industries of the 1960s and 1970s did not come here to the extent that they went to other places. The explanation is complex but seems to combine patriarchal and capitalist structures. The cotton towns were never given development-area status and the economic assistance connected with this, although reductions in employment were as large as in the coal-mining districts that received such a status. The reason could be that women's unemployment is not considered as serious as male unemployment, and a self-confident, independent female workforce is similarly unlikely to attract new investment. Finally, in Hackney, London, the home-sewing trade is still pursued but is now in capitalist competition with cheap products from the Third World. The women of Hackney have become, in part, victims of the changing international division of labour and have to produce more for less to remain in business. If suitably educated, they may have the possibility of taking other jobs, but many are still caught in traditional gender traps and work conditions.

These examples show that societies change but that local conditions continue to be of importance.

Source: Massey and McDowell, 1994

NEW TOOLS IN GEOGRAPHICAL RESEARCH: SATELLITE PHOTOS AND GIS

The technological revolution in mapping began with early satellite photos and was connected with **remote sensing** techniques, in the first instance developed in the 1960s and 1970s for military surveillance. When first introduced, remote sensing proved to have a great many advantages over traditional mapping methods. First, it simplified by spatial resolution (the size of the pixel to be used) the identification of objects that were to be placed on the map at a certain scale. Secondly, it allowed maps to be revised much more frequently. Thirdly, remotely sensed images could be used directly in the computer-assisted map production systems developed in the 1970s and 1980s.

Different satellite sensors produce different images, and the range of these is expanding with each new satellite sent into space. Thousands of images are sent back to the earth each minute, and the usefulness of these images has long since been recognized as covering much more important ground than simple military surveillance. We now rely on remote sensing to a great extent for weather forecasting, and images of changing vegetation patterns are an important means of monitoring ecological changes: 'remote sensing allows **resources** to be identified and measured at the same time as greatly aiding in the monitoring of environmental degradation', note Dorling and Fairbairn (1997, p. 106).

Developments in **GIS** were relatively unimportant until the 1980s. In 1982, Jack Dangermond launched the first successful application package, ARC/ INFO. Dangermond (1992) maintains that the most important function of GIS technology is to provide one mechanism by which people of different organizations, different levels of government, different countries and different disciplines can come together to solve common problems. In this way GIS would serve the purpose of 'uniting the world'. It is true that GIS databases require large quantities of information which obviously need to be based on substantial cooperation. Dorling and Fairbairn (1997), however, express some doubt as to whether this 'coming together' will actually mean solving problems for those outside the ring of computerized power. Dangermond (1992) poses the idea that GIS may help in the development of an 'electronic democracy', as people increasingly gain easy access to databases held by governmental and other institutions. It is certainly the case that it is becoming increasingly difficult for any political, top-down organization to control access to data if it does not have overall technical control. Dangermond's argument, however, was made before Bill Gates founded the Microsoft Corporation, which has created a monopoly that makes it very expensive to be technologically up to date and which may represent a new technical superpower.

> In essence, some GIS hold their data as a series of layers, and the creation of new information is achieved through the construction of new layers derived from the processing of one or more of existing layers. For instance, a layer of roads (represented as lines) could be used as an input into a process which output a layer of road corridors (represented as polygons 'buffering' those lines). ... The cartographic possibilities of adding value to existing data through the use of GIS are not difficult to imagine. (Dorling and Fairbairn, 1997, pp. 128–9)

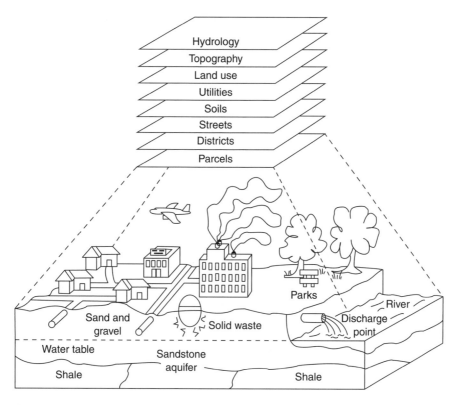

Figure 6.6   The standard layer mode

Source: Dorling and Fairbairn, 1997

In the geosciences, the three-dimensional display of geological and hydrological data is of great interest: GIS in these fields makes it possible to construct 'block diagrams' from contour maps and simple surface data, representing two-dimensional pictures of a three-dimensional scene (see Figure 6.6). By superimposing different layers of maps (including data on slope gradient, vegetation cover, amount of precipitation and exposure to the sun and dominant wind directions) it is now possible to forecast with much more accuracy areas that are prone to avalanches. In human geography, demographic research using census data about the population living in each census district has made it possible to create extremely detailed maps of the social structure of cities. In addition to its usefulness in mapping, GIS can also be applied more generally as a medium of scientific analysis.

GIS have in the new millennium had a fundamental impact as a major new tool in the discipline. And as GIS is used extensively by public administrations, for instance in local planning, geography students who take exams in GIS and have used the tools in their dissertations have a major asset when approaching the job market.

The technological research associated with the development of GIS is computer science, but the information it produces and the methods by which it can be manipulated are far more than yet another technical tool for geographers. As GIS offers a major change in the technology of mapping and the manipulation of map data, it has provoked new geographical thinking and the development of new forms of analysis (see Box 6.4).

Box 6.4	**Geographical Information Systems (GIS)**

A reading of any introductory text on GIS or of one of the many magazines devoted to GIS might promote the expectation that GIS can be used by almost anyone to solve almost any kind of problem. This is because GIS as a software product is heavily marketed as a tool for spatial data management, data analysis, data visualization and map production. However, users and potential users need to be fully aware of the limitations to the use of GIS as well as its capabilities.

The fundamental construct behind the current generation of GIS products is that the world is full of features that can be described appropriately and discretely as one object: one of point, line, polygon or grid cell, or one of their derivatives. Many artificial features, such as telephone poles, roads and property boundaries, fit nicely into such discrete spatial descriptions. Many natural features or conditions (such as land cover) can be similarly described, although natural boundaries tend to have a fuzziness that requires special consideration. If features are determined through either digital air photographs or satellite images, the typical representation is as a homogeneous grid cell. However, data commonly associated with the social sciences may be more difficult to fit into a GIS framework without sacrificing some of their features. Such features as territories, neighbourhoods or families are delimited by imprecise spatial boundaries although they may be well defined in terms of **relational space**. Such objects are awkward to encode (without substantial loss or alteration in meaning) when employing the rigid GIS data structure, where geometric space dominates. Hence, while GIS can offer an alternative perspective to social science research, much research remains to be done before GIS can be considered a universal tool.

One typical GIS application is as a spatial database containing a rich store of information pertaining to environmental conditions. Planners, managers and decision-makers can draw upon these data to assess, monitor and predict conditions before, during or after a planned development (e.g. an oil and gas exploration), a natural event (e.g. a flood) or a human-induced disaster (e.g. an oil or chemical spill). There exist many implementations of such GIS in use at various levels of government and for different components of the earth–environment system. But these implementations all have one thing in common: the data contained in the database must be representative of the prevailing conditions. Without reliable, up-to-date information, any resulting decision would be suspect.

In recent decades there has been a growing awareness of the need for improved monitoring of fragile Arctic areas in order to protect and conserve them, together with an improved understanding of the needs of conservation management, regulations and practices. In addition, there has been an acknowledgement of the growing threat on the quality of the Arctic environment from air- and water-borne pollutants from industrial activity in southern regions. This includes deleterious impacts on human health as well as on plant and animal life. Under the umbrella organization of the AEPS (Arctic Environmental Protection Strategy) (as signed by the eight circumpolar nations – Canada, the USA, Denmark/Greenland, Russia, Norway, Sweden, Finland, Iceland), a number of international and multilateral programmes have been established to conserve, protect, monitor and assess environmental conditions in the Arctic. An international GIS database is developed at UNEP-GERID Arendal in collaboration with AEPS projects to achieve a harmonized set of Arctic data to meet present and future assessment needs.

A glance through the associated web pages (http://vvww.grida.no/) shows the range of participating projects. However, the management of a project of this magnitude requires careful consideration and compromise in many different aspects of its implementation. In some academic institutions, issues of GIS management and construction are treated as research themes in their own right (http://ncgia.ucsb.edu/ncgia.html); elsewhere they are considered engineering or implementation problems that simply have to be overcome. To name but a few, these potential research issues include the following:

1) Meta-data, whereby data users are provided with adequate information about the source, quality and appropriate use of the data.
2) Data harmonization, or the combination of data from different sources that have different levels of generalization or different definitions (i.e. each country may use a different definition of 'Arctic').
3) The incorporation of traditional knowledge, or the integration of knowledge or lifestyle information from indigenous peoples, into a structured framework.
4) Cooperative spatial decision-making, where GIS acts as a focal point for discussion.
5) Data access or the distribution of data through technology (e.g. the World Wide Web).
6) Cross-disciplinary research (i.e. looking for relationships between ecosystem and/or societal components, such as environmental pollutants and health).

In the case of cross-disciplinary research, GIS itself cannot be used explicitly to answer cause–effect questions. At best, the co-location of numerous attributes can indicate a spatial correlation between the attributes that suggests a starting point for more detailed analyses containing alternative approaches.

(Continued)

(Continued)

However, even the presentation of a view of what are considered to be by some researchers well understood themes can be problematic.

One of the data layers that would be useful in assessing any potential relationships between water-borne pollutants and the threat to health (human or ecosystem) is the one that contains information about ocean and nearshore circulation patterns. A cartographic view (such as found in an atlas) of such phenomena typically represents ocean currents by various sizes of blue or red arrows that indicate flow direction, magnitude and water temperature. In GIS terms, the arrow is a symbol rather than data and it needs to be converted (either explicitly or implicitly) to one of the standard data models – either raster or vector. And while the cartographic view presents a spatial and temporal generalization that can be interpreted easily for qualitative assessment, it is not *detailed* or *specific* enough for GIS-based analysis. Herein lies the problem.

The coastal ocean is a four-dimensional entity, with variation in x, y, z (depth) and time dimensions. This variation is continuous (i.e. the ocean never stops moving). The metaphor for the current generation of GIS is one in which map layers (variation in x, y) are stored as layers (either depths or time slices). To input such an entity into a GIS, a compromise must be made in order to deal with the mismatch between the complexity of reality and the data structure required by the GIS. Typically, data are generalized to present monthly, seasonal or annual averages. In the z direction, data are similarly averaged on to specified depth planes (e.g. 1 m, 5 m or 20 m depths).

While such averaging is necessary and relatively easy to carry out in a GIS, in both cases information about environmental processes acting at finer spatial or temporal scales is lost and therefore cannot be integrated into a GIS-based analysis. For example, seasonal averages do not allow the GIS analyst access to information about the process of spring-ice breakup in coastal waters. The presence or absence of ice could be a controlling factor on the distribution of oil or water-borne pollutants. And, unfortunately, it is often only after the database has been built and analysis has begun that the 'missing' information is identified.

What this means is that the GIS designer must work closely with domain specialists in order to ensure that appropriate information is included in the GIS database, and that it is represented in an appropriate manner.

Source: The material for this box was kindly supplied by Anne Lucas.

Johnston (1997, p. 315) notes that the arguments of Openshaw (1991) and other GIS enthusiasts have been met with counter-arguments that have clarified many of the 'differences between "social theory geographers" and "GIS-quantifiers"'. Social geographers argue that the data available for GIS manipulations do not just 'exist' as valuable sources of information; as they have been obtained for the most part for political, military and commercial uses rather than for intellectual ends, they tend to be biased. As pointed out by Dorling and Fairbairn (1997), there is no such thing as a 'free' data set. In much of the world outside the USA, where government data are freely available, data are copyright and large amounts even secret or confidential. The data that are available are, to a large extent, still concentrated in industrialized countries and, in particular, in North America. In Third World countries, on the other hand, most of the data needed for GIS analysis have not been collected. The nearest we get to free data is information available through the World Wide Web and particularly Google World Maps.

Another social-science criticism of GIS is that it increases the level of surveillance of the population by those who already possess power and control. GIS concerns the precise location of land rather than people and, when people are mapped, it is to ascertain where they live and to obtain quantitative data on their living conditions. The more fundamental critique raised against **spatial science** (see pp. 142–3) is also relevant to the debate on GIS. With this in mind, however, we should accept that GIS offers geography a powerful new tool for description and analysis, particularly for **physical geography** and **ecogeography**. GIS will in particular be useful in, for instance, the prediction of environmental futures.

GIS is directly linked to Earth Observation (EO), an alternative term for satellite remote sensing. EO consists of sets of instruments or sensors, their carriers, aircraft or satellites and the data processing techniques that can be used to gather information about the earth's surface from a distant location. This provides an important source of data for GIS which now present a huge number of taken-for-granted practical applications, for instance GPS navigation in cars. Google Earth now provides an accessible set of satellite images for fast overview of local and global geography to everybody. For research, it is now possible to analyse the clearance of rainforests in the Amazon, desertification processes in the SAHEL (Box 3.4, p. 96–7) and changes in ice covers and glaciers. This has given man–environment studies in geography very important new tools.

A special case is the desiccation of the Aral Sea pointed out by Matthews and Herbert (2008). By comparing satellite images, the dramatic reduction of the Aral Sea can be described and mismanagement identified. In 1960, the Aral Sea was the fourth largest inland water body on the earth. By 2003, it was only half that size. Water is mainly used for irrigation and currently the rivers rarely reach the Aral Sea. Enormous salt deserts make up the former seabed. The same happens with the Dead Sea in Israel, which is getting smaller and saltier. These are only one type of example of 'creeping environmental problem induced by human action' (Matthews and Herbert, 2008, p. 123).

THE REDISCOVERY OF NATURE: ACTOR-NETWORK THEORY AND HYBRIDITY

Johnston (1986c, p. 450) maintained that natural and social sciences cannot be integrated because they have different **epistemologies** – they are different forms of science. There certainly is a fair gap between certain positivistic natural science methods and postmodernist approaches in social sciences, but there is also a range of choice in between. And Johnston seems, 20 years later (Cloke and Johnston, 2005), to have found a middle way. Cloke and Johnston's main aim is to deconstruct human geography's binaries; thinking in binary categories is necessary to simplify the world in order to understand it, but 'breaking down binaries is continually necessary, therefore, and [their] book is intended as a contribution to that continuing process' (Cloke and Johnston, 2005, p. 5). They also point out that realism provides a possible basis for dialogue between physical and human geography (ibid., p. 9). Also in terms of science theory, the **actor-network theory** has provided a new basis for breaking down the nature–culture binary, maintains Watts (2005).

The unity of the discipline is discussed in a broad way in Matthews and Herbert (2004). They point out that increasing specialization within the discipline is occurring to the extent that some consider that human and physical geography are 'splitting apart' (Thrift, 2002). Despite these trends, the collection of contributions in Matthews and Herbert (ibid.) demonstrate the abundance of a variety of traditional and new unifying themes that characterize recent geographical research.

Since the early 1990s human geographers have performed something of a volte-face regarding nature. For over a decade, it has been 'on the agenda' in a way one would scarcely have anticipated in the 1980s (Castree, 2005, p. 89). However, Castree, in his book *Nature* (2005), points out that this renewed focus appeared in 'unconventional an unexpected ways'. The focus both in human and physical geography was increasingly triggered by the power of humanity to create not only local, but global environmental problems. Yet human geographers were, in general, eager to show that 'in both representational and physical terms, the non-human world is in some measure a *social construction*' (ibid., p. 90 original emphasis), In a way, human geographers rediscovered nature in a 'de-naturalizing' way, while physical geographers continued to produce 'scientific' knowledge of nature, but increasingly focusing and the effects of human influence (see Box 6.6, pp. 207–9).

'The history of human geography, at least over the past 20 years or so, has been one in which particular articulations of the agency/structure binary have prevailed over others', points out Gregson (2005, p. 22), with **agency** in much of the debate still meaning **human agency**. However, there is a strong minority of geographers – Castree describe them as *relational thinkers* – who resist talking about 'socially constructed nature' as this means that society is a self-sufficient domain that can 'construct' something external to it. There are in fact internal relations between nature and society and we need to get to grips with these relations. Castree uses the concept **postnaturalism** on these forms of analyses as its focus is neither natural, nor social.

> Nothing exists in isolation, which is why it is mistaken to separate
> out different classes of phenomena, like 'social' and natural' ones.
> All there are intimately related 'actants' whose existence and
> effects depend upon those of all living and inanimate things in the
> network, past and present. (Castree, 2005, p. 227)

Gregson (2005) points out, that one of the most critical steps in recent years
has been the acknowledgement of the *agency of things* and the contributions of
actor-network theory (ANT). Actor-network theory orginates in analyses
of how power and knowledge developed in science and technology is transforming contemporary society. It was found that this could only be understood
in terms of 'complex alignments of heterogeneous entities that allow powerful
scientific networks to emerge in the world' (Murdoch, 2006, p. 58). In network
analyses it has become increasingly clear how processes of spatial demarcation
take place within network formations and that 'hybrid' networks are needed
in which people and things are relentlessly 'mixed up'. Actor-network theory
therefore gives clear arguments why the binary nature/culture in scientific and
practical terms is not given. Actor-network theory uses the concept **actant**
derived from **semiotics** for all phenomena that are active and defined through
their relations to other phenomena in networks. The world is not singularly
socially constructed; natural phenomena are to a large extent actants and play
an important role in human life and development. Watts (2005, based on Pollan,
2001) raises the question of whether humans invented agriculture or if it was
certain plants and animals that 'tamed us'. Some types of grass had edible seeds.
They became actants in the development of agriculture. According to recent
debates in the press, we are now living in the 'age of the chicken'; in its meeting
with technology, the natural creature 'chicken' has become one of the most
important sources of food in modern society, and as such is an actant.

In his PhD thesis on fishery management regimes, Holm (2001) found in
actor-network theory the only useful approach to his analyses. He points out that
social scientists think that reality is only based on social relations. They refuse to
engage themselves in direct 'dialogue' with the fish, rather thinking that the fish
is a form of social construction in the heads of the fishermen. But in reality the
fish – where it prefers to spawn and the quantity of its occurence – is the most
important actant for the management regime.

Sarah Whatmore, in *Hybrid Geographies* (2002), has provided an important
contribution in the same debate, stating that nature and culture are not
antitheses, but closely interconnected. She argues for a larger geographical
commitment to **hybrid geography**, mainly by studies of the dependencies
between man and nature.

> At its most skeletal, 'hybrid geographies' involve a radical
> approach to social agency manoeuvring between two theoretical
> commitments. The first is to the de-centring of social agency,

apprehending it as a 'precarious achievement' spun between
social actors rather than a manifestation of unitary intent (Law,
1994: 101). The second is to its de-coupling from the subject/
object binary such that the material and the social interact in
all manner of promiscuous combinations (Thrift, 1996: 24).
(Whatmore, 2002, p. 4)

This type of study is exemplified in the case studies in Whatmore's book, for
instance in a section on 'The Wild' which analyses the ways in which animals
are managed in nature. What does it mean to be 'wild'? Is it possible to talk
about 'wild elephants' when, they are managed in national parks, circuses or
zoological gardens? The management of 'wilderness' may be based on natural
science approaches, but needs to be mixed with social science-based management techniques. In national as well as international policies, 'hybrid geography' approaches are needed. Whatmore points out the boundary disputes in
governance of plant genetic resources in which the Food and Agricultural
Organization (FAO) and Convention on Biological Diversity (CBD) seem to
articulate contradictory understandings. Whereas the CBD presents an understanding cast in wholly biological terms, the FAO articulates diversity as a
heterogeneous achievement in which human being and doing is inmeshed in
a long association and influence with all wildlife (Whatmore, 2002, p. 92). The
word 'hybrid' is in general understood as 'offspring of mixed breed' or a
composite formed or composed of heterogeneous elements. In scientific terms
we can understand it as cross-breeding of two different cultures or traditions.
Whatmore uses the term in this connotation, relating it also to a case study
analyses of 'hybrid maize' and 'hybrid soyabeans' which are far off from natural
food or plants, but are rather industrial products of major agrobusiness firms.
She urges geographers to involve themselves in such issues, which in practice
means a greater focus on concrete problems across the nature/culture divide.
Whatmore gives some credit to ANT approaches, but is in general less focused
on science theory than on interesting themes for pratical reasearch.

  Gregson (2005) presents some other examples of natural phenomena that
set in motion a chain of actions in networks and hierarchies of human
agencies. The 'foot and mouth' outbreak in animal populations in the UK in
2002 had dramatic consequences. The disease was the primary actant, but led
to actions by farmers, veterinaries and in the last instance by the government.
The **tsunami** that hit South East Asia in December 2004 is another example
of a natural phenomenon becoming an important actant in the life of a region.
An actant can thus be literally anything – animate or inanimate – but still we
will have to consider the difference that **human agency** makes. In Figure
6.1 (p. 161) it seems appropriate to draw an arrow from natural processes
to agency, and if we consider **global warming** as a natural process caused by
human agency, we may even draw an arrow the other way, from agency to
natural processes.

Castree (2005, p. 236) maintains that it is possible to sort out a quartet of new approaches that challenges traditional definitions of nature, that is 'nature as the non-human, nature as the essence of something and nature as an overarching force'. He lists these as actor–network theory (see above), non-representational theory, new dialectics and new ecology. It is, he says, inappropriate to use the word 'theory' in relation to **non-representational theory**, which is linked to newer works by Nigel Thrift (1996), who presents a set of general principles and arguments on alternative understanding of how society and nature intertwine. A main point here is that all representations arise from and affect our practical engangements with the biophysical world, be it natural or humanly altered (Castree, 2005, p. 230). **New dialectics** is most clearly voiced by David Harvey. In *Justice, Nature and the Geography of Difference* (1996), Harvey criticizes the view that relations between human and non-human phenomena are external ones that play no role in constituting those phenomena. Harvey adopts an internal relations perspective, for instance that people (workers) and non-humans (factory-farmed chickens) become 'arteries' through which an invisible process of value expansion flows. Particular human and non-human things are, in this context, expressions of general, capitalist processes (Castree, 2005, pp. 234–6). **New ecology**, which has been advocated by biologists and environmental geographers like Botkin (1990) and Zimmerer (2000), challenges the 'old' ecolgy's equilibrium assumptions and 'accents disequilibria, instability, and even chaotic fluctuations in biophysichal environments, both "natural" and human-impacted' (Zimmerer, 1994, p. 108). In such a system, human actors are intrinsic parts of complex and changeable biophysical environments.

There are strong resemblances between these four approaches, points out Castree (2005, p. 236). They all lead to a rejection of former definitions of nature as the non-human, as the essence of something or as an overarching force. All approaches cross the social–nature divide, but are also still trends of thought rather than an ultimate solution for a unified geography.

VERNACULAR AND ACADEMIC DEFINITIONS OF GEOGRAPHY

We are still making geography, but if we now step aside and look at the millennium-long history of the discipline, we realize that in the last decades or so academic geography has developed into a theoretical discipline that is not readily understood by the ordinary citizen. To succeed in academic geography, a student needs years of professional training. Geography clearly has academic and theoretical obligations in the world of learning, but does it also have other obligations, obligations in the general education of the population at large?

As has been pointed out by Asheim (1990, p. 290), Johnston (1986c) makes a distinction between a **vernacular** and an **academic** definition of geography. Asheim would prefer the discipline to develop along the lines of its purely academic definition. This would mean a discipline that is constantly changing and developing in conjunction with research problems, philosophies and methods that academic researchers currently regard as interesting and rewarding. Such a stance would give the academic full freedom to take up any kind of research theme, with no regard for the history, traditions or public expectations of geography as a discipline. The present author cannot support such a purely academic definition of geography. He believes we have to regard the vernacular definition (the public expectations of our discipline, its history and traditions) as an important reason for its existence. Academic disciplines can be compared to political parties. Both compete in public markets: political parties compete with each other for political power and votes, and academic disciplines compete with each other for research funds and commissions that will attract increasing numbers of able students. Thus every discipline needs a 'party programme', a vernacular definition, which functions outwards as the discipline's uniting programme.

We also have to realize that there are basic differences between geography as a 'school discipline', as a 'university study' and as a 'research discipline'. The school discipline will not only be defined by academic geographers but, to a large extent, also by ministries of education, general educationalists and school politicians. The themes of knowledge and the school hours allocated to geography are dependent upon the roles of other disciplines and the public's expectations of the contribution geography is conceived as making to general education. University study at BA level is structured by academic university teachers, and principally it has three aims: to give prospective schoolteachers a general geographical education that must somehow cover the discipline's field as taught in schools; to form the basis for further studies and research; and to provide relevant education for the increasing job market for geographers in public administration, planning, consultancy firms, etc.

Today, it is a general requirement that university teaching should be research based. It is thus rather tempting for a professor to focus lectures around his or her specialist research activities, forgetting that most of the students will need jobs as generalists in schools or public planning. Lecturing based on personal research experiences might be very inspiring to the students but, as a consequence, important themes that are not currently the focus of research at a particular university may be left out. This is a basic conflict in any university discipline, but it may be particularly acute in geography because of geography's broad scope of themes. It is here that university teachers need to consider the discipline's vernacular side, without compromising academic standards and requirements. The term 'research based' also includes research done by others outside one particular limited specialism: university study cannot be structured solely on any one specific current departmental research activity.

The research discipline (in which departmental staff, PhD and, to some extent, MA students take part) has to be constantly changing and developing in line with research problems currently regarded as most promising by academic researchers. There should, in principle, be complete freedom to take up any kind of research theme, but this could create problems for the discipline if no regard is taken as to the history, traditions and public expectations of the subject.

This means that, on the one hand, we have to strengthen public understanding of our discipline, its developing research themes and knowledge base and, on the other, in some way adapt our academic research to public expectations. It may not be easy to strengthen public understanding if we have to start from scratch, which is the case in many countries where high school geography is very rudimentary (for instance, in the USA and Norway). The situation is much better in the UK and eastern Europe because of the traditionally strong position geography holds in the school system. In any case, to be able to create a link between the vernacular and the academic we must take the discipline's traditional focal points as starting points. This is even more true because

> these focal themes arguably underpin much subsequent debate, and in large part set many of these parameters within which contemporary research is conducted. These dual edifices, then, on which geography was built, are the human–environment relationship (or man–environment relationship to use the vernacular of the day), and the regional concept. (Cloke et al., 1991, p. 4)

Geography has traditionally been the one discipline to bridge the division between social and natural sciences. It seems suicidal to discard that position today when there is a public need for both educational efforts and research to analyse natural and social factors affecting the relationship between humanity and the environment. It is this author's experience (as an author of high school textbooks) that it is possible in schools to assess the effects of social and physical factors at one and the same time. In academic research however, it is, necessary to specialize to create something worthwhile.

Matthews and Herbert (2008, p. 90) point out that earlier attempts by geographers to conceptualize and theorize how the environment interacts with society have had mixed success. They illustrate the different approaches in Figure 6.7, in which (A) envisages environmental determinism and (B) the opposite understanding that man can control the environment, that is the belief in a 'technical fix'. Today geographers have a much more refined understanding of the complex relations between man and the environment and we have developed analytic tools to cope with complicated **adaptive systems** (C).

Other reasons for disregarding the idea that there is an unsurmountable barrier between human geography and the geography of nature can be summed up as follows:

1) In agreement with Cloke et al. (1991, p. 2) and Matthews and Herbert (2004), much of the debate has rested upon unduly dogmatic assertions of points of difference, and that this has been to the detriment of many of the continuing threads of geographic endeavour.

(A)   Environmental determinism

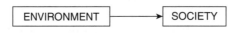

(B)   Technological materialism

(C)   Adaptive systems

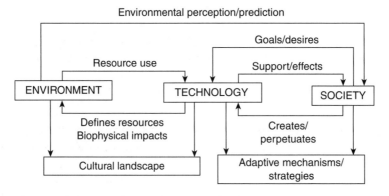

Figure 6.7   Three models of environments–human interaction.
(A): Environmental determinism, (B): Technological materialism,
(C): Adaptive systems.

Source: From Matthews and Herbert, 2008, p. 91

2) The assertion that human geography should be developed solely as a
social science may well lead to its demise as an independent discipline:
'Human geography as an exclusively social science loses its distinctive
identity – it competes with sociology, economics, anthropology – but on
their ground, not on ours' (Stoddart, 1987/1996, p. 471). If it were to become
a common misconception that geographers are only undertaking social
research that could be carried out in any social science department, how
can geography then claim the right to an independent status in university
budgets? Both in the USA and some European countries there are examples
of formerly prestigious geography departments that have been closed as a
result of such factors.

3) For more than 100 years, geographers have tried to build up both an
academic and a vernacular definition of geography as a science that bridges
the gap between the social and the natural sciences: Some parts of the
world are virtually empty of people, others are desperately overcrowded

and becoming more so. Geography is about precisely this: earth's diversity, its resources, man's survival on the planet.

An 'authoritarian' definition of geography pinpoints this:

(a)   Geography explores the relationship between the earth and its people through the study of *space*, *place* and *environment*. Geographers ask the questions *where* and *what*, but also *how* and *why*.

(b)   The study of *place* seeks to *describe* and *understand* not only the location of the physical and human features of the earth, but also the processes, systems, and interrelationships that create and influence those features.

(c)   The study of *space* seeks to explore the relationships between places and patterns of activity arising from the use people make of the physical settings where they live and work.

(d)   The study of the *environment* embraces both its physical and human dimensions. Thus it addresses the resources, sometimes scarce and fragile, that the earth provides and on which all life depends; the impact on those resources of human activity; and the wider social, economic and cultural consequences of the interrelationship between the two. These three elements form the core of geography. Uniquely, they create a bridge between the humanities and the physical sciences.

(National Curriculum Geography Working Group, 1989)

This might be seen as a 'party programme' or a *vernacular* approach to a definition. As it is meant as a framework for the discipline in schools, some might also discard it as irrelevant to academic research. However, the academic discourses around the 28th International Geographical Congress in The Hague in The Netherlands in 1996 resembled this programme to a great extent (Box 6.5).

Box 6.5	Land, sea and human effort

'Land, sea and human effort' was the main theme of the 28th International Geographical Congress in The Hague, 4–10 August 1996. The theme seems to have two connotations, one general and one more special. 'Land, sea and human effort' is, in general, what geography is about. In The Netherlands, however, this theme has a special meaning, depicting in some way the core of Dutch identity: the human effort to build up land through centuries of

(Continued)

(Continued)

struggle with the forces of the sea. The opening focus of the conference was on this theme – The Netherlands as created and formed in a tedious, ever-lasting struggle with the forces of the sea and the rivers. Geography is an important university discipline in The Netherlands; at Utrecht University there is even a Faculty of Geographical Sciences, not merely a department. This faculty has courses that cover geology, geophysics, cartography, GIS and natural and cultural landscape studies, as well as cultural, economic and social geography. Dutch geographers are practical people and have been very active in the development of the Dutch planning discipline: *Planologie*. In planning their country, the Dutch have always needed a thorough understanding of both the forces of nature as well as of transforming human agency. Even though there is a strong tradition of social geography in The Netherlands, the humanity–land–sea relationship cannot be forgotten as it is so strikingly present in everyday life and survival.

This author had the privilege of editing a special issue of *GeoJournal* for the 28th International Geographic Congress. This issue also took the main theme of the Congress as its leading thread. Geographically, the contributions covered the North Sea and the northern Atlantic, including their coastal areas, and the thematic focus was on coastal zone management, management of ocean resources and the pollution of the seas. The intention was to present geography's integrative possibilities by inviting contributions from both physical and social scientists and from ecogeographers.

Some general lines of thought can be traced through the articles published in the journal:

1) *General geographic structures activate a set of mechanisms in local contexts which create specific localities.* Localities are not singular and we should not fall into the **singularity trap**; neither should we fall into the **generalization trap**, since general structures are always filtered through local evaluations and conditions. When it comes to considering physical structures, this is very obvious: the sea as a general **geomorphologic** agent works differently on a debris coast (as in The Netherlands and Denmark) than it does on a rocky coast as in Norway. This makes human efforts to protect coasts necessary in The Netherlands and Denmark but almost superfluous in Norway (see Figure 6.8).

   On the human side, structures are adapted to local conditions in other ways. In the fishery sector, modernization is a general structural process, but it has effectively been modified in many fishing communities along the North Atlantic shores. Coull (1996), for instance, demonstrates how the Shetlanders have tried to counteract general trends by exerting stronger control over local natural resources in an effort to develop a

Figure 6.8   Air photo from the 2007 Limfjord entrance at Thyborön in Denmark, with town, harbour, dykes and groynes. The photo demonstrates the human efforts to control natural processes; strengthening of dykes, dredging of the ship channel is continuously going on to keep the land and the fishing town intact.

Photo: Thyborön Port Authorities, Denmark

sustainable island economy. In analysing coastal zone management, Bennett (1996) found that the local cultural context (particularly common codes of communications and traditions of cooperation) is of crucial importance for the success of local coastal planning. Lundberg and Handegård (1996) found when analysing local farming practices in the Norwegian coastal zone that even at the individual level of the single farmer there has been relative autonomy in relation to socioeconomic structural forces. Spatial activity is governed by individual mental schemata, which are based on social norms and relations, knowledge and experience of resource use, and adaptations to (or protests against) general economic and political forces.

2) *The local processes of change from vertical to horizontal linkages in resource use and dependency: the 'change of modernity' or 'threat of modernity'*. Lundberg and Handegård (1996) demonstrate how farming practice, land use and vegetation have changed in Norwegian coastal

(Continued)

(Continued)

landscapes over 250 years, having adapted to shifting dependencies on local resources. Most coastal settlements grew up to harvest local fishery and land resources – the vertical (local) connections. Modernization has led to specialization as either farmers or fishermen. In Denmark, as discussed by Meesenburg (1996), larger boats that fish in more distant waters have led to a concentration of fishing activity in a few deep harbours like Thyborön (Figure 6.8). The settlements that previously depended on open-shore fishing are now given over to tourists. The depletion of fishery resources has meant that coastal communities have had to find new sources of income to survive. Tourism has been an obvious solution for Danish and other attractive, former fishery-based settlements around the North Sea and the northern Atlantic. In both the Shetland Islands and in Norwegian fishery communes, fish farming has become a means of preserving local settlements. Salmon from the Shetland and Norwegian fish farms finds markets in Paris as well as in Tokyo. Horizontal dependencies are much stronger now than when the settlements were established, but the local environment and local resources are still important for both tourism and fish farming.

3) *The feeble balance between humanity's actions and their effects on natural processes and sustainability.* Over-harvesting of fishery resources in the North Sea and the northern Atlantic and discussion of different measures and methods to regulate harvesting were naturally a core theme of the contributions to this special issue of *GeoJournal*. It is a theme to which biogeographers, physical geographers, social geographers and economic geographers can all contribute. We need to understand the social structure of fishing communities as well as the economic and social effects of such measures as 'tradable fish quotas'. And we need to understand the changing oceanographic and biological factors that influence the developments of fish populations and make them active actants in the management of fisheries.

CONCLUSIONS

A geographical **synthesis** remains as difficult to achieve now as at any earlier period in the history of the subject. Granö (1987) believes that the difficulties we have had in establishing a clear-cut disciplinary matrix may be due to the way in which the discipline was institutionalized by political decisions in the universities during the late nineteenth century. It was only then that the first professors gave geography a cognitive content. They defended the infant discipline by trying in every way to emphasize the distinctions between geography and other subjects. With this in mind, the history of geography was extended backwards in time, with particular reference to its cosmographic roots. This was in line with the political expectations of governments and leading members of the geographical societies who had supported the establishment of geography at universities. At the same time the professors sought to prove their scientific abilities in relation to other scientists through advanced and specialist studies into such fields as glacial morphology and rural settlement patterns. The monistic unity of geography, observes Granö, was absolutely indispensable in order to justify its existence alongside other disciplines, but it did not suit the thematic, discipline-orientated structure of the universities. Geography itself gradually developed into a heterogeneous group of people comprising subdisciplines with no single theoretical framework, although they all maintained to aim at geographical synthesis in order to justify geography's separate existence. One of the most difficult problems in geography has been to create an exemplary scientific model to treat humanity–environment relationships.

For a long time the discipline-orientated structure of the universities functioned well. The institutions were small and they trained specialists to become university teachers and for entry into certain professions (law, medicine, etc.). They also supplied qualified schoolteachers for disciplines in schools corresponding to those at university. It was hence primarily in countries where geography became an important school subject that it achieved academic status and the respect of the general public.

Since the Second World War, traditional university research (constrained as it is within the framework of its separate disciplines) has been increasingly supplemented by problem-orientated or applied research. Applied research often reflects the organization of government funding bodies rather than the traditional university subject. A new and interdisciplinary job market has been created at the same time as the number of traditional, discipline-orientated posts in both universities and schools is declining. In planning, for example, posts are advertised at both national and local levels that do not require training in any one specific discipline at the same time as the number of staff employed in many university departments is being reduced. Consequently, the discipline-orientated structure of the universities has come under severe stress. The essentially democratic decision-making processes of European universities have, to some extent, fended off these developments, but the hierarchical structure of, particularly, American universities has led to the closure of many single-subject departments and has encouraged the establishment of sector-orientated centres such as in regional and environmental studies. To an increasing extent, the European universities – challenged by sector-orientated education in other higher education institutions (the former polytechnics in the UK, district high schools in Scandinavia) – are lowering the barriers between their disciplines and establishing new, integrated patterns of study.

Granö (1987) argues that these developments should suit geography very well, since geography has less easily adapted itself to discipline-orientated research than to the problem-orientated research the learned geographical societies always supported. To the extent that geography has maintained its cosmographic structure within university institutions, it may be able to play an effective role in modern problem-orientated contract research, provided that geographers are outward-looking, active and ready to cooperate with colleagues who can offer specialisms different from their own.

The tendency of physical geography to become more involved in applied research is particularly promising in this context. Orme (1985, p. 264) points out that physical geography (while lacking any distinct status in so far as its raw materials are shared by other natural sciences) can still play an important role through its emphasis on synthesis. The task is to shape a working synthesis of data (from geomorphological, climatological and biogeographical studies) into a comprehensive expression of the physical environment. However, it would not be enough to stop there: 'The physical geographer must also be practical and keen to apply findings to such areas as resource management, regional development and urban planning' (ibid., p. 265).

Since Orme wrote this in 1985, substantial global changes have taken place. 'The global extent and rate at which human activities, ranging from pollution of the natural environment to the organization of society, have transformed the world and its functioning systems means that there are few, if any, past analogues to guide future action' (Matthews and Herbert, 2008, p. 98). Although the task is overwhelming, integrated geography has a major role and task to play in the interface between the biophysical and human dimensions of global change.

In the latest contributions to the geographical discipline four conclusions become very clear:

1) Geography has developed a multi-faceted supply of interesting branches with a wide spectrum of theoretical choices.

2) The newest trends, such as postmodernism, poststructuralism and feminist geography, combine idealistic and materialistic views, the binary positivism/critical theory is fading, but still relevant if we are to understand the theoretical underpinnings of the present scientific progress within geography.

3) New technical developments, particularly within GIS and satellite mapping, have provided the discipline with new tools for research. As important is that candidates with an ability to use these tools will be very much in demand in the labour market.

4) The binary nature/culture is fading as research projects across the traditional divide have become more and more important (for instance, research into processes of global warming and social responses to it) and as new theoretical approaches (as actor-network theory) break down academic barriers.

New fundamental changes in the world today are challenging the scope and focus of geographical investigation. We remember how the market economy changed the basis for regional studies from a focus on vertical land/man relations in self-sufficient regions to horizontal market relations in nation-states after the 1850s. Many maintain that a much more fundamental change has taken place in recent decades. A global **space–time compression** and an economic, cultural and political globalization changes the objects of geographical inquiry in fundamental ways. With a focus on the binary concepts global/local, is geography disappearing in a globalizing world? What interesting contributions can geography bring in the future?

The electronic revolution and the globalization of the economy have tremendously weakened the power of nation-states. A former superpower (USSR) has collapsed, and the USA is in a much weaker position than it used to be (even though it is the home of Microsoft). Whether the world will be ruled increasingly by big multinational consortia that provide information and consumption or by rising new powers (e.g. the European Union, China or India) remains to be seen.

Changing hierarchic structures, the impacts of globalization and the modernization of society are the main sources of inspiration for current geographical research. In this book we have mainly discussed geographical research that is concerned with the local effects of general processes. This emphasis on changing life-worlds in local places and on comparative case studies will probably remain a principal focus for geography into the future, but we also need to focus on the global changes and challenges. An example of the relations between global processes and local impacts is presented in Box 6.6, in which global warming is discussed in a local study of South Georgia.

Box 6.6	South Georgia in the Southern Atlantic – a laboratory for global climate change

South Georgia (54° S, 37° W) is a British possession west of the Falkland Islands in the Drake Passage region in the Southern Atlantic. The Drake Passage is a stretch of ocean between South America and the northernmost peninsula of Antartica. Most of the island (Figure. 6.9) is covered by permanent ice, particularly its western shore as precipitation mainly comes with the predominating westerly winds. South Georgia became part of the British Falkland Island Dependencies in 1908, but a Norwegian whaling company established the whaling station Grytviken at the eastern Cumberland Bay in 1904. The station was important till whaling was stopped in 1965. Presently, a research station of importance for the study of global climate change is located at Grytviken.

The Drake Passage region and South Georgia represents a key for understanding the polar processes responsible for inter-hemispheric

(Continued)

(Continued)

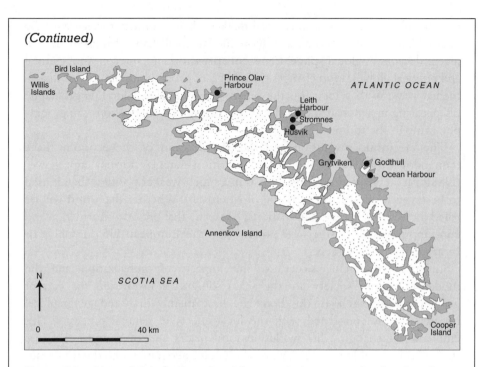

Figure 6.9   Map of South Georgia with summer ice cover dominating the western part of the island

climate change on **decadal** to millennial timescales. The southern westerly winds are supposed to affect the earth's climate both through their influence on ocean circulation and on the atmospheric concentration of carbon dioxide (CO_2). Due to their position over the zonally unbound circumpolar ocean, the southern westerly winds play a key role in modern ocean circulation via their support of the strong Antarctic Circumpolar Current. The Antartic Circumpolar Current, in turn, plays a central role in ocean ventilation as it constitutes the primary mechanism by which water, heat and other properties are exchanged between the ocean's basins – acting as the flywheel prescribing the mode of ocean circulation. These inter-ocean exchanges, along with the conversion of dense deep waters into intermediate waters via Southern Ocean air–sea–ice interactions, help close the **global thermohaline circulation** loop. Furthermore, the shoaling of intermediate and deep density layers across the Antartic Circumpolar Current zone provides atmospheric access to the ocean interior and affects the ocean's ability to absorb heat and CO_2. Indeed, new modelling studies suggest that the southern westerly winds shifts may play a central role in driving CO_2 variability over glacial-interglacial timescales. Furthermore, computer simulations of ocean circulation have been instrumental in highlighting the importance of both the strength and position of the southern westerly winds in determining global deep water mass distributions and overturning. Palaeoclimatic reconstructions in this region address several of the fundamental questions at the heart of current polar climate change research. For example, what is the scale expression of natural variability in the ocean-atmospheric system on longer timescales? How do Antarctic intermediate water masses respond to shorter and longer timescale climate changes and feedback on the global thermocline? How have the southern westerlies varied with climate and impacted Antarctic Circumpolar Current transports through Drake Passage?

To solve these fundamental research questions geographers aim to reconstruct terrestrial glacier records in southern South America and South Georgia which document climate variability across the Drake Passage during the late glacial and postglacial periods up to the present time. Further, geographers aim to document at decadal-millennial resolution the physical and chemical evolution of surface to deep water masses, sea ice extent, frontal positions and transports within the Drake Passage from high accumulation rate marine sediment sequences. By combining data from the terrestrial and the marine realms, the aim is to reconstruct intermediate, mode, and surface water properties for simultaneously resolving intermediate water changes and meridional shifts in westerly wind and ocean frontal systems. To synthesize the work, it is a goal to use climate models of intermediate complexity as well as a fully coupled Global Circulation Model (GCM) in order to identify physical mechanisms behind low frequency climate oscillations and elucidate the coupling between upper and intermediate water properties, sea ice, glacier extent and atmospheric circulation. These local studies in the Drake Passage region will potentially provide good evidence of the local oceanic and climatic processes and hopefully make a valuable contribution to the understanding of global climate change.

This box was kindly contributed by Jostein Bakke.

My belief is that geography through this millennium will be an increasingly more important discipline if we manage to analyse the physical, economic, social and environmental challenges of globalization and analyse in a proper way the possible local responses and obligations versus the global processes. We have an ample store of geographical tools and theoretical approaches, as I have hopefully demonstrated throughout this book. But we should also add that the geographer will never be able to define the future assignments and projects and keep this within a preordained frame. We should be happy for this and hope that the geographer's eternal curiosity will urge her to run into the unknown and unforeseen land and seek adventures through which she learns new things. So, then, it is only to follow Alice in her geographical fieldwork!

Questions for Discussion

1. Discuss the difference between structuralism and structuration theory. What is meant by 'duality of structure'? What are the relations between time–space geography and structuration theory?
2. Discuss realism and different types of research on the basis of Figure 6.2. Give some examples of concrete intensive research and how contingent conditions influence the empirical results.
3. Discuss different interpretations of the terms poststructuralism and postmodernism.
4. To what extent is discourse analysis, semiotics and the semiotic triangle relevant for geographic research? Discuss this in relation to a specific research project in geography that you know of.
5. To what extent has 'power relations' got a new meaning in geographic research projects through new conceptual understanding of habitus, social capital and the development of poststructuralism?
6. Discuss to what extent postmodernism has influenced recent geographical research. Some geographers argue that postmodernism is at the core of geographic thinking and can not be ignored whereas others warns against it. Why?
7. Discuss the major contributions provided by feminist geography in recent decades. Discuss whether men and women have different understandings of 'landscapes of fear'. Find research projects at your university which expose geographical differences in gender relations and discuss these.
8. Define 'diaspora culture' and discuss concrete examples in your neighbourhood in which conflicting cultures of gender relations have been exposed. To what extent is this a conflict between generations rather than a conflict between diaspora and mainstream cultures and to what extent are such gender relations important in geographic research?
9. Discuss to what extent 'social reproduction' is an important element in social urban or rural geography. How can we use time–space geography to expose the role of 'social reproduction'?
10. 'My home is my castle' may be seen as a slogan for the protection of one's private life, but it has been criticized by many researchers. Why?
11. Discuss the role of fieldwork in geography. How important is it? Are gender relations important in fieldwork? Discuss some examples.
12. Discuss some examples of how gender relations have changed over time and differ from place to place within your own country.
13. Explain what is meant by satellite photography and GIS analysis. Look at a research project in your department that has utilized GIS. What problems and benefits were connected to this?

14. Give an account of actor-network theory (ANT). Discuss whether ANT has given us a new understanding in the debate on the binary physical/human geography.
15. Discuss the relations between a vernacular and an academic definition of geography. Which is most crucial for the future of our discipline?
16. What types of research task in geography is Alice most likely to encounter in future decades?

GLOSSARY AND SUBJECT INDEX

abduction   a scientific method (combining elements of *induction* and *deduction*) that is often applied in case study-based social research. The empirical study of a particular case may lead to surprising results. We try to formulate a tentative theory or *hypothesis* that, if correct, will explain the case-study results. However, such a tentative theory or hypothesis must be tested, corroborated or refuted through further case studies. The most crucial phase in abduction is the 'lift' from empirical results to tentative theory (see also Figure 4.5)   110, 111

abiotic   pertaining to or characterized by the absence of life or living organisms   15, 17

absolute space   an understanding of space as a distinct, physical and imminently real or empirical entity. Traditional *regional geography* studies the empirical entities, dependencies or vertical connections between humanity and the environment within the 'container space' of a particular region   2, 30, 116, 120

abstract theory   the isolation conceptually of a *partial* aspect of an object, or a conception that represents an ideal view of reality. In *spatial science* abstraction is the starting point of model-building. In *realism*, however, it is the identification of the *essential* characteristics inherent in the constitution of structures and the construction of the ideal types of relationship between structures, mechanisms and events which, ultimately, have to be tested through concrete research   166, 167

academic (in the sense of the definition of a discipline)   a discipline defined purely on the basis of what the 'avantgarde' of researchers find rewarding and interesting (often in contrast to what a *vernacular* definition implies)   197

actant   term for an influencing element in an ANT-network   195

actor-network theory (ANT)   a theoretical approach that maintains there is an indivisibility of human and non-human agents or *actants*. Both abiotic and biotic components in nature as well as humans are enrolled in networks and influence the development in our world   169, 194, 195, 197

adaptive systems   system models for the relations between man and environment which take into account reciprocal relationships with feedback and feed-forward loops between natural, social, cultural, economic and political factors. The adaption reflects the ability of society to develop alternative strategies and adapt to environmental challenges   199

agency   see *human agency*   23, 29, 30, 161, 162, 167, 194

Allgemeine Geosynergetik   synergistic – working together, being cooperative. The term is used by Schmithüsen (1976) as an underlying philosophical premise in regional geography where human and natural factors work together in complex unities (regions)   7

Annales School   a school of history that aimed to study the history of ordinary people rather than the history of governments, kings, wars, etc.   67, 69

Anthropogeographie   a German term denoting human geography   63

applied geography   the application of current geographical knowledge and analytical techniques to solving contemporary problems in society   80

a priori model   a model that exists in the mind prior to being tested scientifically   106

axiom   a universally accepted principle or rule; an elementary statement; a basic building block in scientific work   128

base   see *economic base*   132

behavioural geography   a form of geography that regards the knowledge and perceptions of decision-makers as equally or more important than the physical and economic conditions of the environment. *Cognition* is considered to be the key to understanding human spatial behaviour   150, 158

Berkeley School   a school of geography closely associated with Carl Sauer when he was chairman of the Geography Department at the University of California, Berkeley. Although the school admitted to no doctrinaire positions with regard to methods or subject-matter, it was associated with *cultural geography*, the *diffusion* of cultural traits and *cultural landscape* and the role of *human agency* in its creation. This school had a marked predeliction for *fieldwork*   74

binaries   in linguistics, a binary opposition denotes a pair of distinctive features such that one is the absence of the other, as voice and voicelessness, or that one is at the opposite pole from the other. In scientific discourse, binaries are often set up as a pedagogical device (global/local, place/placelessness, positivism/critics of positivism, nomothetic/idiographic), most often with the aim to modify or break down the opposition between the binaries. This implies an exercise in *dialectics*   125

biogeography   the systematic geographical study of plants and animals   46

biotic   pertaining to life   15, 17

case study   a social investigation – for example, of a single tract within an urban area selected *not* to provide statistical representativeness but rather to provide a typical (or revealing) account of the local pattern of everyday life   166, 167

causal explanation   all observed facts have causes and, hence, science should look for causes not purposes. Science should set up hypotheses for possible causes that can be tested in a rigid scientific procedure; the hypothetic-deductive method   113

central place theory based on the work of Walter Christaller. The development of systems of central places within a settled area, the distribution of consequent tributary areas and the hierarchical relations between them 84, 85, 86, 98

chorography (*choros* = place; *graphos* = to draw, describe) the description of places and regions; of things occurring in the same place 35, 39, 66

chorology (*choros* = place; *logos* = rational structure, explanation) the scientific study of the relationships between phenomena that occur in the same place 39, 66

chronology the study of events that follow each other in time 39

climatology the study of the prevailing weather conditions in a region throughout the year, most often focusing on a 30-year average 46

cognitive description a description of what is known or understood; rational ordering; the classification and analysis of data that have been collected 95

cognized environment the environment as perceived and consciously understood 148, 149

collaborative planning a planning process characterized through a balanced participation of all relevant stakeholders in an area, public authorities as well as local inhabitants and developers 58, 171

comparative method the systematization and comparison of data, region by region 45

concrete research empirical study of events and contingent conditions in *realism* 166, 167

contingency a contingent event; a chance, accident or possibility that is conditional of something uncertain. In a simplified form of *realism*, a contingency is often understood as special (or accidental) local conditions that promote deviations from general trends 184

contingent condition see *contingency* 165, 166

corroborate make more certain, confirm 110

cosmography (*cosmos* = the world or universe conceived as an orderly system; *graphos* = to draw, describe) a term used in the seventeenth and eighteenth centuries for the scientific description of the universe. Cosmography encompasses the sciences of cartography, geography, biology, geophysics and also anthropology 4, 38, 39, 60, 113

crisis phase a term employed by Thomas Kuhn to describe a phase in the development of scientific theory when new thinking forces a reappraisal of the significance of objective data and a vigorous debate among the scientists concerned 103

critical rationalism the philosophy of science as developed by Karl Popper. Critical rationalism is based on the principle of falsification – a process of error elimination, critical testing and the possible corroboration of preconceived theories   108, 126, 158

critical theory   associated with the Frankfurt School and the later contributions of Jürgen Habermas. Critical theory criticizes *positivism*. Its central concern is the historicity of social action, particularly how human agency is influenced by modern capitalism. Critical theory goes beyond Marx's critique of political economy as it also includes elements of the hermeneutic tradition   124, 125, 129–31, 134, 140

cultural geography   a subfield of human geography that focuses on the material and non-material aspects of human culture (e.g. the study of the agricultural practice of growing paddy rice and the cultural traits of the religious beliefs that underlie such practice). Cultural geography was particularly associated with the *Berkeley School*. Today, it has been revitalized through 'new cultural geography', which focuses on the cultures of everyday life and the relationships between dominant and subordinate cultures   74

cultural globalization   denotes an increasing western dominance of culture all over the world, through pop music, Hollywood (or Bollywood) film industry, modernistic architecture (McDonald's Huts)   9

cultural landscape   the landscape as influenced through time by the technology and attitudes of the human cultural groups who have inhabited it   11, 29, 68, 80, 138

cultural trend (in human geography)   see *cultural geography*   155

cycle of erosion   the regular changes of landforms through time. Landscapes are uplifted as a result of forces within the earth and the movement of continents. They are later eroded by water, ice and wind until further uplifts renew the cycle. Uplift and erosion can take place simultaneously   61, 62

Darwinism   the application of the theories of evolution proposed by Charles Darwin that involve the development from simpler to more complicated lifeforms, the struggle between different species of plants and animals, natural selection and the random character of the many variations observed in nature   52, 53

dasein (being here)   an awareness of the conditions of one's existence   24

decadal   refers to periods of ten years, in climate studies average changes from decade to decade, levelling out changes from year to year   208

deconstruction   a method of analyses that seeks to critique and destabilize systems of meaning that seems stable. The discourse aims at pointing out contradictions, paradoxes and contingencies in the system of meaning under analyses   174

deductive reasoning   the derivation of a particular truth from a more general statement. Starting from a general statement (e.g. the *hypothesis* that 'all swans are white'), the truth of this statement is tested by empirical observation. The opposite of *inductive reasoning*   55, 105–10

deep structures   the structures that underlie observed patterns   155, 169

desertification   a process which leads to increasing areas of deserts, often caused by unwise human actions   19, 96, 97

determinism   see *environmental determinism*   43, 44, 64, 113, 138

deterministic model   a model that will produce only one particular result when a set of inputs is applied to that model   88

dialectic   a form of critical examination that is to be found in Plato and that was developed by Immanuel Kant to show the mutually contradictory character of scientific principles when these are applied to determine objects beyond the limits of experience. Georg Hegel applied the dialectic to the processes of thought through which such contradictions (theses and antitheses) eventually appear to be resolved within a higher truth   122, 131, 132

diaspora   any cultural group living as a minority among people of a majority culture. Originally used for Jews who were scattered outside Palestine but who retained their Jewish culture   151, 182, 185

diffusion   the spread of domesticated animals and crops, ideas and techniques over space and through time. The concept is particularly associated with studies undertaken by the *Berkeley School* (Carl Sauer) and the Lund School of Geography in Sweden (Torsten Hägerstrand)   82, 89

disciplinary matrix   an interpretation of the concept of a *paradigm* whereby a particular scientific community at a particular period of time shares an understanding of its discipline's tasks, special character and methods, which delimit it from other disciplines   102, 115

discourse analyses   a formal or scientific discussion in speech or writing to find out whether arguments are valid and testable. One aim is to enable us to reveal hidden motivations behind a text or a method that has been used to interpret it   174

discursive consciousness   the type of knowledge we can explain and discuss in words; connected to Giddens' *structuration theory*   162

double hermeneutics   the process by which people who are the subject of an attitudinal survey may change their views after having considered how the results of the study will be interpreted. A process of ongoing interaction and interpretation   134

duality of structure   structures set the conditions for human action, but humans are skilled agents who can mould the institutions and other structures of society through their conscious and unconscious actions. Connected to Giddens' *structuration theory*   161, 162

ecogeography   the study of the systems of *geofactors* that arise as a result of the interaction between people and their environments   18, 19, 95, 193

ecological analysis   the study of the connections between environmental variables as well as between human and environmental variables   16, 72

economic base   industries or other forms of production upon which complex economies are thought to be dependent   157

economic globalization   the global economic dependencies increasingly dominated by large multinational firms and funds which have their headquarters in a small number of global cities   9

economic man   a model of human behaviour that assumes that the decision-maker has a perfect knowledge of cost factors and an ability to use that information to maximize returns and minimize costs. The use of this model in *location theory* made it possible for analysts to predict outcomes without reference to human behaviour. The use of the model in *spatial science* produced normative models of a highly mechanical nature   94, 150

ecosystem   a mutually dependent system of plants, animals and organic and inorganic processes that exists in a specific area or place   95–7

empirical-analytical science   a science (particularly a natural science, such as physics) that can be substantiated through the use of a precise scientific language and that can engender predictive knowledge for the technical control of society   106, 138–9

empirical generalization   a generalization based on facts concerning the here and now and, as such, that is only valid for a particular time and place. In positivistic terms, an empirical generalization is more scientific than factual statements or systematized descriptions   106, 116

empirical question   a question about factual content; on what *is* rather than what *ought* to be   128, 156

empiricism   the belief that our sense experiences provide us with the only true basis for knowledge   126–8, 137, 138

Enlightenment movement   a philosophical movement of the seventeenth and eighteenth centuries that is particularly associated with Voltaire, Rousseau and other French thinkers. It was characterized by its belief in the power of human reason and of universal education   127

environment   the aggregate of surrounding things, conditions or influences   200

environmental determinism   the belief that human activities and cultures are profoundly influenced and constrained by the natural environment   43, 53, 63, 65

episteme   according to Michel Foucault, a regime of true or a 'general politics of truth' that is defined and accepted within a society in order to reinforce the power relations within that society   105, 133

epistemology   the application and development of knowledge; a theory of knowledge that seeks to determine correspondence between the realm of knowledge (concepts, propositions) and the realm of objects (experiences, things). An epistemology guides the formulation of research problems   142, 146, 147, 160, 168, 193

error elimination   in Popper's *critical rationalism*, the empirical testing of tentative theories to determine which theories have weak explanatory value   109

evolution   the gradual transformation of organisms from lower and simpler to higher and more complicated forms   53

eugenics   the 'science' of improving the qualities of the human race by the careful selection of 'suitable' parents   54

exemplar   a *paradigm* in the form of an *exemplary model*   101, 103, 115, 120

exemplary model   a particular piece of scientific work that is used as a model for subsequent research   52

existentialism   an individual's essential 'being in the world' and the irreducible personal dimensions of human life (see Box 1.7)   21

factor analysis   a quantitative method of transforming a data matrix so that the variables in the new matrix are uncorrelated. The relative importance of each factor in explaining a certain phenomenon can hence be elucidated   89

falsification   the possibility of proving a scientific theory to be false. Karl Popper would not accept a theory as scientific if it was not conceivably possible to falsify it   107, 108, 126

feminist geography   research that seeks to explore how gender relations differ throughout the world, influence or have important bearings on the social structure and geography of an area   158, 181–7

fieldwork   a term traditionally used in geography for the methods by which primary data are obtained through observation in the place of study. Fieldwork became less important in human geography when secondary data (from censuses, etc.) became the focus of quantitative analysis. However, it was revitalized in the *case studies* typical of contemporary *cultural geography*   3, 36, 43, 74, 113, 184

Fliese   a mosaic tile; a term applied to the smallest category of subregions that form the building blocks of landscape morphology (see Figure 2.2)   76

formal logic   the use of logic in *logical positivism*, by which rules are set for scientific reasoning. Built on certain given and universally accepted elementary statements or *axioms*, further statements of knowledge may be derived through empirical investigations and/or logical steps of argumentation or chains of evidence   128

Frankfurt School   a school of thought that was founded in Frankfurt in 1923 and that was re-established in New York in 1934. It later came to be associated with Jürgen Habermas, among others (see *critical theory*)   125, 134

functional region   a region defined by its function (e.g. a city and the hinterland that uses the city as its service centre)   77, 91

Ganzeit   totality   44

Garden City movement   town planning ideas particularly connected to Ebenezer Howard   58

Gemeinschaft   a much-used German term that denotes the close, local relations between people in traditional, rural societies and the strict social control of, and care for, all members of that community   153

gender   social sex, behaviour, attitudes and opportunities that depend on socially constructed views of femininity and masculinity   182, 183

general geography   a term used by Varenius to denote systematic geography   40

generalization trap   the failure to recognize unique features – local conditions – in geographical study   202

genius loci   a concept used by Norberg-Schultz for the 'spirit of place' – the *phenomenological* understanding of the physical meaning and characteristics of a place   21

genre de vie   a central concept in traditional French regional geography. The way of life characteristic of a human group who have organized themselves to exploit the resources of the land on which they live   68

geofactor   a factor that influences geographical distributions   15, 17, 73

geographical law   see *scientific law* 100

geographical societies   national and local societies, mostly founded in the nineteenth century, for the promotion of geographic knowledge, expeditions and national interests   4, 46, 47

geographical synthesis   combination of factors working together to create particular geographical features (see Figure 1.7)   4

geomorphology   the study of landforms   61, 62, 113

geopolitics   political geography based on Nazi ideology and Darwinistic ideas of the survival of the fittest. Hence the strongest, fittest nations have the right to rule over other, less strong and less fit nations   63, 66

geosphere   the round earth, the surface of the globe   17

Gesellschaft   a much-used German term that describes role-directed relationships in modern, urban societies. People have relations with other people in the same workplace as themselves or in a club of mutually shared interests, but not with their neighbours   153

GIS (Geographical Information Systems)   computer programs that make it possible to store map and other geographical data in a digitalized form and that facilitate the analysis of these data   3, 187–93

glacial morphology   study of landforms created by glaciers in present or former times   61

globalization   the spread of industrial economies and technologies and the establishment of multinational firms across the world. Globalization has also come to mean the spread of a universal culture fostered through the modern mass media, which has created 'placeless' features – both physically and socially   21

global thermohaline circulation   describes the global circulation pattern in the world's oceans and is driven primarily by the formation and sinking of deep water (the Weddel Sea in Antarctic, the Greenland Sea and the Nordic Seas in the North Atlantic Ocean). This circulation is thought to be responsible for the large flow of upper ocean water from the tropical Pacific to the Indian Ocean through the Indonesian Archipelogo. The sinking of water (due to high density caused by low temeratures and high salinity) is the main process but also windstress is an important driver of the circulation   208

global warming   the proved increasing mean temperature on the globe caused by human burning of fossil fuels and destruction of vegetational cover, particularly rain forests   9, 196

governance   cooperation between different public and private actors to improve economic and social development, for instance in a neighbourhood. The broad participation is in contrast to government, i.e. the formal govering body of an organization.   58

gravity model   a mathematical model that is used to study patterns of inter-action. The model assumes that the interaction of people and goods between centres is generally proportional to the product of their populations (or output of goods) and inversely proportional to the distance between them   87, 88, 155

grounded theory   a theory of science that is based on a reaction to crude positivism. Grounded theory is based on pragmatism, social relevance and *idiographic, case study*-based indepth qualitative research rather than on quantita-tive, representative data sets. However, grounded theory supports, the positivis-tic ideal of scientific objectivity and the possibility of separating theory from empirical data   139

habitus   embodied as well as a cognitive *sense of place*. We can understand habitus as social space, as a sense of one's place and sense of other's place in the world   21, 170, 185

'hard' science   a popular concept used for sciences which can be carried out with the help of measurements and quantitative data   97

hermeneutic approach   an interpretative (rather than explanatory) approach to understanding (*verstehen*) and to clarifying meaning   130, 139, 144, 145

historical geography   research that aims to recapture or understand the geographic features of a region in former times   144

historical-hermeneutic science   arts and sciences that, as the history of art and the analysis of poetry, have to base their approach on the interpretation of meanings. A hermeneutic approach is used rather than an approach based on measurements and data analysis   144

historical materialism   a programme of historical research propounded by Karl Marx and Friederich Engels based on the productive powers of societies and their tendency to outgrow current systems of social relationships. When this occurs, contradictions between the organization of production and society can be expected to lead to periods of social revolution, such as the rise of capitalism and its predicted replacement by socialism   132, 157

holism (holistic)   a belief that a whole (for instance, an organism or a region) is more than the sum of its parts and that it is the task of science to grasp this totality   44

horizontal connections/linkages   the links and dependencies between places (particularly in terms of goods and money), as between a centre and its market hinterland   117, 118

human agency   in Giddens' *structuration theory*, the relations between intentions and actions, including the reflexive monitoring of action, the rationalization of action and the motivation for action. Human agency refers more to the agent's capabilities for action and the action itself than to the agent's intentions   160, 182, 194, 196

human ecology   the study of the spatial aspects of human relations, particularly humanity–environment relations; closely related to the functional approach in geography   72

human geography   geography of human settlements and activities   15, 18, 19

humanistic geography   a term used by Yi-Fu Tuan to mean geographies based on the methods of the humanities that strive to synthesize subjective and objective studies and that lay particular importance on human creativity   19, 26, 145

hybrid geographies   a term used by Sarah Whatmore (2002) in arguing that nature and culture are not anthitheses but closely related. The hybridity is underlined in case studies presented in the book   195

hypothesis   a statement established for the purpose of empirical testing   106

hypothetic–deductive method   this method sets up hypotheses to be tested in order to see how far they can explain observed reality. Satisfactory explanations lead to the formulation of scientific laws   55, 100, 106–11, 128

idealism   the view that the things we perceive to be real are in fact contained within our own minds. As a philosophical stance, it is opposed to *materialism* and *realism*. As a concept, however, it has different meanings. For instance, when used to describe science, it implies that science is led by the high, noble principles of individual scientists, not by the material interests and forces in society. Idealism can also mean the tendency to represent things in an ideal form (or as they might be or should be), rather than as they are   46, 132, 150

idealistic viewpoint   science is led by the achievements of individual scientists   122

identity of place   in geography, identity of place has come to mean place as experienced by human beings – their evaluation of physical setting, human activity and meaning   21

ideological base   religion, culture of a society (see also *superstructure*)   157

Ideologiekritik   critique of prevailing doctrines of societies, to support the enlightenment of people to their own true interests   134

idiographic   an explanation or description of unique or particular phenomena or connections. The opposite of *nomothetic*. An idiographic science searches for explanations of the single instance, such as a historic event that is not thought to be the result of general trends or the laws of history   7, 82, 100, 116, 130

inductive reasoning   reasoning in which a conclusion is based on observed empirical data. Induction often leads to unfounded generalization: all swans I have seen are white; therefore all swans are white. The opposite of *deductive reasoning*   55, 68, 105–7, 110, 111, 141

innovation   the introduction of a new phenomenon, for instance a new farming practice. Geographical studies of innovations have focused on their origins and spread (*diffusion*) through time and over space   18, 88

insidedness   as opposed to the *outsidedness* in a place and often related to the study of the *identity of place*   26

institutionalization (of a scientific discipline)   the establishment of scientific departments in order to educate students to prepare them to take part in a profession   46, 52, 57

instrumentalism   models and laws concerned with the technical control of the environment that manipulate rather than explain   142

intensive concrete research   a *realist approach* to research, as recommended by Sayer, in which a limited number of indepth, empirical *case studies* are undertaken to achieve an understanding of the functions of *necessary* and *contingent relations*   166

interpretant   the participants in the *semiotic triad*. The people who communicate personal interpretations and understandings in the form of *signs*, such as words   171

isomorphic   different but seemingly having the same form. Humans seem to act in the same manner as some of the primitive laws of physics (see *gravity model*)   87

karst morphological features in limestone regions, including caves and subterranean rivers   61

laissez-faire   the idea that governments should interfere as little as possible in economic affairs; 'the survival of the fittest' will secure economic growth and general welfare   54

Lamarckianism   a thesis connected with the French naturalist, Jean Baptiste Lamarck. Lamarck maintained that hereditary changes were the result of organisms' efforts to adapt themselves to the changing conditions encountered in their environments, that learnt abilities are passed on to the next generation by heredity. This is proved not to be true   53, 165

Länderkunde   regional geography. The geographical study of particular areas that are differentiated from each other through the synthesis of their individual physical and human features   15, 66, 70, 83

Länderkundliches Schema   a method in regional geography devised by Hettner in which a region is defined via a definitive order of succession of the different physical and human geographic features that constitute that region   115

landscape chronology   the scientific reconstruction of former landscapes or attempts to explain landscape evolution   71

landscape ecology   the study of the connections between biological communities and their environment in a particular section of a landscape   71

landscape geography   the study of cultural and natural landscapes, their particular features and their evolution   15, 16

landscape morphology   the study of the visible phenomena on the earth's surface, both natural and manmade   72, 84, 114, 115

Landschaftskunde   a term developed by Siegfried Passarge to describe the geography of landscapes as created through time by the interaction of human and physical forces. *Landschaftskunde* involves the study of descending hierarchies, from major natural regions (that owe their identities to climatic and physical features) to subregions that are largely differentiated as a result of human activity   15, 71

land use   actual use of land areas for different agricultural uses, transport, housing, industries, recreation, etc.   80

Land Use Survey   registration of actual land use on maps   80

locale   a concept used by Giddens to denote a meaningful setting for social interaction   163

localization   in geographical terms, locating spatial phenomena on a map   8, 12

location theory   a theory that seeks to account for the location of economic activities   82, 86, 94, 150

logical classification   in Immanuel Kant's categorization, the orderingm of phenomena according to their nature: plants are different from stones, etc.   41

logical positivism   an elaboration of *positivism* associated with the Vienna Circle. Unlike Comte's positivism, logical positivism admits that some statements can be verified without recourse to empirical experience. Encompassing the rules of *formal logics*, it is possible to distinguish between analytical statements (i.e. a priori propositions whose truth is guaranteed by their internal definitions, as in mathematics) and synthetic statements (whose truth has to be established by *hypothesis* testing)   126, 128, 129, 138, 142

Marxism   see *historical materialism*   133

Marxist geography   a trend in geography based on *historical materialism*, concerned particularly with the ways in which the production of space, place and landscape is a reflection of specific social formations (capitalism, feudalism, socialism) (see also *radical geography*)   157

materialistic viewpoint   the material base governs the development of society as well as scientific knowledge (in opposition to *idealism*)   122

mechanical explanation   phenomena and observations are understood as outcomes of given causes. Mechanical explanation can be considered as the opposite to *teleological explanation*   44

mental map   the mentally stored images individuals have of spaces and places which they draw upon in their interpretations of spatial desirabilities and in the organization of their spatial routines. Behavioural geographic research has tried to show, for instance, how the mental maps of one particular city differ according to the city dwellers' different ethnic origins   141, 151

metaphor   a word or phrase applied to an object or concept it does not literally denote in order to suggest a comparison with the other object or concept (as in 'mighty fortress is our God'). Metaphor is also used to describe the situation where a group of people try to give a new phenomenon meaning by relating it to or comparing it with something already well known to them   25, 171, 172

metaphysics   the consideration of first principles, including the nature of being and knowing (*ontology* and *epistemology*). These first principles lie outside our sense perceptions or, rather, cannot be tested by *empirical* investigations. *Logical positivism*, therefore, regards metaphysical statements as unscientific   127

method triangulation   the evaluation of (and often the combination of) different methods to solve a defined research problem. Triangulation is used here as a *metaphor* – finding something unknown from the basis of something known: when you know the length of one side of a triangle and two of its angles, you can work out the length of the remaining two sides   147

model   an idealized or simplified representation of reality that seeks to illuminate some of its characteristics   120

modernization   a process of change based on *diffusion* and adoption. Apparently, less developed societies adopt the characteristics of apparently more advanced – in economic terms – societies   177

morphology   the science and study of form (see also *geomorphology* and *landscape morphology*)   60, 61

morphometric analysis   the measurement and analysis of shape. A form of description using geometric, spatial coordinate systems when systematizing and classifying   95

multi-attribute region   region based on a synthesis of a number of *geofactors*   81

ontology   the theory of being and the nature of existence. Empiricism and realism may be regarded as two ontological traditions   142, 146, 147, 160, 168

organism analogy   something which seems to be similar to an organism, a 'whole'   54

outsidedness   as opposed to a person's *insidedness* in a place; an outsider may be a visiting tourist or a researcher   26

palaeontology   the science of the forms of life existing in former geologic periods as represented by fossils, animals and plants   60

paradigm   the academically accepted understandings within a discipline of the discipline's field (aims and tasks) and scientific procedures (exemplary research methods)   27, 99, 101, 102, 103, 104, 111, 115, 122, 174

partial–general reasoning   the study of particular phenomena but with the ultimate aim of presenting general statements (as in the laws of physics)   7, 48

partial–special reasoning   the explanation of individual phenomena that are thought to be unique; *idiographic* reasoning   7

participant observation   a qualitative research approach in which the researcher observes the subjects' everyday lives by participating in those lives. An attempt to acquire insider understanding   113

peneplain   according to W. M. Davis, the flat plain created as the end result of the cycle of erosion   62

perceived environment   the subjective perception of the phenomenal environment that surrounds a human being. As presented by Olavi Granö, the perceived environment is converted (on the basis of an individual's beliefs, knowledge, experience and intentions) to a cognized *environment*, which forms the basis for action   148, 149

perception   the subjective evaluation of the world around us   151

permanent revolution   in scientific theory, the idea that an active science should always fight against the establishment of ruling *paradigms*   105

phenomenology   a philosophy that tries to capture the universal and general structures of the world as it exists in our minds prior to any (*empirical*) scientific investigation   144, 150

physical classification   in Immanuel Kant's categorization, the grouping together of phenomena according to their position in time or place. Phenomena that follow each other in time are studied by history (*chronology*). Phenomena grouped together in the same place are studied by geography (*chorography*)   41

physical geography   the study of the physical features of the earth, their causes and relations to each other   15, 19, 43, 60, 62, 95, 193 *physikalische Geographie* one of the three-fold divisions of the natural sciences proposed by Alexander van Humboldt 43

physiography the description of nature. A term widely used for the geography of nature, wider in scope than physical geography 43, 60, 61, 62

place a portion of geographical space. Often defined as 'territories of meaning' or 'a node of activities' 5

placelessness non-local, international general features created throughout the world by globalization, modernization and internationalization 180

plastic space space whose perceived size or travel-time distances are constantly changing as a result of changes in technological progress and socioeconomic demands 118

political geography spatially informed political studies, including welfare geography and electoral geography 175, 178

polymath a person with knowledge and scholarly training in many disciplines 43

positive theory descriptive theories that seek to account for what is, was or will be on the basis of empirical observation. In contrast to *normative theory*, which is used to promote an 'ought-to-be', rational perspective on the world 126, 142

positivism a philosophical system developed by August Comte which claims that science provides the only valid form of knowledge and that sense perceptions of observable phenomena provide the only possible road to scientific knowledge. It is directly opposed to *metaphysics*, and further developed in *logical positivism* 59, 124–9, 132, 135, 158

possibilism a concept first developed by Lucien Febvre in opposition to environmental determinism. Possibilism emphasizes the importance of choices in human activity rather than the limitations to choice 53, 65, 66, 113

postindustrialism modern society in which a majority of the workforce is employed in tertiary and quartenary industries 168

postmodernism a philosophy of science that is related to *poststructuralism* but, more directly, that was established as an (empirical) reaction to modernist changes *in* societies. Postmodernism advocates pluralism and, in geography, the place-specific in contrast to the *placelessness* of modern societies 21, 178, 179, 180, 181

postnaturalism a term used by Castree (2005) to characterize the new trends in geography, in which we see no clear difference between nature and human society 194

poststructuralism a philosophy of science related to *postmodernism* but, more directly, based on a (philosophical) critique of modern knowledge (as, for instance, of the hyper-reality created by the modern mass media). It has fundamental scepticism towards any form of *structuralist* explanation, capitalist as well as Marxist. Methodologically, it emphasizes the need for a critical understanding of texts and language and the crucial importance of *self-reflection*   140, 158, 168–78

practical consciousness   knowledge we see as more or less self-evident, which we use in our daily lives and which we cannot necessarily explain in words. It is connected to Giddens' *structuration theory*   162

preparadigm period   according to Kuhn, the first phase in the model of the development of science, in which there are different schools of thought clustered around different scientists   103, 120

probability model   a model based on the probability that a given cause will have given effects   88

problem formulation   the crucial start of any scientific investigation   108

process model   a model based on current trends and processes   88, 112

professionalization   the process of making a job market open only to those who have special educational qualifications   52, 103

projection (in cartography)   a systematic two-dimensional transformation of the three dimensions of the spheric globe   35, 38

pseudo-constraints   assumptions, taken-for-granted rules of society, that can and may be changed   134, 143

puzzle-solving   a term used by Kuhn for achieving (anticipated) results within the framework of a ruling paradigm   103, 120

qualitative methods   methods used to examine the social world, in which the central focus is on the definitions, behaviour and intentions of the agents studied. Used particularly in *fieldwork* and in *case studies*, the methods employed vary widely: from empirical approaches (e.g. *grounded theory*) and *hermeneutic analysis* to approaches connected with *critical theory* and *poststructuralism*   26

quantitative methods   statistical and mathematical methods used to analyse quantifiable data sets and to build and analyse *models* and systems   26, 114, 120, 139

quantitative revolution   a widely used but rather misleading term for the transformation that occurred in the 1950s and 1960s in Anglo–American geography in particular. The quantitative revolution led to the establishment of the *spatial science* school   118

Quarternary period   the last of the major subdivisions of the geological scale of time, including pleistocene (1,000,000–10,000 years before present time with a number of glacial periods) and the recent epoch (10,000–present time)   61

quasi-determinism (*quasi* = resembling or seemingly)   a polemic concept that was used to argue against the Marxist view that individual actions are unconsciously (in reality, only *seemingly*) manipulated by the ruling economic forces   157

radical geography   the study of the radical changes that may occur in the way societies are organized. The objective is to foster changes in current society and therefore in its social geography. Some radical geographers advocate revolutionary change (see also *Marxist geography*)   121, 155, 156

rational   agreeable to reason; rationalism implies that reason is the supreme source of knowledge   144

realism   a philosophy of science that uses abstraction to identify the *necessary* causal powers and the conditionalities of the structures that are realized under specific *contingent* conditions. Realism occupies a position between classical *empiricism* and transcendental idealism. While empiricism-positivism collapses the world into a singular plane of space–time events in its study of empirical regularities, realism seeks to recover the connections between different dimensional domains in order to identify the relations between structures, mechanisms and events   132, 163–8, 181

real level   the structural level, for instance the *economic base* in *structural Marxism*, which in reality is ruling the outcomes at the empirical level   156

realm   a domain or field, used by Sack in four connotations: realms of nature, meaning, social relations and *agency*, in the conceptualization of *relational space*   23

region   a distinct segment of the earth that, in the traditional sense of the word, has developed a particular character through a long process of interaction between humanity and nature (*vertical connections*). Regions have also been defined on the basis of interactions between centres and hinterlands (*horizontal connections*)   54, 68

regional complex analysis   according to Haggett, a combination of the results of spatial and ecological analysis   16

regional geography   the study of an area that takes into account an area's total composition or complexity. Alternatively, regional geography may focus on a particular aspect of an area in order to illuminate its special character   5, 6, 15, 16, 40, 46, 66, 114, 116

regionalization   the delimitation of regions   75, 77, 81

regional monograph   a geographical dissertation that analyses a particular region   69, 102

regional planning   application of scientific knowledge to promote the development of a region   76, 80

regional science   a discipline concerned with the theoretical and quantitative analysis of regional economies and problems that combines economics, geography and planning   83

regional studies   a general term including a description and analysis of regions, regionalization, a researcher's devotion to regional specialization   75

regional survey   observation and recording in the field, particularly connected to the approach recommended by Patrick Geddes   76, 80

regional synthesis   an account of an area's special character, with a focus on the relations between humanity and the natural environment   4, 5, 71

relational space   space and place are intrinsic parts of our being in the world – we relate to other people and the physical environment. Thus relational space is consciously or unconsciously embedded in our intentions and actions   1, 20, 23, 25, 153, 190

relative space   the location of, and distance between, different phenomena (*horizontal connections*) as the focus of geographical inquiry. Distance, as measured in terms of transport costs, travel time and the mileage within a network, as well perceived distance, is given explanatory power   12, 30, 118, 120

remote sensing   obtaining images by devices placed far off from objects, that is in satellites, etc.   187

resource   a source of human satisfaction. Natural resources are the things or forces in nature that, at the present level of technology and economic demand, can be exploited to serve human needs   162, 188

revolutionary phase   in Kuhn's *paradigm* model, the phase when one paradigm is overthrown and replaced by another   103

scientific law   according to one definition, a generalization of unrestricted range in time and space. Other definitions accommodate as scientific laws *empirical generalizations* that are valid only for a specific time and space   55, 106

self-reflection   in scientific work, the need for a researcher to reflect on his or her own role and impact within the research process   140, 171

semiotics   research into *signs* and meanings in order to uncover the underlying cultural codes that determine how people interpret the spoken word and other forms of human interaction   140, 171, 195

semiotic triad   a model of the relations between objects, signs and interpreters that is used to underline the relevance of semiotics in a research process   171, 172

sense of place   an individual awareness of the 'spirit' or identity of a place. Sense of place may be related to physical properties (landscape, urban history), to practical layout and organization (traffic links, location of services), social relations (family, friends) and roots (personal history at this location)   145, 154, 170

sequent occupance   stages in the development of a region, often brought about by a new immigrant culture   71

sign   a symbol (such as a word), an icon (such as map made to signify an object) or an index (a sign that relates to an object in the same way as smoke relates to fire). *Metaphor* is also a type of iconic sign   171

simulation   through the use of a computer, modelling all the possible outcomes of a process while deploying all the rules that are considered to be decisive in that process's possible outcomes. Monte Carlo simulation models were used by Hägerstrand to solve the problems of the *spatial diffusion* of *innovations*   88

single-attribute region   a region delimited on the basis of one geofactor, for example vegetation   81

singular   the only one of its kind   16

singularity trap   the failure to recognize generalities – the results of general structural forces – in the study of a particular geographical area   202

social anarchism   as proposed by Peter Kropotkin, if the political structures of dominance and subordination were removed from society, better societies would develop through a process of cooperation. Centralized institutions limit economic progress and promote inequality. The ideas of social anarchism are opposed to both *social Darwinism* and to state socialism, as promoted by Lenin and Marx   55–8

social capital   features of social organization, such as trust, norms and networks that can improve the efficiency of society by facilitating coordinated action. It consists of resources that are built in a society by trust, shared norms and network relations. Social capital is not something that can be owned by the individual, but an individual can benefit from it as a partner in the collective. The benefits of social capital are very much related to power, class relations and economic resources in society   170

social Darwinism   originally proposed by Herbert Spencer. Human societies must struggle with their natural environments and with each other in order to survive. The fittest individuals survive best within an economic system founded on free enterprise   54, 58

social exclusion   in geographic terms, the concentration of economic, political and cultural *outsidedness* in certain localities, which excludes the people living in those localities from participating in mainstream society   137, 151, 152–5

social geography   in German usage the term often refers to an integrated human geography; in Anglo-American usage, it refers to a branch of systematic geography that deals with the geography of social groups   15, 57, 72

social mobilization   planning paradigm based on actions from below; local interest groups mobilize to develop plans for their environment   155

social physics   uses analogies from the physical world to describe or analyse aggregate human behaviour   87

social relevance   the notion that research should not only be carried out for its own sake, but be relevant for the social improvement of society   57

social reproduction   a term used in a wide conceptual way for household activities not directly connected to paid work, including shopping, foodmaking, housekeeping, sports and other leisure activities which all need time–space resources and so influence the formation of geographic space   181, 182

space   a central concept in geography, used in the form of *absolute, relative* and *relational space*   21

space–time compression   a term used both for the increasing interdependencies between all parts of the globe and for the shrinking world in time and economic distance. Inexpensive and fast transport has been a major feature in the economically shrinking world. With increasing oil prices, this has recently had some setbacks so that food with low 'air miles' has got a new merit   207

spatial analysis   the study of the relative localization and distribution of a significant phenomenon or group of phenomena   16, 120

spatial diffusion   see *diffusion*   91

spatial exclusion   a social practice in which certain social groups are excluded from, or confined to, certain living quarters or activity spaces. This creates 'ghettos' of poor as well as 'gated neighbourhoods' of rich people. Its most extreme form was the former apartheid system of South Africa 152–55

spatial factor   a factor that has an influence depending on its relative location in space   8

spatial science   a definition of geography as the science of relations in space or as the science of spatial distributions. It is connected to the so-called 'quantitative revolution' and to the concept of relative space   10, 12, 28, 89, 90, 91, 92, 118, 120, 123, 142, 193

special geography   a term first used by Bernhard Varenius to describe what is now called regional geography   40

stochastic model   a mathematical-statistical model that describes, in probability terms, the outcomes from a series of trials. Sometimes a distinction is made between probabilistic models (in which the outcome of an individual trial is predicted as probable) and stochastic models (in which the development of a series of outcomes is modelled). Stochastic models stand in contrast to *deterministic models*   88

structuralism   the study of the theory of the processes and structural forces that underlie and determine empirical events. We may distinguish between structure as construct type (as in structural linguistics), in which structures are seen as more or less permanent, and structure as process type (including *structural Marxism*), in which structures change through time   156

structural Marxism *see* historical materialism 159, 160

structuration theory as developed particularly by Giddens, a focus on the role of *agency* in interpreting, transforming and perpetuating structures. In contrast to *structuralism*, structures are not seen as determining empirical events but are regarded as resources as well as rules for actions 158, 160–3

structure the underlying and enduring driving forces within society, defined in a number of different ways in *structuralism, structuration theory* and *realism* 161, 164

subjectivity internal reality, or reality as experienced within one's own mind 131

sufficient conditions see *necessary conditions* 164

superstructure in Marxism, the legal, political, religious and other ideological forms of domination. These forms of domination are guided by the 'infrastructure' or the economic base of production 132

surface appearance what is observable; empirical facts and results of underlying structures 155

symbolic capital the abilities, social and cultural capital that secure you a position in your society. Money or economic capital is not necessarily of major importance to secure your belonging and position 170

synthesis a complex whole formed by the combination of its constituent elements 4, 16, 204

systematic geography branches of geography characterized by their theme of study, that is economic geography, population geography, geomorphology 5, 6, 16, 40, 46, 114, 116

systems analysis the analysis of the structure and function of identifiable systems (see Box 3.4) 95, 96

tectonics refers to the forces or conditions within the earth that cause movements of the crust, such as earthquakes, folding, faulting, etc. 19

teleological explanation (*teleos* = purpose) an understanding of events and phenomena in relation to their supposed underlying purposes in some predetermined design. Regarded as the opposite of *mechanical explanation* 44, 55

temporal analysis procedures for describing or explaining phenomena in relation to their development over time 68, 69, 71

territory see *territoriality*

territoriality the geographical exercise of power. An individual or a group influences or establishes control over an area 1, 21, 22, 178

thematic map a map presenting a special thematic feature, such as a vegetation map, geological map, population map 3

theory   a coherent group of general propositions used to explain a class of phenomena (Newton's theory of gravity), or a proposed explanation whose status is still unproven. Theory and *hypothesis* are often used in the same way to mean an untested idea or opinion   108, 109

thing language   the language of positivism, and basically natural sciences, that would supposedly unify science. It is based on empirical observations and definitions, and formal logics   128, 131

time–space geography   (also termed time-geography)   as developed by Hägerstrand and associates, time and space are regarded as limited *resources* on which individuals have to draw in order to realize particular projects. Time–space geography is considered to be central to Giddens' *structuration theory*, as time–space geography's graphical representations make it possible to appreciate the logics of structuration   89, 151, 163, 183

topography   the description of places in some detail. In antiquity, topographical description meant general descriptions of places; today, topography is understood as the relief features or surface configurations of an area   33

total–general reasoning   the nature or essence of scientific objectives. This concept (as employed by Schmithüsen) is a bit vague, but may be regarded as the reasoning concerned with both *epistemology* and *ontology*   7

total–special reasoning   the analysis of the complex features of particular unities, such as landscapes and regions in geography   6, 7

tsunami   an unusually large seawave produced by undersea volcanic eruption or earthquake   196

universal theoretical law   scientific law with universal validity, for instance the physical law of gravitation   106

urban ecology   urban geography and sociology using analogies from ecology in analysing city growth and structures   72

urban morphology   the study of forms of and within urban landscapes   114

Utopia   a place or state of ideal (unattainable) perfection; a concept derived from the society described in Sir Thomas More's *Utopia* (1516)   127

validity   logical soundness. To maintain that a scientific theory is valid implies that it is not proven to be true, but that it is sound and useful for the time being   106

vegetation geography   the part of biogeography that studies geographical patterns of plant cover and its composition of species   5

verification   the confirmation of a hypothesis through a series of experiments. Verification or rejection have been regarded as the logical outcomes of a test of a scientific theory. Others would argue that absolute verification is, in most cases, impossible   106, 126

vernacular (definition of a discipline)   a definition based on ordinary people's everyday or common understandings. For a school discipline, this will often mean, in practical terms, a field of learning that is given in the school curriculum by school politicians. This may contrast with an academic definition of the discipline   197

verstehen   implies both understanding and empathy; putting oneself in the other person's shoes   130, 144

vertical connections/linkages   the dependency of people on their local, natural resources   30, 117

Vienna Circle   established in 1907 and later led by Moritz Schlick. The circle developed *logical positivism*, which emphasized the need for the *verification* of any statement if it were to be acceptable scientifically. They opposed other approaches to knowledge, which they regarded as *metaphysical*   126, 127

welfare geography   the study of spatial variations in the quality of life and, as proposed by some practitioners, the setting out of proposals for social and spatial policies aimed at reducing inequalities in the quality of life   121, 151, 155

Wissenschaft   a wide definition of scientific knowledge that includes all forms of methodological study (several of which are regarded as 'arts' in English-speaking countries)   130

REFERENCES AND BIBLIOGRAPHY

Aasbø, S. (1997) Landskap på Bortasiao. Landskapsidentitet og modernisering i et ruralt utkantområde. MA thesis Bergen, Dept. of Geography.

Aase, A. (1970) Geografi og samfunn. Noen tendenser og problemer i dagens samfunnsgeografi, *Norsk Geografisk Tidsskrift*, Vol. 24, pp. 1–21.

Aase, T. H. (1999a) The theological construction of conflict: Gilgit, northern Pakistan, pp. 58–79 in L. Manger (ed.), *Muslim Diversity: Local Islam in global contexts*, Curzon Press, London, pp. 59–78.

Aase, T. H. (1999b) The use of metaphor in Himalayan resource management, in S. Toft Madsen (ed.), *State, Society and the Environment in South Asia*, Curzon Press, Honolulu, HI.

Ackerman, E. A. (1945) Geographic training, wartime research and immediate professional objectives, *Annals of the Association of American Geographers*, Vol. 35, pp. 121–43.

Ackerman, E. A. (1958) *Geography as a Fundamental Research Discipline*, University of Chicago, Department of Geography, Research Paper No. 53.

Ackerman, E. A. (1963) Where is a research frontier?, *Annals of the Association of American Geographers*, Vol. 53, pp. 429–40.

Adams, J. D. (1968) *A Review of Behaviour and Location*, LSE Graduate School, Discussion Paper No. 20, London.

Aitken, S. and Valentine, G. (eds) (2006) *Approaches to Human Geography*, Sage, London.

Alvesson, M. and Sköldberg, K. (1994) *Tolkning och reflektion. Vetenskapsfilosofi och kvalitativ metod*, Studentlitteratur, Lund.

Andrews, H. F. (1986) The early life of Paul Vidal de Blache and the makings of modern geography, *Transactions, Institute of British Geographers* NS, Vol. 11, pp. 174–82.

Appleton, J. H. (1975) *The Experience of Landscape*, Wiley, Chichester.

Åquist, A. C. (1981) *Kuhns paradigmteori. Ett försök till tillämpning på kulturgeografi*, Rapporter og notiser 61, Institutt för Kulturgeografi, Lund.

Asheim, B. T. (1990) How to confuse rather than guide students: a review of Holt-Jensen's Geography – History and Concepts, *Progress in Human Geography*, Vol. 14, pp. 281–92.

Axelsen, B. and Jones, M. (1987) Are all maps mental maps? *GeoJournal*, Vol. 14, pp. 447–64.

Bagrow, L. (1945) The origin of Ptolemy's 'Geographia', *Geografiska Annaler*, Vol. xx, pp. 318–87.

Banse, E. (1924) *Die Seele der Geographie Geschiehte einer Entwicklung*, Braunschweig und Hamburg.

Barber, B. R. (1995) *Jihad vs McWorld: How Globalism and Tribalism are Reshaping the World*, Ballantine Books, New York.

Barrows, H. H. (1923) Geography as human ecology, *Annals of the Association of American Geographers*, Vol. 13, pp. 1–14.

Bartels, D. (1968) *Zur wissenschaftstheoretischien Grundlegung einer Geographic des Menschen*, Beihefte zur geographische Zeitschrift 19 F Steiner, Wiesbaden.

Batterbee, R. W., Flower, R. J., Stevenson, J. and Rippey, B. (1985) Lake acidification in Galloway: a palaeological test of competing hypotheses, *Nature*, Vol. 314, pp. 350–2.

Baudrillard, J. (1987) *Forget Foucault*, Semiotexte, New York.

Beck, H. (1982) *Grosse Geographen: Pioniere–Aussenseiter–Gelehrte*, Dietrich Reimer Verlag, Berlin.

Bennett, R. G. (1996) Challenges in Norwegian coastal zone planning, *GeoJournal*, Vol. 39, pp. 153–65.

Bennett, R. J. (1985) Quantification and relevance, in R. J. Johnston (ed.), *The Future of Geography*, Methuen, London.

Beresford, M. (1951) The lost villages of medieval England, *Geographical Journal*, Vol. 117, pp. 129–47.

Berry, B. J. L. (1973a) A paradigm for modern geography, in R. J. Chorley (ed.), *Directions in Geography*, Methuen, London.

Berry, B. J. L. (1973b) *The Human Consequences of Urbanization*, Macmillan, London.

Berry, B. J. L. (1974) Review of D. Harvey, *Social Justice and the City*, *Antipode*, Vol. 6, pp. 142–5, 148.

Bhaskar, R. (1975/1978) *A Realist Theory of Science*, Leeds Books, Leeds (reprinted 1978 by Harvester, Brighton).

Bhaskar, R. (1979) *The Possibility of Naturalism*, Harvester Press, Brighton.

Biilmann, O. (1981) *Geografi, tradisjoner og perspektiver*, Geografforlaget, Brenderup.

Bird, J. (1975) Methodological implications for geography from the philosophy of K. R. Popper, *Scottish Geographical Magazine*, Vol. 91, pp. 153–63.

Bird, J. (1977) Methodology and philosophy, *Progress in Human Geography*, Vol. 1, pp. 104–10.

Bird, J. (1979) Methodology and philosophy, progress report, *Progress in Human Geography*, Vol. 3, pp. 117–20.

Bird, J. (1993) *The Changing Worlds of Geography* (2nd edn), Oxford University Press, Oxford.

Bjørlykke, C. (1996) Islands and oil – locality and structure, *GeoJournal*, Vol. 39, pp. 221–7.

Bobek, H. and Schmithüsen, J. (1949) Die Landschaft im logischen System der Geographie, *Erdkunde*, Vol. 3, pp. 112–20.

Bonnett, A. (2008) *What is Geography?* Sage, London.

Botkin, D. (1990) *Discordant Harmonies*, Oxford University Press, Oxford.

Bourdieu, P. (1977) *Outline for a Theory of Practice*, Cambridge University Press, Cambridge.

Bourdieu, P. (2000) *Pascalian Meditations*, Polity Press, Cambridge.

Bourdieu, P. and Wacquant, L. J. D. (1992) *An Invitation to Reflexive Sociology*, Polity Press, Cambridge.

Bowler, P. (1992) *The Fontana History of the Environmental Sciences*, London: Fontana.

Braithwaite, R. B. (1953) *Scientific Explanation*, Cambridge University Press, Cambridge.

Breitbart, M. M. (1981) Peter Kropotkin, the anarchist geographer, in D. R. Stoddart (ed.), *Geography, Ideology and Social Concern*, Blackwell, Oxford.

Broek, J. O. M. (1965) *Geography, its Scope and Spirit*, Merrill, Colombus, OH.

Broek, J. O. M. and Webb, J. W. (1973) *A Geography of Mankind*, McGraw-Hill, New York.

Brunhes, J. (1912) *La geographie humaine, essai de classification positive, principes et exemples*, Paris.

Bunge, W. (1962) *Theoretical Geography* (2nd edn, 1966), Lund Studies in Geography, Series C1, Gleerup, Lund.

Bunge, W. (1966) Annals commentary: locations are not unique, *Annals of the Association of American Geographers*, Vol. 56, pp. 375–6.

Burton, I. (1963) The quantitative revolution and theoretical geography, *The Canadian Geographer*, Vol. 7, pp. 151–62.

Buttimer, A. (1978) Charisma and context: the challenge of la Géographie Humaine, in D. Ley and M. S. Samuels (eds), *Humanistic Geography, Prospects and Problems*, Maaroufa Press, Chicago, IL.

Buttimer, A. (1981) On people, paradigins and progress in geography, in D. R. Stoddart (ed.), *Geography, Ideology and Social Concern*, Blackwell, Oxford.

Buttimer, A. (1983) *The Practice of Geography*, Longman, London and New York.

Buttimer, A. and Seamon, D. (eds) (1980) *The Human Experience of Space and Place*, Croom Helm, Beckenham.

Capel, H. (1981) Institutionalization of geography and strategies of change, in D. R. Stoddart (ed.), *Geography, Ideology and Social Concern*, Blackwell, Oxford.

Capelle, R. B. Jr (1979) On the periphery of geography, *Journal of Geography*, Vol. 78, pp. 64–8.

Carlstein, T. et al. (1978) *Timing Space and Spacing Time* (3 vols), Arnold, London.

Carroll, L. (1872) *Through the Looking Glass and What Alice Found There*. Wildside Press.

Castree, N. (2003) Geographers of nature in the making, in K. Anderson, M. Domosh, S. Pile and N. Thrift (eds), *Handbook of Cultural Geography*, Sage, London, pp. 168–83.

Castree, N. (2005) *Nature*, Routledge, London.

Chisholm, M. (1975) *Human Geography: Evolution or Revolution?* Pelican, Harmondsworth.

Chorley, R. J. (1973) Geography as human ecology, pp. 155–69 in R. J. Chorley (ed.), *Directions in Geography*, Methuen, London.

Chorley, R. J. (1976) Some thoughts on the development of geography from 1965 to 1975, in D. Pepper and A. Jenkins (eds), *Proceedings of the 1975 National*

Conference on Geography in Higher Education: Oxford Polytechnic Discussion Paper in Geography, Oxford Polytechnic Press, Oxford.

Chorley, R. J. and Haggett, P. (eds) (1965) *Frontiers in Geographical Teaching*, Methuen, London.

Chorley, R. J. and Haggett, P. (eds) (1967) *Models in Geography*, Methuen, London.

Christaller, W. (1933) *Die zentralen Orte in Süddeutschland*, Jena (English trans. C. W. Baskin (1966) *Central Places in Southern Germany*, Prentice-Hall, Englewood Cliffs, NJ).

Christaller, W. (1968) Wie ich zur der Theorie der zentralen Orte gekommen bin, *Geographische Zeitschrift*, Vol. 56, pp. 88–101.

Clarke, D. B. (2006) Postmodern geography and the ruins of modernity, in S. Aitken and G. Valentine (eds), *Approaches to Human Geography*, Sage, London, pp. 107–21.

Claval, P. (1980) Epistemology and the history of geographical thought, *Progress in Human Geography*, Vol. 4, pp. 371–84.

Claval, P. (1996) From a 'cultural' world to a 'political' one, in I. Douglas, R. Huggett and M. Robinson (eds), *Companion Encyclopedia of Geography*, Routledge, London.

Cloke, P. and Johnston, R. (eds) (2005) *Spaces of Geographical Thought*, Sage, London.

Cloke, P., Philo, C. and Sadler, D. (1991) *Approaching Human Geography: An Introduction to Contemporary Theoretical Debates*, Paul Chapman, London.

Coates, B. E., Johnston, R. J. and Knox, P. L. (1977) *Geography and Inequality*, Oxford University Press, Oxford.

Coates, B. E. and Rawstron, E. M. (1971) *Regional Variations in Britain*, Batsford, London.

Collingwood, R. (1946) *The Idea of History*, Oxford University Press, Oxford.

Cooke, P. (ed.) (1989) *Localities: The Changing Face of Urban Britain*, Unwin Hyman, London.

Cornu, A. (1955) *Marx et Engels*, Presses Universitaires de France, Paris.

Cosgrove, D. (1984) *Social Formation and Symbolic Landscape*, Croom Helm, London.

Cosgrove, D. (1993) On the 'reinvention of cultural geography' by Price and Lewis: commentary, *Annals of the Association of American Geographers*, Vol. 83, pp. 515–16.

Cosgrove, D. and Daniels, S. (1988) *The Iconography of Landscape*, Cambridge University Press, Cambridge.

Coull, J. R. (1996) Towards a sustainable economy for the Shetland Islands: development and management issues in fishing and fish farming, *GeoJournal*, Vol. 39, pp. 185–94.

Dangermond, J. (1992) What is a geographical information system?, in A. I. Johnson, C. B. Petterson and J. L. Fulton (eds), *Geographic Information Systems and Mapping Practices and Standards*, Philadelphia, American Society for Testing and Materials.

Darwin, C. (1859) *The Origin of Species*, London.

Davies, W. K. (1972) *The Conceptual Revolution in Geography*, University of London Press, London.

Dear, M. (1988) The postmodern challenge: reconstructing human geography, *Transactions of the Institute of British Geographers*, Vol. 13, pp. 262–74.

Demangeon, A. (1905) *La Picardie et les régions voisines: Artois, Cambresis, Beauvaises*, Armand Colin, Paris.

Dicken, P. (1986/1998/2003/2007) *Global Shift* (3rd edn), Sage, London.

Dickinson, R. E. (1939) Landscape and society, *Scottish Geographical Magazine*, Vol. 55, pp. 1–14.

Dickinson, R. E. (1969) *The Makers of Modern Geography*, Routledge & Kegan Paul, London.

Dixon, D. P. and Jones III, J. P. (2006) Feminist geographies of difference, relation and construction, in S. Aitken and G. Valentine (eds), *Approaches to Human Geography*, Sage, London, pp. 42–56.

Dorling, D. and Fairbairn, D. (1997) *Mapping: Ways of Representing the World*, Longman, Harlow.

Dray, W. H. (1966) *Laws and Explanation in History*, Oxford University Press, Oxford.

Dunbar, G. S. (1981) Elisée Réclus, an anarchist geographer, in D. R. Stoddart (ed.), *Geography, Ideology and Social Concern*, Blackwell, Oxford.

Duncan, J. S. (1985) Individual action and political power: a structuration perspective, in R. J. Johnston (ed.), *The Future of Geography*, Methuen, London.

Duncan, N. (ed.) (1996) *Body Space: Destabilising Geographies of Gender and Sexuality*, Routledge, London.

Duncan, S. S. and Goodwin, M. (1988) *Uneven Development and the Local State*, Polity Press, Cambridge.

Engels, F. (1969) *The Conditions of the Working Class in England*, Panther, St Albans.

Entrikin, N. J. (1976) Contemporary humanism in geography, *Annals of the Association of American Geographers*, Vol. 66, pp. 615–32.

Fawcett, C. B. (1919) *The Provinces of England* (rev. edn, 1960), Hutchinson, London.

Febvre, L. (1922) *La terre et l'evolution humaine*, in the series *L'Evolution de l'Humanité, Paris*, English trans. 1925, *A Geographical Introduction to History*, Knopf, London.

Fischer, E., Campbell, R. D. and Miller, E. S. (1969) *A Question of Place: The Development of Geographic Thought*, Beatty, Arlington, VA.

Fleure, H. J. (1919) Human regions, *Scottish Geographical Magazine*, Vol. 35, pp. 94–105.

Fochler-Hauke, G. (ed.) (1959) *Geographie*, Das Fischer Lexikon, Frankfurt.

Forer, P. (1978) A place for plastic space, *Progress in Human Geography*, Vol. 2, pp. 230–67.

Foucault, M. (1972) *The Archaeology of Knowledge*, Tavistock, London.

Foucault, M. (1980) *Power/Knowledge: Selected Interviews and Other Writings, 1972–1977*, C. Gordon (ed.), Harvester Press, Brighton.

Foucault, M. (1986) Of other spaces, *Diacritics*, Vol. 16, pp. 22–7.

Freeman, T. W. (1961) *A Hundred Years of Geography*, Duckworth, London.

Freeman, T. W. (1980) The Royal Geographical Society and the development of geography, in E. H. Brown (ed.), *Geography, Yesterday and Tomorrow*, Oxford University Press, Oxford.

Friedmann, J. (1992) *Empowerment*. Blackwell, Oxford.

Friedmann, J. (2005) Place-making as a Project? Habitus and Migration in Transnational Cities, in J. Hillier and E. Rooksby (eds), *Habitus: A Sense of Place* (2nd edn), Ashgate, Aldershot, pp. 315–33.

Garrison, W. L. (1959–60) Spatial structure of the economy, *Annals of the Association of American Geographers*, Vol. 49, pp. 232–9, 471–82; Vol. 50, pp. 357–73.

Gerland, G. (1887) Die wissenschaftliche Aufgabe der Geographie, ihre Methode und ihre Stellung im praktischen Leben, *Beiträge zur Geophysik*, Vol. 1, pp. 4–54.

Gibson-Graham, J. K. (2000) Postructural interventions, in E. Sheppard and T. Barnes (eds), *A Companion to Economic Geography*, Blackwell, Oxford, pp. 95–109.

Giddens, A. (1979) *Central Problems in Social Theory*, Macmillan, London.

Giddens, A. (1984) *The Construction of Society*, Polity Press, Oxford.

Gilbert, A. (1988) The new regional geography in English- and French-speaking countries, *Progress in Human Geography*, Vol. 12, pp. 208–28.

Goudie, A. (1990) *The Human Impact on the Natural Environment* (3rd edn), Blackwell, Oxford.

Gould, P. (1979) Geography 1957–1977: the Augean period, *Annals of the Association of American Geographers*, Vol. 69, pp. 139–51.

Gould, P. (1985) *The Geographer at Work*, Routledge & Kegan Paul, London.

Gould, P. and White, R. (1974) *Mental Maps*, Penguin, Harmondsworth.

Gourou, P. (1936) *Les Paysons du delta Tonkinois*, École Française d'Extrême-Orient, Paris.

Gradmann, R. (1931) *Süd Deutschland* (2 vols), J. Engelhorn, Stuttgart.

Granö, J. G. (1929) Reine Geographie, *Acta Geographica*, Vol. 2, pp. 1–202.

Granö, O. (1981) External influence and internal change in the development of geography, in D. R. Stoddart (ed.), *Geography, Ideology and Social Concern*, Blackwell, Oxford.

Granö, O. (1986) *Finnish Geography 1880–1980: Highlight of the Decades*, University of Turku (*mimeo*).

Granö, O. (1987) Vetenskapens institutionella struktur och geografins utvekling, *Nordisk Samhällsgeografisk Tidsskrift*, Vol. 5, pp. 3–8.

Greene, T. M. (ed.) (1957) *Kant Selections*, Scribner, New York.

Gregory, D. (1978) *Ideology, Science and Human Geography*, Hutchinson, London.

Gregory, D. (1989) Areal differentiation and post-modern human geography, in D. Gregory and R. Walford (eds), *Horizons in Human Geography*, Macmillan, London.

Gregory, D. (1994) *Geographical Imaginations*, Blackwell, Oxford.

Gregory, K. J. (1985) *The Nature of Physical Geography*, Edward Arnold, London.

Gregson, N. (2005) Agency: structure, in P. Cloke and R. Johnston (eds), *Spaces of Geographical Thought*, Sage, London, pp. 21–41.

Grigg, D. (1965) The logic of regional systems, *Annals of the Association of American Geographers*, Vol. 55, pp. 465–91.

Guelke, L. (1974) An idealist alternative in human geography, *Annals of the Association of American Geographers*, Vol. 64, pp. 193–202.

Guelke, L. (1977) Regional geography, *The Professional Geographer*, Vol. 29, pp. 1–7.

Guelke, L. (1978) Geography and logical positivism, in D.T. Herbert and R.J. Johnston (eds), *Geography and the Human Environment, Progress in Research and Applications* (Vol. 1), Wiley, Chichester.

Guelke, L. (1981) Idealism, in M. E. Harvey and B. P. Holly (eds), *Themes in Geographic Thought*, Croom Helm, Beckenham.

Guelke, L. (1982) *Historical Understanding in Geography: An Idealistic Approach*, Cambridge University Press, Cambridge.

Guess, R. (1981) *The Idea of a Critical Theory: Habermas and the Frankfurt School*, Cambridge University Press, Cambridge.

Hägerstrand, T. (1953) Innovations – förloppet ur korologisk synpunkt, *Medd. Från Lunds Universitets Geografiska Institution. Avhandling* nr. 25 (trans. A. Pred (1967) *Innovation Diffusion as a Spatial Process*, University of Chicago Press, Chicago, IL).

Haggett, P. (1965) *Locational Analysis in Human Geography*, Arnold, London.

Haggett, P. (1972/1983) *Geography: A Modern Synthesis* (3rd edn), Harper & Row, New York.

Haggett, P. (1990) *The Geographer's Art*, Blackwell, Oxford.

Haggett, P. (1996) Geographical futures: some personal speculations, in T. Douglas, R. Huggett and M. Robinson (eds), *Companion Encyclopedia of Geography*, Routledge, London and New York.

Haggett, P. (2001) *Geography: A Global Synthesis*, Prentice-Hall Pearson Educational, New York and London.

Haggett, P., Cliff, A. D. and Frey, A. (1977) *Locational Analysis in Human Geography* (2nd edn.), Arnold, London.

Haines-Young, R. and Petch, J. (1986) *Physical Geography: Its Nature and Methods*, Paul Chapman, London.

Hannerberg, D. (1961/1968) *Att Studera Kulturgeografi*, Scandinavian University Books, Stockholm.

Hansen, F. (1994) Analyseramme – fagopfattelse og geografi, in J. Öhman (ed.), *Traditioner i Nordisk kulturgeografi*, Nordisk Samhällsgeografisk Tidskrift, Uppsala.

Hard, G. (1973) *Die Geographie, eine wissenschaftstheoretische Einfürung*, DeGruyter, Berlin.

Harding, S. (1991) *Whose Science? Whose Knowledge? Thinking Women's Lives*, Open University Press, Milton Keynes.

Harding, S. (2001) A response to Walby's 'Against epistemological chasms': a standard misreading, *Signs*, Vol. 22, pp. 367–74.

Harris, C. D. and Ullman, E. L. (1945) The nature of cities, *Annals of the American Academy of Political and Social Sciences*, Vol. 242, pp. 7–17.

Harrison, P. (2006) Poststructuralist theories, in S. Aitken and G. Valentine (eds), *Approaches to Human Geography*, Sage, London, pp. 122–35.

Hartshorne, R. (1939) The nature of geography: a critical survey of current thought in the light of the past, *Annals of the Association of American Geographers*, Vol. 29, pp. 173–658.

Hartshorne, R. (1955) 'Exceptionalism in Geography' re-examined, *Annals of the Association of American Geographers*, Vol. 45, pp. 205–44.

Hartshorne, R. (1959) *Perspective on the Nature of Geography*, Rand McNally, Chicago, IL.

Harvey, D. (1969) *Explanation in Geography*, Arnold, London.

Harvey, D. (1973) *Social Justice and the City*, Arnold, London.

Harvey, D. (1982) *The Limits to Capital*, Blackwell, Oxford.

Harvey, D. (1984) On the history and present condition of geography: an historical materialist manifesto, *The Professional Geographer*, Vol. 36, pp. 1–11.

Harvey, D. (1985a) *The Urbanization of Capital*, Blackwell, Oxford.

Harvey, D. (1985b) *Consciousness and the Urban Experience*, Blackwell, Oxford.

Harvey, D. (1989) *The Condition of Postmodernity: An Enquiry into the Origins of Cultural Changes*, Blackwell, Oxford.

Harvey, D. (1996) *Justice, Nature and the Geography of Difference*, Blackwell, Oxford.

Harvey, D. (2006) *Spaces of Global Capitalism: Towards a Theory of Uneven Geographical Development*, Verso, London.

Harvey, M. E. and Holly, B. P. (eds) (1981) *Themes in Geographic Thought*, Croom Helm, Beckenham.

Hassinger, H. (1919) Über einige Aufgaben geographischer Forschung und Lehre, *Kartogrophische and Schulgeographische Zeitschrift*, Vol. 8, pp. 65–76.

Healey, P. (1997) *Collaborative Planning: Shaping Places in Fragmented Societies*, Macmillan, London and BC Press, Vancouver.

Healey, P. (1998) Institutional theory, social exclusion and governance, pp. 53–73 in J. Allen, G. Cars and A. Madanipour (eds), *Social Exclusion in European Cities*, Jessica Kingsley, London.

Healey, P. (2005) Place, identity and governance: transforming discourses and practices, in J. Hillier and E. Rooksby (eds), *Habitus: A Sense of Place* (2nd edn), Ashgate, Aldershot, pp. 189–218.

Hegel, G. W. F. (1975) *Lectures on the Philosophy of World History* (new edn), Cambridge University Press, Cambridge.

Henderson, G. and Sheppard, E. (2006) Marx and the spirit of Marx, in S. Aitken and G. Valentine (eds), *Approaches to Human Geography*, Sage, London, pp. 57–74.

Henriksen, G. (1973) *Grunnlagsproblemer og interaksjon – en metageografisk anolyse, Hovedfagsoppgave i geografi*, Geografisk Institutt, Universitetet i Bergen.

Hettner, A. (1927) *Die Geographie, ihre Geschichte, ihr Wesen and ihre Methoden*, Ferdinand Hirt, Breslau.

Hettner, A. (1929) Methodische Zeit- und Streitfragen, Neue Folge, *Geographische Zeitschrift*, Vol. 35, pp. 264–86, 332–44.

Hettner, A. (1930) Zur 'Stellungnahme von Seiten der Schulgeographie', *Geographische Anzeiger*, Vol. 31, pp. 353–6.

Hillier, J. and Rooksby, E. (eds) (2005) *Habitus: A Sense of Place* (2nd edn), Ashgate, Aldershot.

Holm, P. (2001) *The Invisible Revolution: The Construction of Institutional Change in the Fisheries*, PhD dissertation, Norwegian High School of Fisheries, University of Tromsø, Norway.

Holt-Jensen, A. (1986) *Konsentrasjon og spredning: Studier i det norske bosettingsmønsterets historie, med en spesialstudie i Kristiansandområdet, Dr.Philos* Universitetet i Bergen, Bergen.

Holt-Jensen, A. (1988/1999) *Geography: History and Concepts* (2nd and 3rd edns), Paul Chapman/Sage, London.

Holt-Jensen, A. (2006) Vidal de la Blache's regionalgeografiske modell, in S. U. Larsen (ed.), *Teori og metode i geografi*, Fagbokforlaget, Bergen, pp. 134–51.

Holt-Jensen, A. (2007) *Hva er geografi?*, Universitetsforlaget, Oslo.

Holt-Jensen, A., Henu, E., Romice, O., Kährik, A. and Liias, R. (eds) (2004) *New Ideas for Neighbourhoods in Europe: NEHOM Handbook*, Department of Geography, Bergen and TUT Press, Tallinn, Estonia.

Hosseini, K. (2007) *A Thousand Splendid Suns*, Bloomsbury, London.

Howard, E. (1902) *Garden Cities of Tomorrow*, London.

Huggett, R. J. (1993) *Modelling the Human Impact in Nature: Systems Analysis of Environmental Problems*, Oxford University Press, Oxford.

Huntington, E. (1915) *Civilization and Climate*, Yale University Press, New Haven, CT.

Huxley, T. H. (1877) *Physiography*, Macmillan, London.

International Geographical Union (1992) *International Charter on Geographical Education*, Washington, DC, National Geographic Society.

Jackson, P. (1989) *Maps of Meaning: An Introduction to Cultural Geography*, Unwin Hyman, London (reprinted 1992 and 1994 by Routledge, London).

James, P. E. (1972) *All Possible Worlds: A History of Geographical Ideas*, Odyssey Press, Indianapolis, IN.

Jarvis, H., Pratt, A. C. and Wu, P. C.-C. (2001) *The Secret Life of Cities: The Social Reproduction of Everyday Life*, Pearson Educational/Prentice Hall, Harlow.

Johannessen, K. S. (1985) *Tradisjoner og skoler i moderne vitenskapsfilosofi*, Sigma, Bergen.

Johansson, I. (1973) Anglosaxisk vetenskapsfilosofi, in *Positivismn, Marxism, kritisk teori*, Pan/Nordsteds, Stockholm.

Johnston, R. J. (1978) Paradigms and revolutions or evolution, *Progress in Human Geography*, Vol. 2, pp. 189–206.

Johnston, R. J. (ed.) (1985) *The Future of Geography*, Methuen, London.

Johnston, R. J. (1986a) *Philosophy and Human Geography* (2nd edn), Arnold, London.

Johnston, R. J. (1986b) *On Human Geography*, Blackwell, Oxford.

Johnston, R. J. (1986c) Four fixations and the quest for unity in geography, *Transactions of the Institute of British Geographers*, New Series, Vol. 11, pp. 449–53.

Johnston, R. J. (1991) *A Question of Place: Exploring the Practice of Human Geography*, Blackwell, London.

Johnston, R. J. (1997) *Geography and Geographers: Anglo-American Human Geography since 1945* (5th edn), Arnold, London.

Jones, M. (1988) Land-tenure and landscape change in fishing communities on the outer coast of central Norway, *c.* 1880 to the present, *Geografiska Annaler*, Vol. 70B, pp. 197–204.

Kant, E. (1946) Den indre omflyttingen i Estland i samband med de estniska städernas omland, *Svensk Geografisk Årsbok*, Vol. 22, pp. 83–124.

Kant, E. (1951) Omlandsforskning och sektoranalys, in G. Enequist (ed.), *Tätorter och Omland*, Lundequistska Bokhandelen, Uppsala.

Keltie, J. S. (1886) Geographical education: report to the Council of the Royal Geographical Society, *Supplementary Papers of the Royal Geographical Society*, No. 1, pp. 439–594.

Keltie, J. S. (1921) Obituary for Peter Alexievich Kropotkin, *Geographical Journal*, Vol. 57, pp. 316–19.

Kidd, B. (1894) *Social Evolution*, Macmillan, London.

Knox, P. L. (1975) *Social Well-being: A Spatial Perspective*, Clarendon Press, Oxford.

Knox, P. L. and Pinch, S. (2006) *Urban Social Geography: An Introduction* (5th edn), Pearson Educational/Prentice-Hall, Harlow and New York.

Kropotkin, P. (1885) What geography ought to be, *Nineteenth Century*, Vol. 18, pp. 940–56.

Kropotkin, P. (1924) *Ethics: Origin and Development*, New York.

Kropotkin, P. (2008) Mutual aid among the barbarians, in *Political History and Culture of Russia*, 24, 4, Nova Science Publishers, Happauge, New York, pp. 489–511 (excerpted from Kropotkin, P. (1902) *Mutual Aid: A Factor of Evolution*).

Kuhn, T. S. (1962/1970a) *The Structure of Scientific Revolutions*, University at Chicago Press, Chicago, IL.

Kuhn, T. S. (1970b) Reflections on my critics, in I. Lakatos and A. Musgrave (eds), *Criticism and the Growth of Knowledge*, Cambridge University Press, Cambridge.

Lange, G. (1961) Varenius über die Grundfrage der Geographie, *Petermanns Geographische Mitteilungen*, Vol. 105, pp. 274–83.

Lash, S. and Urry, J. (1987) *The End of Organised Capitalism*, Polity Press, Cambridge.

Law, J. (1994) *Organizing Modernity*, Basil Blackwell, Oxford.

Leser, H. (1980) *Geographie, Das Geographische Seminar*, Westermann, Braunschweig.

Lévi-Strauss, C. (1969/1949) *The Elementary Structures of Kinship*, Beacon Press, Boston, MA.

Livingstone, D. N. (1992) *The Geographical Tradition*, Blackwell, Oxford.

Löfgren, A. (1996) *Om kvalitativ metod och fältarbete i geografi. Arbeider fra Geografisk Institutt, Universitet i Trondheim*, New series C, No. 4, Universitetet i Trondheim, Trondheim.

Lowenthal, D. (1985) *The Past is a Foreign Country*, Cambridge University Press, Cambridge.

Lowenthal, D. (1996) *Possessed by the Past: The Heritage Crusade and the Spoils of History*, Free Press, New York.

Lukermann, F. (1958) Towards a more geographic economic geography, *The Professional Geographer*, Vol. 10, pp. 1–10.

Lundberg, A. and Handegård, T. (1996) Changes in the spatial structure and function of coastal cultural landscapes, *GeoJournal*, Vol. 39, pp. 167–78.

Lyotard, J. -F. (1984) *The Postmodern Condition: A Report on Knowledge*, Manchester University Press, Manchester.

Mabogunje, A. (1976) Systems approach to a theory of rural–urban migration, in J. Beishon and C. Peters (eds), *Systems Behaviour* (2nd edn), Harper & Row/Open University Press, London.

Mackinder, H. J. (1911) The teaching of geography from an imperial point of view, and the use which could and should be made of visual instruction, *Geographical Teacher*, Vol. 6, pp. 79–86.

Mair, A. (1986) Thomas Kuhn: and understanding geography, *Progress in Human Geography*, Vol. 10, pp. 345–69.

Malmberg, T. (1980) *Human Territoriality*, Mouton, The Hague.

Marsh, G. P. (1864) *Man and Nature, or Physical Geography as Modified by Human Action*, Schribners, New York.

Martin, G. J. (1985) Paradigm change: a history of geography in the United States 1892–1925, *National Geographic Research*, Spring, pp. 217–35.

Massey, D. (1984) *Spatial Division of Labour: Social Structures and the Geography of Production*, Macmillan, London.

Massey, D. (1994) *Space, Place and Gender*, Polity Press, London.

Massey, D. and Allen, J. (eds) (1984) *Geography Matters: A Reader*, Cambridge University Press, Cambridge.

Massey, D. and McDowell, L. (1994) A woman's place, in D. Massey, *Space, Place and Gender*, Polity Press, London.

Matthews, J. A. and Herbert, D. T. (eds) (2004) *Unifying Geography: Common Heritage, Shared Future*, Routledge, London and New York.

Matthews, J. A. and Herbert, D. T. (2008) *Geography: A Very Short Introduction*, Oxford University Press, Oxford.

May, J. A. (1970) *Kant's Concept of Geography and its Relation to Recent Geographical Thought*, University of Toronto Press, Toronto.

McDowell, L. (2003) Geographers and sexual difference: feminist contributions, in R. Johnston and M. Williams (eds), *A Century of British Geography*, The British Academy/Oxford University Press, Oxford, pp. 603–23.

Mead, W. (1954) Ridge and furrow in Buckinghamshire, *Geographical Journal*, Vol. 120, pp. 34–42.

Meesenburg, H. (1996) Man's role in changing the coastal landscapes in Denmark, *GeoJournal*, Vol. 39, pp. 143–52.

Meijer, H. (1981) *Zuyder Zee–Lake Ijssel*, Haag: IDG, Utrecht.

Minshull, R. (1970) *The Changing Nature of Geography*, Hutchinson, London.

Morrill, R. L. (1965) *Migration and the Growth of Urban Settlement, Lund Studies in Geography*, Series B, 24, Gleerup, Lund.

Morrill, R. L. (1984) Recollection of the 'quantitative revolution's' early years: the University of Washington 1955–65, in M. Billinge, D. Gregory and R. Martin (eds), *Recollection of a Revolution*, Macmillan, London.

Morrill, R. L. (1974) Review of D. Harvey, *Social Justice and the City*, Annals of the Association of American Geographers, Vol. 64, pp. 457–477.

Morrill, R. L. and Wohlenberg, E. H. (1971) *The Geography of Poverty in the United States*, McGraw-Hill, New York.

Murdoch, J. (2006) *Post-structuralist Geography*, Sage, London.

Myrdal, G. (1953) The relation between social theory and social policy, *British Journal of Sociology*, Vol. 23, pp. 210–42.

National Curriculum Geography Working Group (1989) *Interim Report*, Department of Education and Science and the Welsh Office, Brighton.

Neef, E. (1982) Geographie-einmal anders gesehen, *Geographische Zeitschrift*, Vol. 70, pp. 241–60.

Newcomb, R. M. (1979) *Planning the Past: Studies in Historical Geography*, Dawson/Archon, London.

Norberg-Schultz, K. (1984) *Genius Loci: Towards a Phenomenology of Architecture*, Rizzoli, New York.

Olsson, G. (1974) Servitude and inequality in spatial planning: ideology and methodology in conflict, *Antipode*, Vol. 6, pp. 16–21 (reprinted in R. Peet (ed.) (1977) *Radical Geography*, Methuen, London).

Olsson, G. (1975) *Birds in Egg*, Michigan Geography Publication No. 15, Ann Arbor, MI.

Olsson, G. (1978) Of ambiguity or far cries from a memoralising mamafesta, in D. Ley and M. Samuels (eds), *Humanistic Geography: Prospect and Problems*, Croom Helm, Beckenham.

Olwig, K. (1984) *Nature's Ideological Landscape: A Literary and Geographic Perspective on its Development and Preservation on Denmark's Jutland Heath*, Allen & Unwin, London.

Olwig, K. (1996) Recovering the substantive nature of landscape, *Annals of the Association of American Geographers*, Vol. 86, pp. 630–53.

Openshaw, S. (1991) A view of the GIS crisis in geography: or, using GIS to put Humpty-Dumpty back together again, *Environment and Planning A*, Vol. 23, pp. 621–8.

Orme, A. (1985) Understanding and predicting the physical world, in R. J. Johnston (ed.), *The Future of Geography*, Methuen, London.

Overå, R. (1998) *Partners and Competitors: Gendered Entrepreneurship in Ghanian Canoe Fisheries*, PhD dissertation, Department of Geography, University of Bergen, Norway.

Paffen, K. H. (1955) Die natürlichen Landschaften und Ihre raümliche Gliederung, *Forschungen zur deutschen Landeskunde 68*.

Peet, R. (ed.) (1977) *Radical Geography*, Methuen, London.

Peet, R. (1985) The social origins of environmental determinism, *Annals of the Association of American Geographers*, Vol. 75, pp. 309–33.

Peet, R. (1996) Structural themes in geographic discourse, in I. Douglas, R. Huggett and M. Robinson (eds), *Companion Encyclopedia of Geography*, Routledge, London.

Peet, R. (1998) *Modern Geographical Thought*, Blackwell, Oxford.

Peet, R. and Watts, M. (eds) (1996) *Liberation Ecologies: Environment, Development, Social Movements*, Routledge, London.

Penck, A. (1894) *Morphologie der Erdoberflache*, Stuttgart.

Penck, A. (1901–9) *Die Alpen in Eisalter, Vols 1–3*, Stuttgart.

Penck, A. (1928) Neuere Geographie, in *Zeitschrift de Gesellschaft für Erdkunde zu Berlin*, Berlin, pp. 31–56.

Peschel, O. (1870) *Neue Probleme der veigleichenden Erdkunde als Versuch einer Morphologie der Erdoberfläche*, Duncker & Humblot, Leipzig.

Pickles, J. (1985) *Phenomenology, Science and Geography*, Cambridge University Press, Cambridge.

Pollan, M. (2001) *The Botany of Desire*, Knopf, New York.

Popper, K. (1970) Normal science and its dangers, in F. Lakotos and A. Musgrave (eds), *Criticism and the Growth of Knowledge*, Cambridge University Press, Cambridge.

Popper, K. R. (1972) *Objective Knowledge*, Oxford University Press, Oxford.

Poster, M. (1984) *Foucault, Marxism and History: Mode of Production versus Mode of Information*, Polity Press, Cambridge.

Poulton, M. (1995) Affordable homes at affordable (social) price, pp. 50–122 in G. Fallis, M. Poulton, L. B. Smith, M. Y. Seelig and J. H. Seelig, *Home Remedies: Rethinking Canadian Housing Policy*, C.D. Howe Institute, Toronto.

Pred, A. (1967) *Behaviour and Location. Part I: Foundations for a Geographic and Dynamic Location Theory*, Gleerup, Lund.

Pred, A. (1969) *Behaviour and Location. Part II: Foundations for a Geographic and Dynamic Location Theory*, Gleerup, Lund.

Pred, A. (1984) Place as a historically contingent process: structuration and the time-geography of becoming places, *Annals of the Association of American Geographers*, Vol. 74, pp. 279–97.

Quaini, M. (1982) *Geography and Marxism*, Blackwell, Oxford.

Ratzel, F. (1882) *Anthropogeographie. I. Oder Grundzüge der Anwendung der Erdkunde auf die Geschichte*, Engelhorn, Stuttgart.

Ratzel, F. (1891) *Anthropogeographie. II: Die geographische Verbrietung des Menschen*, Engelhorn, Stuttgart.

Ratzel, F. (1897) *Politische Geographie*, Oldenburg, Munich.

Réclus, E. (1866–7) *La Terre*, Hachette, Paris.

Réclus, E. (1875–94) *Nouvelle Géographie Universelle*, Hachette, Paris.

Réclus, E. (1905–8) *L'Homme et la Terre* (6 vols), Paris.

Reenberg, A. (1982) *Det katastroferamte Sahel*, Geografforlaget, Brenderup.

Relph, E. (1976) *Place and Placelessness*, Pion, London.

Relph, E. (1996) Place, in I. Douglas, R. Huggett and M. Robinson (eds), *Companion Encyclopedia of Geography*, Routledge, London.

Ritter, C. (1822–59) *Die Erdkunde, im Verhältnis zur Natur und zur Geschichte des Menschen, oder allgemeine vergleichende Geographie als sichere Grundlage des Studiums und Unterrichts in Physikalischen und historischen Wissenschaften* (19 vols), Reimer, Berlin.

Ritzer, G. (2007) *The Globalization of Nothing 2*, Sage, London.

Sack, R. D. (1972) Geography, geometry and explanation, *Annals of the Association of American Geographers*, Vol. 62, pp. 61–78.

Sack, R. D. (1980) *Conceptions of Space in Social Thought*, Macmillan, London.

Sack, R. D. (1986) *Human Territoriality, Its Theory and History*, Cambridge University Press, Cambridge.

Sack, R. D. (1992) *Place, Modernity, and the Consumer's World*, Johns Hopkins University Press, Baltimore, MD.

Sack, R.D. (1997) *Homo Geographicus: A Framework for Action, Awareness and Moral Concern*, Johns Hopkins University Press, Baltimore, MD and London.

Sauer, C. O. (1925) The morphology of landscape, *University of California Publications in Geography*, Vol. 2, pp. 19–35.

Sauer, C. O. (1963) *Land and Life* (ed. J. B. Leighley), University of California Press, Berkeley, CA.

Savage, M., Warde, A. and Ward, K. (2003) *Urban Sociology: A Realist Approach*, Hutchinson, London.

Sayer, A. (1984/1992) *Method in Social Science: A Realist Approach*, Hutchinson, London.

Sayer, A. (1985) Realism and geography, in R. J. Johnston (ed.), *The Future of Geography*, Methuen, London.

Sayer, A. (1991) Behind the locality debate: deconstructing geography's dualisms, *Environment and Planning A*, Vol. 23, pp. 283–308.

Sayer, A. (1993) Postmodernist thought in geography: a realist view, *Antipode*, Vol. 25, pp. 320–40.

Schaefer, F. (1953) Exceptionalism in geography, *Annals of the Association of American Geographers*, Vol. 43, pp. 226–49.

Schlüter, O. (1906) *Die Ziele dei Geographie des Menschen*, München, Berlin.

Schlüter, O. (1920) Die Erdkunde im Verhältnis zu der Natur- und Geisteswissenschaften, *Geographische Anzeiger*, Vol. 21, pp. 145–52, 212–21.

Schmieder, O. (1964) Alexander van Humboldt: Persönlichkeit wissenschaftliches Werk und Auswirkung auf die moderne Länderkunde, *Geographische Zeitschrift*, Vol. 52, pp. 81–95.

Schmithüsen, J. (1976) *Allgemeine Geosynergetik*, De Gruyter, Berlin.

Scholten, A. (1980) Al-Muqaddasi *c.* 945–*c.* 988, in T. W. Freeman and P. Pinchemel (eds), *Geographers, Bibliographical Studies* (Vol. 4), Mansell, London.

Schültz, H. D. (1980) Die deutschsprachige Geographie von 1800 bis 1970, *Abhandlung des geographischen Instituts-Antropogeographie* Band 29, Selbstverlag der geographischen Instituts der Freien Universität, Berlin.

Schumacher, E. F. (1974) *Small is Beautiful: A Study of Economics as if People Mattered*, Abacus, London.

Semple, E. C. (1911) *Influences of Geographical Environment*, Henry Holt, New York.

Sheppard, E. and Barnes, T. (eds) (2000) *A Companion to Economic Geography*, Blackwell, Oxford.

Sibley, D. (1995) *Geographies of Exclusion*, Routledge, London.

Simpson, G. G. (1963) Historical science, in C. C. Albritton (ed.), *The Fabric of Geology*, Addison-Wesley, Reading, MA.

Skjervheim, H. (1974) Objectivism and the study of man, *Inquiry*, Vol. 17, pp. 213–39, 265–302.

Smith, D. M. (1979) *Where the Grass is Greener: Living in an Unequal World*, Penguin, Harmondsworth.

Smith, N. (1990) *Uneven Development: Nature, Capital and the Reproduction of Space*, Blackwell, London.

Smith, R. (2005) *The Utility of Force: The Art of War in the Modern World*, Allen Lane/Penguin, London.

Soja, E. (1989) *Postmodern Geographies: The Reassertion of Space in Social Theory*, Verso, London.

Somerville, M. (1848) *Physical Geography*, London.

Sømme, A. (ed.) (1965) *Fjellbygd og feriefjell*, Cappelen, Oslo.

Speak, S., Gilroy, R., Cameron, S. and Woods, R. (1995) *Young Single Mothers: Barriers to Independent Living*, Family Policy Studies Centre, London.

Stamp, D. (1966) Ten years on, *Transactions, of the Institute of British Geographers*, Vol. 40, pp. 11–20.

Steers, J. A. (1946) *The Coastline of England and Wales*, Cambridge University Press, Cambridge.

Steiner, D. (1965) Die Faktorenanalyse: eine modernes statistisches Hilfsmittel des Geographen für die objektive Raumgliederung und Typenbildung, *Geographica Helvetica*, Vol. 20, pp. 20–34.

Stevenson, W. I. (1978) Patrick Geddes 1854–1932, in T. W. Freeman and P. Pinchemel (eds), *Geographers, Bibliographical Studies* (Vol. 2), Mansell, London.

Stewart, J. Q. (1947) Empirical mathematical rules concerning the distribution and equilibrium of population, *Geographical Review*, Vol. 37, pp. 461–85.

Stoddart, D. R. (1966) Darwin's impact on geography, *Annals of the Association of American Geographers*, Vol. 56, pp. 683–98.

Stoddart, D. R. (1975) 'That Victorian science' – Huxley's 'physiography' and its impact on geography, *Transactions of the Institute of British Geographers*, Vol. 66, pp. 17–40.

Stoddart, D. R. (1981) The paradigm concept and the history of geography, in D. R. Stoddart (ed.), *Geography, Ideology and Social Concern*, Blackwell, Oxford.

Stoddart, D. R. (1986) On *Geography*, Blackwell, Oxford.

Stoddart, D. R. (1987/1996) To claim the high ground: geography for the end of the century, *Transactions of the Institute of British Geographers*, New Series, Vol. 12, pp. 327–36 (reprinted in S. Daniels and R. Lee (eds), *Exploring Human Geography: A Reader*, Edward Arnold, London).

Taaffe, E. J. (ed.) (1970) *Geography*, Prentice-Hall, Englewood Cliffs, NJ.

Tatham, G. (1951) Geography in the nineteenth century, in G. Taylor (ed.), *Geography in the Twentieth Century*, Methuen, London.

Taylor, G. (ed.) (1951) *Geography in the Twentieth Century*, Methuen, London.

Taylor, P. J. (1976) An interpretation of the quantification debate in British geography, *Transactions of the Institute of British Geographers*, New Series, Vol. 1, pp. 129–42.

Thrift, N. J. (1986) The geography of international economic disorder, in R. J. Johnston and P. J. Taylor (eds), *A World in Crisis: Geographical Perspectives*, Blackwell, Oxford.

Thrift, N. (1996) *Spatial Formations*, Sage, London.

Thrift, N. (2002) The future of geography, *Geoforum*, Vol. 33, pp. 291–8.

Troll, C. (1947) Die geographische Wissenschaft in Deutschland in dem Jahren 1933 bis 1945, *Erdkunde*, Vol. 1, pp. 3–48.

Tuan, Y.-F. (1971) Geography, phenomenology, and the study of human nature, *The Canadian Geographer*, Vol. 15, pp. 181–92.

Tuan, Y.-F. (1974) Space and place: humanistic perspective, in J. Agnew, D. N. Livingstone and A. Rogers (eds), *Human Geoyaphy: An Essential Anthology*, Blackwell, Oxford (reprinted 1996).

Tuan, Y.-F. (1976) Humanistic geography, *Annals of the Association of American Geographers*, Vol. 66, pp. 266–76.

Tuan, Y.-F. (1977) *Space and Place: The Perspectives of Experience*, University of Minnesota Press/Arnold, Minneapolis, MN and London.

Tuan, Y.-F. (1978) Literature and geography: implications for geographical research, in D. Ley and M. S. Samuels (eds), *Humanistic Geography: Prospects and Problems*, Maaroufa, Chicago, IL.

Tuan, Y.-F. (1980) *Landscapes of Fear*, Pantheon, New York and Blackwell, Oxford.

Uhlig, H. (1967) *Methodische Begriffe der Geographie, besonders der Landschaftskunde. Separat-Vorabdruck aus Westermanns Lexikon der Geographie*, Westermann, Braunschweig.

Uhlig, H. (1971) Organization and system of geography, *Geoforum*, Vol. 7, pp. 7–38.

Uhlig, H. (1973) Landschaftökologie, in *Des Wesen der Landschaft*, Wissenschaftliche Buchgesellschaft, Darmstadt, pp. 268–85.

Ullman, E. (1941) A theory of location for cities, *American Journal of Sociology*, Vol. 46, pp. 835–64.

Unwin, T. (1992) *The Place of Geography*, Longman, Harlow.

van Valkenburg, S. (1952) The German school of geography, in G. Taylor (ed.), *Geography in the Twentieth Century*, Methuen, London.

Varenius, B. (1650) *Geografia Generalis*, Amsterdam.

Vidal de la Blache, P. (1903) *Tableau de la géographie de la France*, Hachette, Paris.

Vidal de la Blache, P. (1917) *La France de l'Est*, Armand Colin, Paris.

Vidal de la Blache, P. (1921) *Principes de la Géographie humaine* (trans. 1926 as *Principles of Human Geography*, Constable, London).

Viles, H. (1992) Physical geography fieldwork, in A. Rogers, H. Viles and A. Goudie (eds), *The Student's Companion to Geography*, Blackwell, Oxford, pp. 187–95.

von Humboldt, A. (1845–62) *Kosmos: Entwurf einer physischen Weltbeschreibung* (5 vols), Cotta, Stuttgart (English trans. E. C. Ohé (1849–58), H. G. Bohn, London).

von Thünen, J. H. (1826) *Der Isolierte Staat in Beziehung auf Landwirtschaft und Nationalökonomie*, Hamburg (English trans. C. M. Wartenburg (1966), *Von Thünen's Isolated State*, ed. P. Hall, Pergamon, Oxford).

Wagner, D. L. and Mikesell, M. W. (1962) *Readings in Cultural Geography*, University of Chicago Press, Chicago, IL.

Waibel, L. (1933) Was verstehen wir unter Landschaftskunde?, *Geographische Anzeiger*, Vol. 34, pp. 197–207.

Walmsley, D. J. and Lewis, G. J. (1993) *People and Environment: Behavioural Approaches in Human Geography* (2nd edn), Longman, Harlow.

Warntz, W. (1959) *Towards a Geography of Price: A Study in Geo-Econometrics*, University of Pennsylvania Press, Philadelphia, PA.

Warntz, W. (1964) A new map of the surface of population potentials for the United States, 1960, *Geographical Review*, Vol. 54, pp. 170–84.

Watts, M. (2005) Nature: culture, in P. Cloke and R. Johnston (eds), *Spaces of Geographical Thought*, Sage, London, pp. 142–74.

Weber, A. (1909) *Über der Standort der Industrien*, Tübingen (trans. C. Friederich (1929) *Alfred Weber's Theory of the Location of Industries*, Chicago University Press, Chicago, IL).

Weichhart, P. (1975) Gesucht: Eine human-ökologisch orientierte Teildisziplin der komplexen Geographie, *Berichte zur deutschen Landeskunde*, Vol. 54, pp. 125–32.

Weichhart, P. (1980) *Geographie im Umbruch*, Franz Deuticke, Wien.

Werlen, B. (1993) *Society, Action and Space: An Alternative Human Geography*, Routledge, London and New York.

Whatmore, S. (2002) *Hybrid Geographies: Natures, Cultures and Spaces*, Sage, London.

White, G. (1973) Natural hazards research, in R. J. Chorley (ed.), *Directions in Geography*, Methuen, London.

White, R. and Gould, P. (1974) *Mental Maps*, Penguin, Harmondsworth.

Whittlesey, D. (1929) Sequent occupance, *Annals of the Association of American Geographers*, Vol. 19, pp. 162–65.

Widberg, J. (1978) *Geografi från naturvetenskap til samhällsvetenskap: En idéhistorisk översikt* (3-betygsuppsats), Institutt för Kulturgeografi och Ekonomisk Geografi, Lund.

Wolpert, J. (1964) The decision process in spatial context, *Annals of the Association of American Geographers*, Vol. 54, pp. 337–58.

Wood, J., Gilroy, R., Healey, P. and Speak, S. (1995) *Changing the Way We Do Things Here: The Cruddas Park Initiative*, Department of Town and Country Planning, Newcastle University, Newcastle upon Tyne.

World Commission on Environment and Development (WCED) (1987) *Our Common Future*, Oxford University Press, Oxford.

Wrigley, E. A. (1965) Changes in the philosophy of geography, in R. K. Chorley and P. Haggett (eds), *Frontiers in Geographical Teaching*, Methuen, London.

Wylie, J. W. (2006) Poststructuralist theories, critical methods and experimentation, in S. Aitken and G. Valentine (eds), *Approaches to Human Geography*, Sage, London, pp. 298–310.

Yeates, M. (1968) *An Introduction to Quantitative Analysis in Economic Geography*, McGraw-Hill, New York.

Zimmerer, K. (1994) Ecology as a cornerstone and chimera in human geography, in C. Earle, K. Mathewson and M. Kenzer (eds), *Concepts in Human Geography*, Rowman & Littlefield, Lanham, MD, pp. 161–88.

Zimmerer, K. (2000) The reworking of conservation geographies: non-equilibrium landscapes and nature–society hybrids, *Annals of Association of American Geographers*, Vol. 90, No. 2, pp. 356–70.

AUTHOR AND PERSONALITY INDEX

Note: the letter 'f' after a page number refers to a figure.